ML

D1170977

FEB - 2018

Poetry and Theology in the Modernist Period

Poetry and Theology
in the Modernist Period

ANTHONY DOMESTICO

JOHNS HOPKINS UNIVERSITY PRESS   BALTIMORE

© 2017 Johns Hopkins University Press
All rights reserved. Published 2017
Printed in the United States of America on acid-free paper
9 8 7 6 5 4 3 2 1

Johns Hopkins University Press
2715 North Charles Street
Baltimore, Maryland 21218-4363
www.press.jhu.edu

Library of Congress Cataloging-in-Publication Data

Names: Domestico, Anthony, 1984– author.
Title: Poetry and theology in the modernist period / Anthony Domestico.
Description: Baltimore : Johns Hopkins University Press, 2017. | Includes
bibliographical references and index.
Identifiers: LCCN 2016051700 | ISBN 9781421423319 (hardcover :
acid-free paper) | ISBN 9781421423326 (electronic)
Subjects: LCSH: English poetry—20th century—History and criticism. |
Modernism (Literature)—Great Britain. | Theology in literature. |
Christianity in literature. | Religion and literature—Great Britain—
History—20th century. | Eliot, T. S. (Thomas Stearns),
1888–1965—Criticism and interpretation. | Jones, David,
1895–1974—Criticism and interpretation. | Auden, W. H. (Wystan Hugh),
1907–1973—Criticism and interpretation.
Classification: LCC PR605.M63 D66 2017 | DDC 821/.9109112—dc23
LC record available at https://lccn.loc.gov/2016051700

A catalog record for this book is available from the British Library.

*Special discounts are available for bulk purchases of this book. For more information,
please contact Special Sales at 410-516-6936 or specialsales@press.jhu.edu.*

Johns Hopkins University Press uses environmentally friendly book materials,
including recycled text paper that is composed of at least 30 percent post-consumer
waste, whenever possible.

The last printed page of this book is an extension of the copyright page.

FOR MEGAN

Contents

Acknowledgments

This book came about by a circuitous route. In 2007, I was re-reading Marilynne Robinson's beautiful novel *Gilead*, and I noticed that the protagonist, John Ames, praised the Protestant theologian Karl Barth on several occasions. Trusting Robinson (and Ames), I checked Barth's *Epistle to the Romans* out of the library. Astonished by the book's ferocious power, I also was struck by how much, in its imagery, it reminded me of *The Waste Land*, so I decided to dig into the archives of the *Criterion* and see if Barth had ever been mentioned in Eliot's little magazine. He had been, and so too had Reinhold Niebuhr, and Jacques Maritain, and Paul Tillich, and many other modern theologians. Down the rabbit hole I went, and the further down I went the more connections I found between modern British poetry and modern Christian theology. Ten years later, *Poetry and Theology in the Modernist Period* is the result of this digging and exploring.

This book and the thinking that has gone into it have been shaped by many such chance encounters—stray conversations, seemingly random but ultimately meaningful book recommendations. It also has been shaped by more sustained relationships. Amy Hungerford and Pericles Lewis served as my dissertation advisors, nurturing and believing in this project from its most formative stages. This book wouldn't exist without their constant and supportive presence. Paul Grimstad, Langdon Hammer, and Justin Neuman offered detailed, generous feedback at various points. While teaching at Purchase College, SUNY, Frank Farrell has been a treasured conversation partner about poetry and sacrament. Kathleen McCormick, Gaura Narayan, Gary Waller, and Louise Yelin have been welcoming colleagues, keeping me sane and happy during the final stages of this project. Looking further back, four teachers at the undergraduate level—Curtis Brown, Philip Fisher, Helen Vendler, and James Wood—taught me how to read and write. In the process, they showed me just how worthy literary study could be.

This book is about conversation and it grew out of conversation. Craig Fehrman helped me think more intelligently about archives and the profession; Griffin Oleynick talked with me about theology, aesthetics, and Russian literature; Bo Li served as a fantastic writing partner; Emily Gustafson and Victor McFarland have been wonderful friends throughout. Thanks also go to Matthew

Boudway, Eric Bugyis, Katie Bugyis, Colleen Carroll, Susan Chambers, Merve Emre, Soren Forsberg, Paul Fry, David Gorin, Len Gutkin, Leslie Jamison, Lawrence Joseph, Jill LaBrack, Jessica Matuozzi, Vittorio Montemaggi, Matthew Mutter, Mollie Wilson O'Reilly, John Rogers, Denys Turner, Grant Wiedenfeld, and Nathalie Wolfram. At Johns Hopkins University Press, Matt McAdam and Catherine Goldstead were strong advocates for the project from the beginning, and Barbara Lamb was a superb copy editor. Thanks also to the anonymous reader whose comments helped greatly in making this book as strong as it could be.

I've also benefitted from institutional help. While at Yale, the Whiting Foundation offered a year of financial support; the Whitney Humanities Center provided delicious lunches and exhilarating interdisciplinary conversation in my time as a fellow. A National Endowment for the Humanities seminar on Herbert and Dickinson helped enrich my thinking on the relationship between poetry and religion. Special thanks are due to Richard Strier for gathering such an interesting group of scholars and writers. At Purchase, a Junior Faculty Leave Award helped me to put the finishing touches on this book.

Portions of this book have been published in slightly different forms. Parts of Chapter 2 appeared as "Editing Modernism, Editing Theology: T. S. Eliot, Karl Barth, and the Criterion," *Journal of Modern Periodical Studies* 3.1 (2012): 19–38. This article is used by permission of The Pennsylvania State University Press. Parts of Chapter 3 appeared as "The Twice-Broken World: Karl Barth, T. S. Eliot, and the Poetics of Christian Revelation," *Religion & Literature* 44.3 (Autumn 2012): 1–26. Reprint permission granted by the University of Notre Dame. Thanks to the anonymous readers of both of these essays; their comments helped clarify and strengthen my arguments. Finally, parts of Chapter 4 appeared as "Words in Action: The Sacramental Poetry of David Jones," *Commonweal* (December 20, 2012): 12–16. Reprint permissions granted by the Commonweal Foundation. The editors at *Commonweal*, especially Matthew Boudway, have offered the greatest gifts a writer could receive: a place to publish and a supportive yet critical editing eye.

Finally, I owe a debt of gratitude to my family. My parents taught me from the beginning that reading could be the greatest of pleasures. It's been a long journey from the Great Illustrated Classics and the "great conversation" to here, and my parents have helped me through it all.

Above all, thanks to Megan—my first, last, best, and most loved reader. As usual, Auden said it best: "My Dear One is mine as mirrors are lonely."

Poetry and Theology in the Modernist Period

CHAPTER ONE

A Conversation between
Philosophers and Artists

Cultured people, to whom, until recently, theological terms were far more
shocking than any of the four-letter words, are now in such danger and have
seen so many of their absolute assumptions destroyed, that they may even
overcome this final prudery. —W. H. AUDEN, "The Means of Grace"

In *The Lives of the Poets*, Samuel Johnson warned against mixing theology and
literature, claiming that "the ideas of Christian Theology are too simple for
eloquence, *too sacred for fiction*, and too majestick for ornament; *to recommend
them by tropes and figures* is to magnify by a concave mirror the sidereal hemi-
sphere."[1] Johnson's warning—that to treat the ideas of Christian theology in
literary form is necessarily to sully them—is a familiar one, though it is advice
more honored in the breach (think of John Milton, George Herbert, and Gerard Manley Hopkins) than in the observance. On the one side, we have sacred
truth, which for the Christian means the revelation of God through the birth,
death, and resurrection of Jesus Christ. On the other side, we have poetry, full
of images and metaphors, figures and filigree, all of which distort the true nature of God's divine grace. The one is defined by simplicity and grandeur, the
other by elaboration and embellishment. For Johnson, theology is theology,
poetry is poetry, and the two should never be—must never be—confused.[2]

Here are some very different words, written by the Catholic philosopher
and theologian Jacques Maritain. In his 1920 work *Art and Scholasticism*—a
work whose very title brings together the two categories, aesthetics and theology, that Johnson said must be held apart—Maritain wrote that European
culture in the years after World War I needed "a conversation between philosophers and artists."[3] In making this claim, Maritain had in mind a specific
kind of philosopher: Catholic neo-Thomists like himself, Etienne Gilson, and
Martin D'Arcy. These thinkers sought to wed traditional Catholic sacramentalism (what Maritain called the "Metaphysics of the ancients") to a critically
realist epistemology, arguing that, because the intellect and that which it per-
ceives arise from and are sustained by God, the world is an "intelligible mystery."[4] Maritain also had in mind a specific kind of artist: post-Impressionist
painters like Pablo Picasso and Paul Cézanne and modernist writers like T. S.
Eliot and James Joyce.

The historical moment at which Maritain was writing seemed ripe for such an interdisciplinary conversation. After the horrors of World War I, Maritain wrote, "All feel the necessity of escaping from the immense intellectual disorder inherited from the nineteenth century."[5] Maritain believed that, just as Catholic neo-Thomists were challenging the "original sin against the light" that was philosophical idealism, so the period's best painters, poets, and novelists were challenging the supremacy of unthinking mimesis in art.[6] Picasso, Joyce, and others realized that "art, as such, does not consist in imitating, but in making, in composing or constructing, in accordance with the laws of the very object to be posited in being."[7] If only theologians and artists would speak with one another, Maritain suggested, then we might be saved from the previous generation's reductive thinking about the world (privileging epistemology over metaphysics) and about art (privileging mimetic convention over formal experimentation).

Maritain knew of what he spoke. He was perhaps the preeminent Catholic public intellectual of the day: writing seminal texts on metaphysics, moral philosophy, and Christian epistemology; shaping the modern Christian Democratic movement; and helping to draft the United Nations' Universal Declaration of Human Rights. He was also, however, a prolific and respected aesthetic thinker. In 1926, he and his friend Jean Cocteau jointly published *Letter to Jacques Maritain* and *Response to Jean Cocteau*, works in which the two men discussed the deep resonances between avant-garde aesthetics and Catholic thinking. Indeed, Maritain engaged with modern art regularly, in both essay form (he contributed a series of reflections on poetry and religion to Eliot's *Criterion* in 1927) and in book form. In *Art and Scholasticism* (1920), *The Frontiers of Poetry* (1935), and *Creative Intuition in Art and Poetry* (1953), Maritain attempted a synthesis of aesthetics and theology, outlining what Rowan Williams calls "a comprehensive theory of artistic labour on the basis of a very ambitious religious metaphysic."[8]

How exactly did Maritain go about connecting "artistic labour" to a "religious metaphysic"? Why did he believe that artists (more specifically, modern artists) and theologians (more specifically, modern theologians) had a great deal to say to one another? In short, because they were engaged in a similar task: trying to show how the everyday, physical world, when seen properly, is shot through with radiance and harmony, *claritas* and *consonantia*; how materiality has a radical openness to that which simultaneously exceeds and sustains it; how the immanent is the route to the transcendent.[9] In *Creative Intuition in Art and Poetry*, Maritain wrote that true art is always fractured and incomplete because it can never fully contain the perfect vision that it seeks. It always possesses "*that kind* of imperfection through which infinity wounds the finite."[10] Both the theologian and the poet inevitably reach a moment when words fail, when the vision so exceeds its expression that an admission of defeat becomes the best and only way to express that vision. On the poetic side, we might think of Eliot's "Burnt Norton," where we hear that "Words strain, / Crack and sometimes break, under the burden."[11] On the theological side, we might think of a claim by the transcendental Thomist Karl Rahner: "Every theological statement is only truly and authentically such at the point at which one willingly allows it to extend beyond his comprehension into the silent mystery of God."[12] In both instances, words fall short of the Word (whether that means poetic truth or divine revelation), yet this falling short is the only means by which the Word and its mysteries might be approached.

Maritain wrote that Cézanne, like other modern artists, was "obdurately and desperately intent on that bound, buried significance of visible things": obdurate because, in modern times, the world didn't seem to offer up hints of divine transcendence quite as easily as it once had done; desperate because this transcendence was necessary if one were to find meaning in existence.[13] The modern theologian was likewise aware of the importance and impossibility of the theological task, and Maritain believed that this shared sense of desperate obduracy meant that the one discipline could—indeed, should—learn from the other. For Maritain, the relationship between literature and theology was not antithetical, as Samuel Johnson claimed, but dialectical: theology tests itself against literature, literature against theology, and the two disciplines are the richer for it.

Taking Theology Seriously

In this volume, I argue that Maritain's hoped-for conversation between literature and Christian theology did in fact occur in the years between the two world wars and that this relationship is a long-overlooked but crucial part of the literary and intellectual history of the period. In the 1930s and 1940s, poets read theologians (and oftentimes wrote about them in essays and reviews), and theologians read poets (and reflected upon them in their own writing). Marianne Moore recommended the work of the Swiss Reformed theologian Karl Barth to Elizabeth Bishop and urged Ezra Pound to read Reinhold Niebuhr; David Jones cited Maritain's *Art and Scholasticism* as a formative influence and looked to *Mysterium Fidei*, Maurice de la Taille's 1921 work of sacramental theology, to help structure his epic poem *The Anathemata*; and W. H. Auden wrote poems in response to Reinhold Niebuhr's theological irony and to Paul Tillich's concept of *kairos*. It is telling that when T. S. Eliot, one of literary modernism's savviest marketers, was trying to drum up interest in the *Criterion* in 1927, he decided to start a controversy over, of all things, the theology of Thomas Aquinas.

That was the kind of world in which modernist poetry was written—a world in which debates over Thomism could grace the pages of a literary review, and in which such debates were thought to be an enticement to potential readers. Several of the period's most important poets regularly read, reviewed, and responded to contemporary Christian theology, and this reading, reviewing, and responding helped to shape the period's very understanding of poetry. That is to say, an important strand of modern British poetry understood itself in and through the theological questions of the time. Karl Barth asked, what is divine transcendence, and how can we truthfully reason and write about it? Jacques Maritain asked, what is the nature of the sacramental, and how does its wedding of the material and the immaterial, the immanent and the transcendent, inform the aesthetic act? Reinhold Niebuhr asked, how should we understand temporal experience, and how can we relate the City of God to the City of Man, eternity to history? For many poets, to write modern poetry was to consider such questions, and to consider such questions was to enter contemporary theological debate.

For a long time, critics tended to treat modernism as primarily secular in nature.[14] This has begun to change in recent years, with scholars emphasizing how Virginia Woolf, Joyce, Pound, and other modernists were haunted by Christianity's cultural traces despite their own lack of belief.[15] Still, these critics tend to argue that, when modernists talk about a religious or theological concept, they are actually talking about something else. When Eliot talks about God, for instance, he is actually talking about the social and intellectual order that belief in God might provide; when Woolf discusses the soul, she really just means the self; when Joyce mentions the Eucharist, he just has the work of art in mind.[16]

John Milbank summarizes this style of thinking nicely. In this "modern mode of suspicion, the problem was, 'isn't religion really x?'. An x which is more basic, though concealed. Isn't it really a function of social control, really a means of discipline for production, really an aspect of the psyche's suppression of the unacceptable?"[17] In this conception, the modernist scholar becomes a decoder, telling us what religion *really* was about for the modernists. But what if we take a radically different tack? What if we assume that, when Eliot talks about a theological term like the Incarnation, he really is talking about the Incarnation; that, for Eliot, the Incarnation is not a concept to be decoded but a concept to be explored on its own theological grounds; that, in writing poetry about the Incarnation, Eliot is taking a serious theological idea seriously?

This is not, of course, to say that thinking about the Incarnation means not thinking about things like politics or aesthetics. Since to be human is to be a political and aesthetic animal, belief in the Incarnation must influence politics and aesthetics. What I am suggesting, then, is a shift in emphasis. For Eliot, the Incarnation specifically and Christian theology generally entailed certain ideas about aesthetics, but that did not mean that theology was ultimately reducible to aesthetics. By reading theology as theology, Eliot believed, we wrestle with God's ultimately unknowable nature—and, in doing so, we necessarily begin to think about how this divine mystery influences art, physical embodiment, and other aspects of human life. Indeed, part of what Eliot and other modern poets so admired about Christian theology was its comprehensiveness—how "God talk," *theo-logos*, has implications for human creativity and practice more generally.

The writers that I consider in this book—T. S. Eliot, W. H. Auden, and David Jones—reacted against what they saw as the emotivism of nineteenth-century religious liberals such as Friedrich Schleiermacher. Instead, these poets emphasized religious thinking over religious feeling. (Or, in the case of Eliot most obviously, they emphasized that religious thinking could be its own form of religious feeling.) They were unembarrassed by theology's epistemological and ontological claims. For them, religion involved intellectual *and* emotional assent, doctrinal articulation *and* ritual practice. In fact, it was largely theology's objective claims about sin and the meaning of human history that so appealed to a group of writers who had grown weary of the fractured subjectivism of early and high modernism. We might even read this poetic interest in the ideas of Christian theology as a reaction against high modernism's absolute elevation of form over content and subjective experience over objective truth claims. Just as modern theology seemed to these poets a way out of the navel-gazing of nineteenth-century religious liberalism, so their own poetry would show self-reflexivity and theological speculation, aesthetic form and intellectual exploration, working hand in hand.

In 1918, Eliot famously claimed that Henry James "had a mind so fine that no idea could violate it." Eliot wasn't saying that James lacked ideas: in the same paragraph, he goes on to claim that James "is the most intelligent man of his generation."[18] Rather, he was arguing that James would never be so clumsy as to express these ideas directly or to let them "run wild and pasture on the emotions."[19] In James's novels, ideas arose from, and seemed embodied by, form itself. By the 1930s, though, Eliot and the other figures I treat were attempting a delicate balancing act: to reclaim ideas—more specifically, theological ideas—as a direct object of literary representation, while refusing to scrap the formal innovations of modernism. In other words, they wanted both Jamesian fineness and theological content; they wanted a literature of ideas that was also modernist. I call the work that resulted from such a desire "theological modernism": a body of poetry that is both theological (it considers, enlivens, and explores theological concepts such as revelation and eschatological hope) and modernist (it employs the forms and tropes of modern poetry).[20]

Theology Generating Poetry

In order to better understand how Eliot and his peers found contemporary theology such a rich source for poetic exploration, it will be helpful to look at Eliot's description of an earlier religious thinker, the seventeenth-century Anglican priest Lancelot Andrewes:

> Reading Andrewes on [the Nativity] is like listening to a great Hellenist expounding a text of the *Posterior Analytics*: altering the punctuation, inserting or removing a comma or a semi-colon to make an obscure passage suddenly luminous, dwelling on a single word, comparing its use in its nearer and in its most remote contexts, purifying a disturbed or cryptic lecture-note into lucid profundity. To persons whose minds are habituated to feed on the vague jargon of our time, when we have a vocabulary for everything and exact ideas about nothing—when a word half-understood, torn from its place in some alien or half-formed science, as of psychology, conceals from both writer and reader the meaninglessness of a statement, when all dogma is in doubt except the dogmas of sciences of which we have read in the newspapers, when the language of theology itself, under the influence of an undisciplined mysticism of popular philosophy, tends to become a language of tergiversation—Andrewes may seem pedantic and verbal.
>
> It is only when we have saturated ourselves in his prose, followed the movement of his thought, that we find his examination of words terminating in the ecstasy of assent. Andrewes takes a word and derives the world from it; squeezing and squeezing the word until it yields a full juice of meaning which we should never have supposed any word to possess.[21]

Here, Eliot identifies what Andrewes does so well by contrasting it with what most modern, nontheological thinkers do so poorly. Where they are "vague" and "undisciplined," having "a vocabulary for everything and exact ideas about nothing," Andrewes is precise and rigorous, even violent, squeezing each word and term for all the meaning it might yield. Andrewes concerns himself with linguistic exactitude; words are used carefully and examined thoroughly. This rigor becomes, for Andrewes's listeners and for Eliot himself, erotically charged, an "ecstasy of assent" that "yields a full juice of meaning."[22] Whatever good is derived from Andrewes—and, according to Eliot, there is much good—comes from his theological precision. You only get the juice after the squeezing; you only get the ecstasy in and through the disciplined examination. Again, religious thinking is not incidental but essential to religious feeling. (Here and throughout, we might notice how gendered theology was for the poets I consider: if nineteenth-century "religious feeling" was too sentimental, too imprecise, too feminine, then twentieth-century "religious thinking" or "theology" would be appropriately intellectual, rigorous, and masculine.)

How does this investment in the joys of theological inquiry make itself felt in the poetry of theological modernism? We might first consider Auden's "Kairos and Logos," a 1941 poem that consists of four sestinas and borrows its title from Paul Tillich's 1936 *The Interpretation of History*—the text in which Tillich first introduced the terms *kairos* and *logos* into modern theology.[23] The concept of *kairos*, as Lewis Hyde has written, "comes from the art of weaving and refers to the brief instant when the weaver may shoot her shuttle through the rising and falling warp threads."[24] *Kairos*, Hyde continues, is the time of potentiality, "a penetrable opening in the weaving of cloth, the weaving of time, the weaving of fate." In theological terms, *kairos* refers to holy time, to those opportune moments when the temporal opens up to the divine. Or, as Tillich puts it, "the moment that is creation and fate . . . the moment of time approaching us as fate and decision."[25]

In Auden's "Kairos and Logos," the time is opportune, at least in the first sestina, because it is so ungodly, so flat. We are in the time of the Roman Empire, where, in lines that echo Kierkegaard's distinction between the aesthetic, the ethical, and the religious, "conscience worshipped an aesthetic order / And what was unsuccessful was condemned"; where "Caesar [rules] with his pleasures, dreading death"; where time is not yet fulfilled or full of meaning and significance; where instead we simply hear "boom . . . the rhetoric of time."[26] Because of these conditions, the age is ripe for a different kind of order—an order in which the unsuccessful are embraced rather than condemned, death is not feared, and time is redeemed. The time is ripe, in other words, for the Incarnation, for the *logos* making itself present in history. Auden describes this divine act with the Protestant language of predestination and condescension: "predestined love / Fell like a daring meteor into time, / The condescension of eternal order."[27] Love falls not towards but into time—a "daring" and unexpected act. At this particular *kairotic* moment, love decides to dwell within time, and, because it has done so, "in little clumps about the world, / The just, the faithful and the uncondemned / Broke out spontaneously all over time." The faithful, those lovers of and within time, "never . . . condemned the world / Or hated time, but sang until their death." Because Christ (*logos*) enters the world at the opportune moment (*kairos*), time is no longer mere rhetoric but holy song.

Each of the following three sestinas varies wildly in style and imagery, but a thematic thread unites them all: each takes as its subject the nature of *kairos* and the relation between time and eternity. The second sestina—a lovely dream vision of unicorns and rose gardens—ends with *logos*, the Word, "still nurs[ing]" the world.[28] The third, in a modern and ironic tone, offers a final vision of a poet who "saw himself there with an exile's eyes, / Missing his Father."[29] The fourth, a dizzying burst of language that describes the "order of the macrocosmic spaces" and the "subatomic gulfs [that] confront our lives," concludes with a "reproach" that is also a "blessing" and that opens up the possibility of salvation.[30] The poem, to summarize, grows out of a theological text (Tillich's *The Interpretation of History*), and it takes as its guiding theme a set of fundamental theological questions: When is time most open to its rupture and fulfillment by eternity? and how might this rupture and fulfillment best be described in language? We are a long way from the compression and indirection of Eliot's *The Waste Land* or the work of the Imagists. Instead, we are in the world of theological modernism, where theological speculation generates and sustains poetic creation.[31]

The same sustaining relationship is posited in David Jones's short "A, a, a, DOMINE DEUS." The poem's opening lines articulate the tight link between Jones's poetic and theological thinking: "I said, Ah! what shall I write? / I enquired up and down."[32] As the rest of the poem illustrates, enquiring up and down means looking and thinking theologically: enquiring how divinity ("up") is present in materiality ("down"); how we hope to find Christ's "Wounds / in nozzles and containers"; how we must look for "His symbol at the door," in the "textures and contours" of the world. In looking for the up in the down, in asking how the eternal might make itself felt in the temporal—in seeing the world as sacramental—Jones comes to write his poem. The answer to Jones's question—What shall I write?—is something like: write of the theological task itself. Indeed, it is likely that Jones's poem arose from his reading of a theological thinker—more specifically, from his reading of Maritain's "The Purity of Art." In that essay, Maritain claims that art "suggests without conveying absolute knowledge, and expresses what our ideas are impotent to signify. *A, a, a*, exclaims Jeremias, *Domine Deus, ecce nescio loqui*. But song begins where speech breaks off, *exsultatio mentis prorumpens in vocem*."[33] As with Auden, we see how the reading of modern theology leads to the writing of modern poetry.

Jones's poem ends with a lament that modern technology cannot truly express "the Living God": "I have said to the perfected steel, be my sister and for the glassy towers I thought I felt some beginnings of His creature, but *A, a, a, Domine Deus*, my hands found the glazed work unrefined and the terrible crystal a stage-paste . . . *Eia, Domine Deus*." The glazed work and terrible crystal of the modern city are but a stage-paste, yet Jones's own poetic creation, unrefined and imperfect as it might be, is at least capable of gesturing towards God. The ellipsis followed by the exclamation of "*Eia, Domine Deus*" opens up a space for divine presence. The poet cannot find God in the nozzles and containers, so he must simply end with an expression of faith and longing for God's presence. For Jones, theology and poetry end up in the same place: charting the relationship between the transcendent and the immanent, believing that the one can house the other. Song begins, for both the theologian and poet, where speech breaks off.

"Ye cannot halve the Gospel of God's Grace"

Why did this particular constellation of poets become so interested in Christian theology at this particular moment in history? Of course, World War I played an important role in encouraging a return to religion, both for literature specifically and for society more generally. The butcheries of the war seemed to show up serious weaknesses in the modern, liberal viewpoint—its faith in the goodness of humanity and in historical progress, for instance. Christianity, with its doctrine of original sin and Christ's redeeming death, seemed both to account for human failure and to offer hope for a more lasting harmony.[34]

The story this book attempts to trace is, however, more complex than a return to religion brought about by cataclysmic world events. After all, the poets that I consider, these theological modernists, were not just interested in "religion," broadly conceived. They were interested in the specific mode of discourse called theology, and they were interested even more specifically in the kind of theology being written by their contemporaries. To understand why this particular kind of religious thinking would appeal to poets of the time, we need to look to intellectual history, moving back from the modernist period to a figure who, though Victorian, presaged in many ways the theological and literary currents of the interwar period: John Henry Newman. Though Joyce and Eliot, among others, admired Newman as a stylist, he would come to influence interwar theology primarily as a controversialist, as someone who stared down, with withering contempt, what Barth, Maritain, and Niebuhr saw as the most dangerous threat to doctrinal Christianity: religious liberalism.

We couldn't find a better place to begin to examine the nature of this purported threat than Newman's straightforwardly titled 1833 poem, "Liberalism." (Later, religious liberalism, at least in Catholic circles, would often be labeled "modernism.") Newman opens by sternly admonishing a growing segment of Christian believers who would winnow God's majesty, "halv[ing] the Gospel of God's Grace."[35] These believers, Newman writes, mark how the Gospel "spoke of peace, chastised desires, / Good-will and mercy," but they ignore its more powerful message of humankind's sinfulness and God's unmerited, transformative forgiveness. They hear, in short, how the Gospel speaks of this world but not how it speaks of the next; they heed its call for liberal kindness "But, as for zeal and quick-eyed sanctity, / And the dread depths of grace, ye pass'd them by."[36] The liberal message, according to Newman, leaches Christianity of both its true vigor ("zeal and quick-eyed sanctity") and its true terror ("dread depths of grace"). We are left with bloodless piety. Desire has been "chastised" but not reborn into holy action.

Why has liberal Christianity lost its pith and vigor? It is not because these liberal believers doubt the order that Christianity has bestowed upon a chaotic world. They have, after all, seen how "the Word refines all natures rude, / And tames the stirrings of the multitude."[37] And it is not, moreover, because they doubt the power and beauty of the Christian narrative. They have, Newman writes, "caught some echoes of its lore, / As heralded amid the joyous choirs." It is rather because these liberals, "in heart, / At best, are doubters whether [the Word] be true." They believe in Christianity's effects but doubt the truth claims from which these effects emerge; they believe in Christianity's aesthetic beauty but not in its doctrinal validity. In his *Apologia Pro Vita Sua*, Newman defines liberalism quite simply as "the anti-dogmatic principle and its developments."[38] Liberals, in Newman's view, refuse not specific dogmatic assertions but dogma as such. For Newman, this privileging of ethics over doctrine is a dangerous, even demonic, way to understand the Christian faith. Liberalism appears the "new-compass'd art / Of the ancient Foe," Satan, who now seems to extend his influence "O'er our own camp, and rules amid our friends."[39]

This liberal tendency to focus on humankind's "Good-will and mercy" rather than "God's grace" only spread in the decades after Newman's anguished poem. Religious thinkers of the nineteenth and early twentieth centuries, believing that the transcendent God of the Bible could not be accounted for in the light of science and biblical criticism, turned their sights to matters of this world. Religious feeling was emphasized over religious dogma. Schleiermacher claimed in *On Religion* that "religion's essence is neither thinking nor acting, but intuition and feeling," while Matthew Arnold echoed this sentiment about sentiment in arguing that "the power of Christianity has been in the immense emotion which it has excited."[40] If God were to be seen and understood, it would be by immersing oneself in human experience and feeling; God was immanent in and through the world, not infinitely above it.

Religious liberals emphasized unity between God and humanity, proclaiming faith in human progress and marginalizing sinfulness: Arnold claimed that the "object of religion is conduct," and William James defined religion as the "feelings, acts, and experiences of individual men in their solitude, so far as they apprehend themselves to stand in relation to whatever they may consider the divine."[41] It seemed that questions of dogma were largely beside the point— or, at the very least, were subservient to the felt experience of divinity. As James C. Livingston writes, "Schleiermacher means that religious feeling is not derived, not the product of ratiocination—it is an immediate *intuition*."[42] And so for religious liberalism as a whole: feeling and ethics displaced dogma and authority as the proper locus of religious investigation. Here, for instance, is how T. S. Eliot summed up the liberal position, as exemplified for him by Arnold: "The total effect of Arnold's philosophy is to set up Culture in the place of Religion, and to leave Religion to be laid waste by the anarchy of feeling. And Culture is a term which each man not only may interpret as he pleases, but must indeed interpret as he can."[43]

Thomas Carlyle's chapter "Everlasting Yea" in *Sartor Resartus* (1836) crystallizes this privileging of religious experience over religious dogma. There, we hear that the true believer must pass through disbelief on his way to belief, and that this movement from negation to affirmation is above all a matter of God's presence "being felt in my own Heart." This affective response to divinity, the character Teufelsdröckh claims, "is Belief; all else is Opinion."[44] Belief does not exist—cannot exist—until it becomes felt experience: "Speculation is by nature endless, formless, a vortex amid vortices: only by a felt indubitable certainty of Experience" does it "find any centre to revolve around."[45] Without grounding in lived experience, speculation is chaotic, fragmented, and ultimately meaningless. With lived experience, speculation is replete with significance, a source of certainty and grounding rather than dizzying formlessness.

If nineteenth-century religious thinking concerned itself with immanence and intuition, then interwar theology marked a return to something very different: absolute transcendence. Religious liberalism, of course, lived on— and continues to live on—both among everyday believers and among preachers, theologians, and artists. But, in the thinking of many philosophical and theological elites, this emphasis on ethics and immanence over theology and transcendence was seriously challenged immediately by and after World War I. In 1917, the German Lutheran theologian Rudolf Otto published *Das Heilige* (translated into English in 1923 as *The Idea of the Holy*). This popular work—it has never been out of print—introduced Otto's famous definition of the "numinous": the nonrational, mysterious force that undergirds all religious experience. Otto describes this feeling as the "*mysterium tremendum et fascinans*": the awful terror and fascination that one feels in the face of the holy. Writing against religious liberalism's focus on immanence, Otto emphasizes that the numinous is a feeling of absolute transcendence. The numinous is "the Wholly Other," "that which is hidden and esoteric, that which is beyond conception or understanding, extraordinary and unfamiliar"—the terrifying, the mysterious, the "aweful."[46] If religious liberalism tried to strip away the mystery of religious experience, then Otto tried to put it back in.

Still, despite Otto's focus on the "Wholly Other" nature of the numinous, his writing, like that of religious liberals, centered on experience and feeling. We feel the numinous in moments of intense rapture, and this feeling, not the transcendent source of this feeling, is the proper subject of religious inquiry. The English title of Otto's book gets at this fact: the book's subject isn't the holy, but the idea or feeling or experience of the holy. The nature of the numinous, Otto writes, "is such that it grips or stirs the human mind with this and that determinate affective state," and Otto's book sought to analyze these affective states.[47] In other words, Otto remained, like Schleiermacher, an emotionalist. (He was also a universalist: according to Otto, people experienced the same feeling of numinousness across cultures and across creeds, in antiquity and in modernity.)

This focus on a feeling of sublime otherness that could be proved on the pulses helps explain Otto's continued popularity, even into the present, and it also sharply differentiates him from another interwar theologian who tried to reclaim the "Wholly Other" for religion: the neo-Orthodox Protestant theologian Karl Barth. Barth, even more than Otto, emphasized that God did not reside in the human breast but was "unapproachably distant and unutterably strange," the transcendent Other who is the ground of humanity's being yet is completely unlike it.[48] Again and again, Barth harshly criticized liberalism's religious subjectivism, defining himself against Schleiermacher and criticizing liberalism's supposed focus on intuition and feeling as the one route to God.[49] In the preface to the famous second edition of his *Epistle to the Romans*, Barth described his theology in this way: "If I have a system, it is limited to a recognition of what Kierkegaard calls the 'infinite qualitative distinction' between time and eternity, and to my regarding this as possessing negative as well as positive significance: 'God is in heaven, and thou art on earth.' "[50] Barth's theology in *Epistle to the Romans* and other early works has been termed "dialectical" because it emphasizes the absolute gap separating creator and creation, a gap that can never be crossed by humanity but only by God in his infinite, unmerited, and unexpected love. Barth's focus on the chasm between a perfect, loving God and his abject, sinful creation was so unrelenting that his theology has often been characterized not just as dialectical but as Manichean. The religious liberal risks losing sight of divinity by halving the gospel of God's grace, Newman argues, but Barth's dialectical theologian risks losing sight of this world by looking exclusively to God's absolute transcendence.

Barth's work fundamentally transformed the theological landscape. Barth is widely considered the most influential theologian of the twentieth century, and one of the most important in the history of Christianity. His first work, *Epistle to the Romans*, fell, as Karl Adam famously put it, like "a bomb on the playground of the theologians."[51] Above all, Barth and his neo-Orthodox followers signaled a return to revelation as the proper subject of religious thought. In order to do real theology, they suggested, you had to take account of the utter strangeness of transcendence. Gone was the moralism of religious liberalism; in its place, Reinhold Niebuhr, for example, claimed that the sinful self must be violently "crucified," "shattered and destroyed."[52] Gone was the vision of man as perfectible; Barth instead proclaimed original sin as "THE DOCTRINE which emerges from all honest study of human history."[53] Barth embraced

St. Anselm's definition of theology as *fides quaerens intellectum*, faith seeking understanding, and Barth emphasized the middle term, "seeking." Theology was a seeking that understood that it would never fully understand; it was "broken thought," in Barth's words, which knew of its brokenness but persisted anyway, anchored by faith in God's revelation; it was a discipline that taught one how to ask the right questions rather than providing the right answers.[54]

Another contemporary theological movement, neo-Thomism, similarly reacted against Schleiermacher and religious liberalism. Catholic neo-Thomists defined themselves as "critical realists": "Against the idealism of Kant," Stephen Schloesser writes, "Thomism promised access to the real, not merely mental constructs; against the naïve realism of Auguste Comte, it promised access to something unchanging beneath the epiphenomena."[55] For Maritain and other neo-Thomists, metaphysics preceded epistemology. They believed that we intellectually intuit "being" from all concrete experience, and this intuition, Maritain writes, "open[s] to the mind an infinite supra-observable field."[56] Thomism's metaphysics of participation suggests that all of creation participates in God and, because of this participation, all of creation communicates God's being—not perfectly or directly, but analogously (hence the *analogia entis*, or analogy of being, that was so crucial to Aquinas and his later followers). In 1953, Maritain published *Approaches to God*, a philosophical primer that builds upon Aquinas's proofs of God's existence and stresses, in each chapter, how the intellect in its various forms—both the prephilosophical intellect and the philosophical intellect—allows us to approach God. But it is always the intellect, not the emotions, that serves for Maritain as the way towards God. Neo-Thomists displayed "an attitude of scepticism towards those who claim that religion is exclusively an affair of religious experience."[57] Exclusively, yes, and even primarily; the neo-Thomists argued that the mind had been neglected for too long by too many. In reviving the writings of Aquinas, neo-Thomists like Maritain and D'Arcy argued that sense and intellect should work together, that religion was not just a matter of feeling but the use of a subjective mind to move towards objective truth.

There are certainly important differences between Protestant neo-Orthodoxy (especially that of early Barth) and Catholic neo-Thomism (especially that of Maritain). Neo-Orthodoxy focused on humanity's fallenness, God's transcendence, and biblical revelation, whereas neo-Thomism stressed humanity's reason, the ways that God could be approached through introspection, and the sacraments. Most dramatically, natural theology—the branch of theology that arises not from revealed truth but from ordinary, earthly experience—was, for Maritain, one of the primary means by which we come to know God. For Barth, it was blasphemy, a category mistake that confused creator with creation.

The similarities between the two movements are also, however, illuminating. Both neo-Orthodox and neo-Thomist thinkers claimed to expose the weaknesses of religious liberalism and the myth of progress. Both criticized subjectivism and a notion of religious experience centered solely in the self. Both emphasized the need for rigorous doctrinal articulation, and both gained admirers in the most sophisticated intellectual and literary circles of the modernist period. If, as Eliot wrote, religious liberalism sought to "divorce Religion from thought," then figures like Barth and Maritain sought to reunite the two again.[58] David Jasper claims that in Barth we see a movement from "theology to theological thinking," from a collection of old texts to be mastered to a vibrant, provisional method of knowing the world.[59] It was this focus on theology as a mode of thoughtful exploration that so appealed to the poetic creators of theological modernism.

Why Theology? Why Modernism?

If theology was so important to modernist poetry, why has it been ignored for so long? Part of this is because of the long critical tendency to see the modernist period as one in which God is finally put to rest and to see all modernist interest in religion as truly an interest in aesthetics. Stephen Dedalus in *A Portrait of the Artist as a Young Man* famously makes this conflation of the aesthetic and the religious explicit when he declares the artist "like the God of the creation," "within or behind or beyond or above his handiwork."[60] Even when Stephen mentions Thomas Aquinas, it is to outline an aesthetic theory rather than to engage theological issues per se: "Aquinas says: *ad pulcritudinem tria requiruntur, integritas, consonantia, claritas.* I translate it so: *Three things are needed for beauty, wholeness, harmony, and radiance.*"[61]

Scholars of modernism have followed Stephen's lead in translating the religious into aesthetic terms ever since.[62] The narrative here is familiar. God/metaphysics dies and the modernist artist steps into the breach, giving meaning to existence through the well-wrought urn of the aesthetic object or through the aesthetic mode itself. God isn't so much killed off as replaced by something else.[63] But such an approach ignores the crucial fact that many modern poets did not see any such substitutionary logic at play in their own work or thinking. For them, theological questions needed to be approached *as* theological questions, and so, if we want to be good historicists, we likewise have to take seriously the intellectual enterprise of Christian theology.[64]

In taking theology as seriously as the modernists took it, this book looks both to the institutions and to individual works of interwar poetry. In Chapter 2, I reconstruct the regular presence of theological discussions within the networks formed by interwar literary periodicals—so regular a presence that, I argue, to be a reader of modernist magazines meant to be a reader of contemporary theological debates. Eliot's *Criterion*, for instance, often seemed as much a theological review as a literary magazine: the works of Karl Barth, Jacques Maritain, and Reinhold Niebuhr were reviewed regularly and with great sophistication, and contributors included prominent neo-Thomist theologians and philosophers like Etienne Gilson, Martin D'Arcy, and Maritain himself. In each subsequent chapter, I pair a writer with a theologian or theologians: Eliot with Barth; Jones with Maritain and Maurice de la Taille; and Auden with Niebuhr, Kierkegaard, and Charles Williams.

These pairings are determined not only by intellectual affinities, though these exist. Nor are they based on stylistic similarities (though a case could be made that, as *The Waste Land* is the great poetic expression of the modernist movement, so Barth's *Epistle to the Romans* is its great theological expression). Rather, in each case the pairing is grounded in personal, though not merely personal, connections. Eliot knew Barth's theology, having helped introduce it to the English-speaking literary world through his editing of the *Criterion*. Jones thanked de la Taille in the acknowledgments of *The Anathemata* and concluded his most direct analysis of the relationship between aesthetics and theology, the 1955 essay "Art and Sacrament," with a quotation from *Mysterium Fidei*. Auden counted Reinhold and Ursula Niebuhr among his closest friends in the United States and claimed that Charles Williams's "personal sanctity," his incapability of "doing or thinking anything base or unloving," helped bring about Auden's own return to the Christian faith.[65]

Moreover, each chapter goes beyond a mere comparison or historical narrative to engage with large-scale questions—about poetic form and intellectual history, about the material circulation of texts and the publics they create. In Chapter 2, this question is: Can theology speak across confessional boundaries? In other words, what can an Anglo-Catholic learn from Protestant theology? It also considers what is at stake in thinking about theology not merely as a series of propositions but also as discourse, as a particular kind of language deployed in reviews, essays, and poetry, and how interwar periodicals like the *Criterion* cultivated both a certain kind of literary reader and a certain kind of theological reader. Chapter 3 asks, what is the relationship between nature and grace, between time and eternity, and how does the notion of revelation affect Christian poetic practice? Chapter 4 asks, what is the nature of sacrament, and how does this relate to the broader project of human sign-making? Chapter 5 asks, what is the relationship between theology and history, and how can irony, as both a mode and a style, serve as the basis for an affirmative poetics and theology?

The answers that each poet offers to these questions vary. Auden, for instance, saw theology primarily as a critical tool, showing up the pretenses of modern liberalism, whereas Eliot saw the "eternal scheme" of Christianity as offering a coherent "framework of mythology and theology and philosophy" for understanding the world.[66] But what these theological modernists all agreed upon was that theology spoke to many of their own formal and thematic concerns. It was, as Eliot put it, "the one most exciting and adventurous subject left for a jaded mind."[67]

Coda

An entirely different study could have been written about modernism's engagement with non-Christian religion. Indeed, many such studies *have* been written.[68] The influence of non-Christian religion on modernism was real and lasting, and to argue for the importance of Reinhold Niebuhr to Auden's late poetry, for instance, is not to say that Martin Buber was unimportant. But there was something particular and compelling about Christian theology for the figures I consider. After all, while their greatest religious poems occasionally alluded to Eastern texts and religions, they centered on things like the Incarnation and the Eucharist—on specifically Christian doctrines and concepts that they read and thought about through the work of Karl Barth, Maurice de la Taille, and others. Christian theology was not the only religious discourse these poets were interested in, but it was the religious discourse that they read most regularly and deeply, and it was the religious discourse that proved most important in their formation as poets and believers.

Finally, what exactly is "theology"? How can we differentiate theology from other areas of religious study: philosophy of religion, for example, or the sociology of religion, or the aesthetics of religion? What marks Barth's claim that "the conception of an indirect revelation in nature, in history and in our self-consciousness is destroyed by the recognition of grace" as a distinctively theological statement?[69]

Throughout, I take theology to mean the systematic investigation of revealed truths; it is the use of human reason to try to understand things beyond human understanding. So, whereas a sociologist might study what effects religious belief have for communal identity and a historian might examine how religious beliefs affected political institutions in a particular period, a theologian asks, given that God has revealed himself in this world, what *is* religious belief? The theologian takes what she sees as revealed truth—Christ's atonement for humankind's sins, for instance—and builds outwards, using the tools of logic and dialectical reasoning: What other beliefs does belief in revealed truth entail? What kind of epistemology is necessary if we are to preserve belief in revealed truth? One way to describe the difference would be to say that religious researchers—sociologists, historians, and political philosophers—study people devoted to God; theologians study God and, given God's nature, articulate what devotion to God should look like.

Even with this relatively narrow definition in place, though, "theology" can be a slippery term. It is safe to say that a papal encyclical or a monograph published by a professor of theology would qualify as "theology." But what of a magazine article that discusses the Incarnation and its effects on artistic creation? or a generalist writing on the relationship between faith and reason? Given these gray areas, it might seem more appropriate to talk about "theological discourse" than about "theology"; to talk about the deployment of language about sin, salvation, and the nature of religious belief not just in work that is recognizable as "theology" (Barth's *Epistle to the Romans*, for instance) but also in various genres and publishing contexts—poetry, novels, reviews, essays, popular music, radio addresses.

I choose to use the word "theology" throughout this book, however, for two primary reasons. First, because the concept of "theology" as its own well-defined, intellectually rigorous discipline, set off from sociological or aesthetic understandings of religion and religious experience, was important to Eliot, Auden, and Jones. These modern poets prided themselves on being readers of theology, in large part because the term "theology" meant for them not just a body of work but a distinctive way of approaching religion: through the intellect and through doctrine. Second, I use the term "theology" because using it helps maintain the distinction between the theology that Eliot, Auden, and Jones were reading and the poetry that they were writing. These writers would have been happy to say that they wrote "theological poetry," but they would have resisted any attempt to describe their poetry as "theology." The border between poetry and theology is sometimes hard to locate in a work like *Four Quartets* or *The Anathemata*. But it is there, and part of the purpose of this project is to chart the points at which these two discourses mix, mingle, and ultimately part ways.

CHAPTER TWO

The "Living Theology"
of the *Criterion*

Nothing will give me more pleasure than to continue this debate; for theology is the one most exciting and adventurous subject left for a jaded mind. —T. S. ELIOT, 1930 letter to Paul Elmer More

T. S. Eliot was a brilliant promoter, possessing a keen sense for how to generate—and then capitalize upon—publicity for his work and that of other, sympathetic artists. Writing in 1919 to his former Harvard professor, J. H. Woods, for instance, Eliot described the current state of his "reputation" in literary London: "There are only two ways in which a writer can become important— to write a great deal, and have his writings appear everywhere, or to write very little. It is a question of temperament. I write very little, and I should not become more powerful by increasing my output. My reputation in London is built upon one small volume of verse, and is kept up by printing two or three more poems in a year. The only thing that matters is that these should be perfect in their kind, so that each should be an event."[1] Here Eliot, at the time an employee at Lloyds Bank, displays his awareness of the importance of supply and demand not just to the financial but also to the literary marketplace. If the poet is to make himself known, then he must either flood the market or starve the market; he must overwhelm with his presence or tantalize with his absence so that each appearance becomes "an event." As Lawrence Rainey puts it, Eliot "understood the protocols of avant-garde publishing" through and through, and he put this understanding to good use.[2]

Three years later, in 1922, Eliot's business acumen with regards to literary matters faced another challenge. *Prufrock and Other Observations* was five years old—ancient, according to the standards of avant-garde publishing. *The Waste Land*, with much help from Ezra Pound, was in its final, chiseled form, but Eliot now had to decide how to share his poem with the world in a way that would maximize readerly interest. Eliot's management of the release of *The Waste Land* provides a master class in literary promotion. First, he did a slow rollout, sharing the manuscript with Richard Aldington, Aldous Huxley, Virginia Woolf and Leonard Woolf, and others. Then, he began contacting American publishers, sussing out interest and playing one publisher against the other.[3] Eventually, the poem would be published in two literary magazines: the

Dial in the United States and Eliot's own *Criterion* in England. Yet Eliot knew that publishing his new work in such little magazines was not enough. As he put it, *The Waste Land* "would make a much more distinct impression and attract much more attention if published as a book."[4] So, in order to generate enough pages for book publication and provide a scholarly apparatus for its interpretation—in other words, in order to insure that the poem's publication would qualify as "an event" and make a "distinct impression"—Eliot went about supplying his famous author's notes. Again, Eliot's business sense is acute. Identifying, cultivating, and then instructing a potential audience was Eliot's way throughout his career as poet, critic, and editor.[5]

But no venture showed Eliot's savvy so clearly as his stewardship of the *Criterion*. From its first issue in 1922 (an issue that made itself an event by featuring the much-anticipated first appearance of *The Waste Land*) to its last in 1939, the *Criterion* prided itself on its small, discriminating readership. Circulation never rose above one thousand, and the magazine's very name indicated that it had little interest in appealing to a mass audience by lowering its exacting (some would say stuffy) standards. But remaining solvent while appealing to such a small readership meant that Eliot often had to be creative. He was a hands-on editor, involved at almost every stage of production: soliciting contributions, editing essays, worrying over layout, wining and dining potential patrons. In December of 1922, he claimed to be so "infernally busy" with the magazine that he was "living a double or triple life."[6] The overlap between these lives—more specifically, between Eliot's life as a banker and his life as an editor—could be productive; the lessons he learned at Lloyds Bank were applied at the *Criterion*. As Jason Harding argues, much of Eliot's editing time was actually spent obsessing over money and "worr[ying] over the commercial imperatives of finance and circulation: cultivating patrons, attempting to promote sales, struggling to reduce expenses, securing copy, and so forth."[7]

In 1927, Eliot's worries over circulation and expenses were at a high point. The *Criterion* was struggling financially, as the magazine's recent shift from a quarterly to a monthly format had caused production costs to balloon. In order to boost interest and sales, Eliot resorted to one of his old tricks: picking a fight with another literary luminary.[8] To do so, he looked to another little magazine that was also troubled financially. At the time, J. Middleton Murry's *Adelphi* was hemorrhaging contributors and money, so much so that Murry considered resigning as editor.[9] The two magazines both needed attention and sales, and a high-stakes literary argument seemed the best way to secure them.

On its surface, the Eliot-Murry debate, which played out over a few months in the pages of the *Criterion*, was about a subject familiar to readers of the time: romanticism versus classicism. Eliot, unsurprisingly, defended the classicist position and criticized Murry as a romantic; Murry, in turn, argued that his position was not in fact that of a romantic and that Eliot's confusion arose from a philosophical and aesthetic misunderstanding. To get at this misunderstanding, Murry looked to three faculties of the mind: reason, intuition, and intelligence. He argued that Eliot's problem lay in his impoverished sense of what "reason" actually meant. Reason is not, Murry argues, pure, cold rationality; it is not the instrumental and calculating mind at work manipulating the world around it. Rather, "reason" should be understood as "generated by the friction between intuition and intelligence," a generative friction achieved not by philosophical introspection but by artistic creation: "In the modern epoch it is not the poet who must study the philosopher, as Goethe knew when he put Kant aside, but the philosopher the poet."[10] Eliot disagreed, arguing that Murry's "reason" was just another way of saying "feeling." It was not a synthesis of intuition and intelligence but a privileging of the former over the latter. Murry's position, Eliot wrote, made "poetry a substitute for philosophy and religion," in the process "falsif[ying] not only philosophy and religion, but poetry too."[11]

This argument over classicism and romanticism, intelligence and intuition, is well known to modernist scholars. But if we actually go back and read the *Criterion* essays in which this particular argument took place, we see something that might surprise us: the bulk of Murry's opening salvo, and much of Eliot's response, concerned not aesthetics but theology.[12] More specifically, Eliot and Murry both seemed to think that, in order to understand what was at stake in describing a writer's sensibility as romantic or classicist, what was needed first was an understanding of Thomism, the philosophical and theological school associated with Thomas Aquinas and reenergized in the twentieth century by Catholic figures like Jacques Maritain and Etienne Gilson. In fact, Murry devoted the first eleven pages of his piece to identifying the problems of "Thomist epistemology" and, at greater length, the errors of "the Thomist metaphysic, the theology and the ontology of the *Summa Theologiæ*."[13] In this argument about modernist self-understanding, more space was given, it turns out, to theology than to poetry.

Our modern understandings of intelligence and intuition have been shaped by Aquinas, Murry argues, and so, if we are to understand these faculties correctly, we have to go back to the source and ask some basic questions: What did Thomism have to say about the relationship between faith and reason? Between what could be perceived and what could be known? Between the material and immaterial worlds? Murry found Aquinas's synthesis of these things—faith and reason, intuitition and intellect—appropriate for the medieval mind but wildly inadequate for the modern mind. Why? As James Matthew Wilson puts it, "precisely because modern man's experience no longer corresponded to the Thomist system of metaphysics, which had been itself only a projection of the subjective experience of medieval man."[14] Murry argues that Thomist epistemology depended upon a Christian metaphysics of Creator and creation (as he puts it, "Thomism without Christian orthodoxy is a tree without a root"), and, since a Christian metaphysics no longer holds water (this seems an obvious point to Murry), neither can Thomist epistemology.[15] To accept Thomism is to accept a "metaphysical theory of knowledge," one that "is remote from the facts of experience."[16]

Though disavowing any expertise in Aquinas or his heirs, Eliot agreed that Thomism was central to the issues at hand.[17] He simply disagreed with Murry's understanding of Thomism and, more generally, with his unsophisticated "attitude toward 'faith.' "[18] If you are going to rule out Thomist epistemology because it depends upon a metaphysical account of existence, Eliot argues, then you are also going to have to rule out "such modern theories of knowledge as those of [Alexius] Meinong, and [Edmund] Husserl, and that which [Bertrand] Russell holds or once held." Why? Because *all* of these systems have a metaphysical grounding of one kind or another: "These theories are neither physical nor psychological, and therefore have singularly little reference to the actual process of knowing in Mr. Murry's experience."[19] Without metaphysics, all you have is "pure naturalism," and Eliot finds such a thing "a *fatalism* which is wholly destructive."[20] Hoping to keep the debate alive, Eliot printed another response to Murry's essay, this time by the Jesuit theologian Martin D'Arcy. D'Arcy, like Eliot, criticized Murry not on aesthetic but on metaphysical and theological grounds. Murry had, D'Arcy wrote, a "very inaccurate definition" of faith, not realizing that modern followers of Aquinas were realists, up "to the task of seizing the concrete reality in all its warm and fresh individuality."[21] In fact, D'Arcy argued, this philosophical realism—a commitment to the concrete existence of the world independent of our perceptions of it—was a foundation of Aquinas's thought and that of his later inheritors. To be a Thomist wasn't, as Murry seemed to suggest, to be an otherworldly mystic, removed from the actualities of sensory experience. Rather, it was to be committed absolutely to the particularities of this world, to perception and cognition in all their concreteness.

Eliot's management of this public quarrel was brilliant and ruthless. He agreed to talk over Murry's essay with him before printing it, but then reneged, fearing that if Murry revised his essay it would not generate enough outrage from D'Arcy and others.[22] One must ask, though. Why would Eliot, a superb marketer, so carefully instigate and prolong this neo-Thomist squabble at a critical moment in his magazine's history? The decision implies, first, that he felt confident in his readers' familiarity with neo-Thomism; and second, that he thought his readers would actually be excited by internal, definitional debates about the nature of this theological movement. Eliot believed, in short, that his readers would be interested not just in purely aesthetic questions, and not just in aesthetic-theological questions, but also in theological questions as such. Was neo-Thomism a unified, rigid body of religious dogma that had to be accepted whole or not at all, as Murry argued? Or was it more a mode than a system, a way of approaching God and the world that, Eliot wrote, is "admirable for me only in so far as I can find some crumbs of truth in it"?[23] Was neo-Thomism a way of reducing religion to intelligence or a way of enfolding intelligence within religion? Did it make holiness reasonable, or did it make reason holy?

It tells us something about this particular moment in literary and cultural history that these were the kinds of questions Eliot posed in an attempt to excite his readership. In the 1930s, to be a reader of the *Criterion*, Britain's most influential literary magazine, was also to be a reader of contemporary theology. Interwar periodical networks oftentimes doubled as interwar theological networks.

"A bomb on the playground of the theologians"

No literary magazine of the 1920s and 1930s cast such a large critical shadow— or displayed such an intense and sustained interest in theological matters—as Eliot's *Criterion*. Jason Harding, in the best book-length study of the magazine, has drawn attention to the *Criterion*'s central place in interwar literary culture: "More responsive than the printed book, the subtle and intricate reciprocity of literary journalism allowed Eliot to address and even, upon occasions, to shape the agenda of inter-war cultural criticism."[24] Even contemporaries frustrated with the stodginess of the *Criterion* could not deny its importance. In a tribute printed in *New Verse* following the *Criterion*'s demise in 1939, the usually hostile Geoffrey Grigson declared that "from *The Criterion* next to no English writer of value was ever excluded. We can be grateful indeed to Mr. Eliot. He was catholic and serious."[25] Most of Eliot's peers—and most later critics—would agree with Grigson that the *Criterion* was above all else serious, both in the kind of writing it published and in the kind of intellectual culture it envisioned.

Many would disagree, however, with Grigson's claim that Eliot's editing practices were catholic—that is, broad and sympathetic—at least in the magazine's final years. Indeed, scholars have echoed Denis Donoghue's claim that the *Criterion* divides "with desolate precision" into two phases. According to this view, from 1922 until around 1930, the *Criterion* gave voice to what Donoghue calls "the general sense of a new literature," publishing Eliot's *The Waste Land*, the first English translation of Marcel Proust, and poems by Yeats, Moore, and Pound.[26] After 1930, though—the year in which Pound himself characterized "Criterionism" as "a diet of dead crow" featuring "dead and moribund writing"—the journal seemed to become a clearinghouse for conservative politics and religious orthodoxy.[27] In particular, the *Criterion* appeared to be an unofficial mouthpiece for Catholic neo-Thomism. The magazine regularly featured essays by Catholic writers, and its book reviews praised the work of such neo-Thomists as Jacques Maritain and Etienne Gilson. By 1930, Laura Riding went so far as to accuse the *Criterion* of being "an exclusive Thomist club," and Eliot felt compelled to respond in print to the charge that his magazine was "an organ for a 'Frenchified' doctrine called neo-Thomism."[28]

This narrative of decline, however, ignores the fact that, in its final years, the supposedly close-minded *Criterion* was open in the deepest sense, displaying a sophisticated engagement with contemporary Protestant *and* Catholic theology, with neo-Orthodoxy *and* neo-Thomism.[29] In this chapter, I trace the presence of neo-Orthodox theology within the *Criterion* throughout the 1930s, showing that Karl Barth, whose radical Protestantism would appear to be at odds with Eliot's orthodox Anglo-Catholicism, was one of the *Criterion*'s major theological interlocutors from 1934 onwards. In particular, the *Criterion*'s "Books of the Quarter" section, a rich and surprisingly understudied resource for scholars interested in modernist culture, reads like a Barthian salon, with the theologian's ideas—about God's absolute transcendence, about original sin, about religious liberalism's many and insidious errors—appearing in issue after issue.

Despite political and confessional differences, *Criterion* regulars like Christopher Dawson (a Catholic) and George Every (an Anglican) looked to Barth to define their own positions on revelation and grace and to reconfigure the place of theology within interwar Europe.[30] They admired Barth's focus on the antithesis between the divine and the human, as well as his vision of theology as a dynamic, inherently unfinishable mode of inquiry—what Barth called the "forming of principally incomplete thoughts and statements, in which every answer is once again a question."[31] In essays, but especially in its "Books of the Quarter" section, *Criterion* writers praised the daring of Barth's dialectical method, celebrated his defiance of Nazism, and reiterated his focus on original sin. The *Criterion*, in short, was a site at which modern Christian theology generally, and not just conservative Anglo-Catholicism specifically, could be discussed alongside literature.

Indeed, the *Criterion* wasn't the only literary periodical to facilitate such theological conversations. In the pages of the *Nation* and the *New Republic*, Auden reviewed Niebuhr and Kierkegaard; in the pages of the *Times Literary Supplement*, Eliot and Murry reviewed Maritain and others. To understand modern poetry, we have to examine the periodical networks out of which modern poetry emerged—the magazines that poets read and wrote for, the journals they published their own creative and critical work in. And to look at this periodical culture in detail is to recover the outsized role that theology played within it.

Paratextual Publics

While Denis Donoghue has identified 1930 as a precise dividing point for the *Criterion*, another year, 1933, could serve just as well. This was the year in which Sir Edwyn Hoskyns first translated Karl Barth's second edition of *Epistle to the Romans* into English. From this point on, the review pages of the *Criterion* facilitated a lively debate in which Barth's theology was frequently quoted, admired, and argued with.

A January 30, 1937, letter from Marianne Moore to Elizabeth Bishop puts this fact into relief. Moore begins her letter by relating the high jinks of a cat owned by Bishop and temporarily cared for by Moore. Moore then describes a coconut given to her by a friend: "Like Friar Tuck's leather bottle, when shaken [the coconut] gurgles in a way that makes me impatient to get to the milk; I removed the last fragment of husk today, but a neighbor said on no account to open the inner nut until it had ripened."[32] Finally, Moore mentions that she is including with her letter a copy of the *Criterion*: "*The Criterion* is not to be returned. The Frank O'Connor story gives me a great deal to think about—perhaps *too* much. Please ignore the review of Karl Barth which seems to me exactly like the fibres that surrounded the cocoa-nut."[33]

A more perfect encapsulation of the *Criterion*'s status at the time would be hard to imagine. There are the casual swipes at the magazine (it is not to be returned; its stuffy reviews obscure whatever nourishing work it might contain), which are in tension with Moore's having forwarded it to another poet and, moreover, her having taken the time to read the 199-page issue. (Maybe even from front to back: O'Connor's story and Barth's review are separated by more than 150 pages.) One is reminded of Ezra Pound, who enjoyed mocking the magazine's theological commitments yet struck up a correspondence with Etienne Gilson after reading a review by the neo-Thomist in the *Criterion*;[34] and of Wyndham Lewis, who likewise complained of the magazine's insufficiencies yet wrote to Martin D'Arcy after reading his theological/philosophical essays in the *Criterion*'s pages.[35]

Moving back to Moore's letter, it is striking that, of all the books reviewed in the issue, Moore singles out a review of Barth's work to mention to Bishop. Her casual reference to Barth belies the relative obscurity of the theologian at the time.[36] In 1937, Barth was a well-known if oft-misunderstood figure in English-speaking theological circles. It was not until 1962, however, when he appeared on the cover of *Time* magazine, that Barth attained truly popular acclaim (or at least some approximation of it). Why does Moore have such confidence in Bishop's familiarity with the Swiss theologian? To what extent did Barth have a public by this time, and to what extent did this public overlap with the public of magazines like the *Criterion*?

A public, Michael Warner argues, is "a kind of practical fiction," a "social entity" that is created precisely in the act of its being addressed *as* a social entity. "Its reality," Warner writes, "lies in just this reflexivity by which an addressable object is conjured into being in order to enable the very discourse that gives it existence."[37] For a magazine to address its public in the form of an editorial, for instance, it must simultaneously imagine that this public exists (after all, an address must be directed towards an addressee) and also forget that this public has been imagined. In the process of addressing and forgetting, the conjuring trick has been pulled off: the public has been made real, or at least as real as it ever can be. Warner goes on to claim that publics necessarily are constituted and defined by textual production and circulation, for "without the idea of texts that can be picked up at different times and in different places by otherwise unrelated people, we would not imagine a public as an entity that embraces all the users of that text."[38] Paratextual elements such as letters to the editor—elements that, through self-reference, describe the magazine as a regular topic of discourse—are an essential means by which a magazine brings its public into existence.[39]

The *Criterion* ably employed both text and paratext to, in Warner's more general terms, "characterize [the magazine's] own space of consumption."[40] Eliot printed essays stoking controversies with other magazines, articles that pointed to previous *Criterion* articles, and advertisements for works by *Criterion* contributors.[41] In fact, it was largely the success of such self-reflexive, public-generating strategies that opened the magazine up to criticism by figures like Pound. Pound could talk about "Criterionism" because the magazine had so effectively imagined the public that consumed and contributed to it. Before examining the actual text of the *Criterion*'s reviews of Barth's theology, then, we might look briefly at the magazine's paratextual elements. These features, which primed contemporary readers before they encountered any content, allow us to see the extent to which the *Criterion*'s public was defined as a Barth-reading public.

Several aspects of the magazine remained consistent from its first appearance, in 1922, to its final issue, in 1939. Each issue contained several essays of 10 to 15 pages as well as a few poems, short stories, and essays. Until January 1931, a "Commentary," written by Eliot, immediately followed the title page. After this issue, Eliot's editorials moved, coming after the opening critical essays and creative work but before the review section. (The magazine was still, of course, publicly associated with Eliot. "Edited by T. S. Eliot" appeared prominently on each issue's cover/title page after 1926.) Despite these regular features, however, one thing did change dramatically over the *Criterion*'s seventeen-year run: the magazine's size. The first volume, published in 1922, offered 102 pages of content, with no advertisements. The final 1939 volume, on the other hand, was a bloated 220 pages, with 10 full pages of advertisements, hawking everything from Faber & Faber's latest publications to luxury cruises. This dramatic growth was largely the result of an ever-expanding review section. The July 1924 issue saw the first "Books of the Quarter" section. Reviews of foreign periodicals soon followed, as did, at various times, a "Music Chronicle," a "Broadcasting Chronicle," and an "Art Chronicle." By the 1930s, reviews often took up close to 100 pages.

The *Criterion*'s title page reflected this change in content. While the first issue's title page was relatively sparse in text, merely listing the titles and authors of the issue's seven major pieces, later editions were text-crammed. The January 1934 cover, for instance, in which a review of Barth appears, lists title and author for the issue's seven major pieces but also for each of its fourteen book reviews. By 1934, the *Criterion* also used more expensive yellow card stock for its cover and better paper throughout. While the first issue promoted a stripped-down aesthetic in both its design and in its masterpiece of compression, *The Waste Land*, later issues revealed a different purpose. By the 1930s, the *Criterion* was less a magazine devoted to publishing a specific type of literature than a magazine devoted to the discussion of a specific view of culture.[42]

With the January 1934 issue, the one in which a review of Barth appears, we immediately see the growing importance of the magazine's "Books of the Quarter" section. As mentioned above, the cover lists fourteen different reviews, each with its own page number. (Other articles do not have such page citations.) The reviews are listed in one large, continuous block, with the reviewers' names in slightly larger font than the titles under review. Generally, the cover did not include the names of the authors to be reviewed. Focusing on the reviewer rather than the reviewed was a shrewd marketing decision on Eliot's part: contributors to the "Books of the Quarter" section included well-known writers such as Pound, Moore, and Auden.

Interestingly, the only reviewed author to be named on the cover of the January 1934 issue is Karl Barth. The final item under "Books of the Quarter" reads, "Barth on The Epistle to the Romans: (page 34) *reviewed by* Norman W. Porteous."[43] What are we to make of the appearance of Barth's name here? When the proper name of the reviewed author was included on the *Criterion*'s title page, it was almost always either a widely recognized literary or cultural figure (A. E. Housman, J. Middleton Murry, and Sir James Frazer, for instance), or a much lesser-known theologian (for example, Etienne Gilson). Three reasons present themselves for the inclusion of Barth's name: first, simply listing *Epistle to the Romans* would make it seem as if the magazine were reprinting the sixth book of the New Testament; or, second and more interestingly, the

Criterion is insinuating that its readers *should be* familiar with Barth; or, third and most interestingly, it is assuming that its readers *in fact are* interested enough in Barth to immediately flip open to a review of his book.

The cover of the January 1937 issue, which also features a review of Barth's work, takes a slightly different format. In 1934, the "Books of the Quarter" section occupied about 3.5 of the available 8.5 inches. In 1937, the section takes up nearly 4.5 inches. The reviews are no longer listed in one continuous block; rather, each review occupies its own line, as if it were a self-sufficient article. These design changes show the *Criterion* as more book review than anything else. In this particular issue, three of the reviewed books include the name of the author: F. R. Leavis, whose *Revaluation, Tradition, and Development in English Poetry* is listed as "Mr. Leavis's Essays"; Reinhold Niebuhr, whose *An Interpretation of Christian Ethics* is listed simply as "Reinhold Niebuhr"; and Karl Barth, whose *Credo* is listed as "Karl Barth's Credo." Again, it seems that readers are either being primed by this offhand mentioning of two relatively unknown theologians ("You know who Leavis is, and you should know who Niebuhr and Barth are"), or it is assumed that readers will recognize and be attracted by the two names ("We know you're interested in Niebuhr and Barth, so flip to the reviews!"), or, most likely, a combination of the two ("These are names that you might not but should know").

Similarly, in both reviews of Barth's work and in the review of Niebuhr's *An Interpretation of Christian Ethics*, the essayists describe these theologians as part of an existing public, as already forming a regular topic of discourse. Porteous opens by describing Barth's book as the "famous commentary on St. Paul's Epistle to the Romans"; George Every claims that "Barth's writings have had sufficient publicity in this country for us" to know of their troubling relation to liberal Anglicanism; finally, Cyril Hudson begins his review by quoting the book jacket of Niebuhr's *An Interpretation of Christian Ethics*, which describes the theologian as "one of the most prophetic voices in modern America."[44] The reviews state explicitly what the covers say implicitly: there is a public for these theologians, and it in large part coincides with the *Criterion*'s readers.

"Living Theology": Karl Barth in the *Criterion*

Actual engagement with Barth's theology occurred not on the cover page but primarily in the "Books of the Quarter" section. The first extended treatment of Barth's dialectical theology came in the *Criterion*'s January 1934 issue, in which Norman W. Porteous reviewed the newly translated second edition of Barth's *Epistle to the Romans*.[45] This was the only time that the little-known Scottish theologian would write for the *Criterion*. It would appear that Eliot chose Porteous rather than someone from his regular roster of reviewers due to his familiarity with the material: Porteous had studied in Münster in the 1920s and described himself as the "first English-speaking student of Karl Barth."[46] This was to be one of the first nonacademic reviews of Barth's seminal text in English, and Eliot's choice of such a sympathetic reviewer all but guaranteed that the *Criterion's* first view of Barth would be a positive one.[47]

Porteous begins by describing Barth's main focus in *Epistle to the Romans*: "The theme of the Epistle to the Romans is God's justifying grace in Christ. Barth attempts to show that the Epistle is a unity throughout and that its paradoxes are to be accepted as the inevitable outcome of that fundamental relation between God and man which is the presupposition of all Paul's thinking."[48] Porteous is at pains to show how this movement from paradox and opposition to unity defines Barth's entire theological project. He emphasizes Barth's dialectical thinking, how Barth shows that "neither positive human activity nor its negation is continuous with divine grace," how the "whole concrete, temporal world of human life and thought" is under God's severe judgment but is also the object of "divine forgiveness," how Barth "deals the shrewdest of blows to left and right."[49]

Barth sets up a series of seeming theological oppositions only to unsettle them. For Porteous, though, the most revolutionary aspect of Barthian theology is its focus on "the metaphysical distinction between the Creator and His creation." (Barth picked up this "qualitative difference" between Creator and creation from Kierkegaard, whose work was being translated into English for the first time during the 1930s.)[50] For Barth, Porteous writes, the Bible shows not that "God exists but what we must do in view of the abyss between man and God which the witness has revealed."[51] The key word here is "abyss": the "fundamental relation between God and man" is one of absolute difference.

Throughout the review, Porteous easily slides from reporting Barth's positions in the third-person—"Barth attempts to show"—to stating, as if in his own voice and with no indication that he is summarizing the reviewed book, many of the tenets of neo-Orthodoxy. Porteous uses the first-person plural throughout: "We are united by our promised membership in the body of Christ"; "What then must we do? Let us cease to mount our little platforms of supposed human superiority and live soberly."[52] Any distance between reviewer and reviewed is collapsed. Porteous's only words of mild censure are for the translator and for those who might misinterpret the book because they "do not read to the end."[53] The piece ends up being less an evaluative review than an explication of Barthian theology that assumes the truth, and interest, of its subject matter. If readers of the *Criterion* had not read Barth before—and surely almost none of them had—then they would emerge from the review sensing that this was a thinker to be reckoned with.

A more distanced but still sympathetic reading of Barth came in George Every's January 1937 review of *Credo*, Barth's clause-by-clause explication of the Apostles' Creed. Every, an Anglo-Catholic, was one of the *Criterion's* most prolific reviewers of religious work; unlike Porteous, he had no affiliation with Barth. Every emphasizes that Barth's theology, in which "we hear again the voices of Luther and Calvin," likely will *not* receive a positive reception among English Protestants (by these, he seems to mean liberal Protestants).[54] Rather, the book "will find English readers chiefly among the younger Anglo-Catholics who have been influenced by Sir Edwyn Hoskyns, Noel Davey, and Charles Smyth."[55] When we consider that Eliot had already publicly declared himself Anglo-Catholic in religion and that Davey and Smyth were contributors to the *Criterion* (Smyth's forty-six reviews made him the magazine's second-most prolific contributor), we see that Every is claiming that Barth's public is the *Criterion*'s public; that those who will be most sympathetic to his theology are those who already are most sympathetic to Eliot's magazine.

Every argues that Anglo-Catholics will be receptive to the work of this radical Protestant theologian due to Barth's deep sense of humanity's sinfulness: "Protestantism was and is a protest against man's claim to be able to achieve any good apart from God's free grace, given to man once and for all in the one sacrifice of the cross, yet still dispensed by God alone, not stored in a tank to which the hierarchical church possesses a key; in other words, a protest against the whittling-down of Original Sin."[56] Every emphasizes what Charles Taylor calls the Protestant "rejection of mediation" as well as its focus on humanity's total depravity.[57] It is not just that humanity cannot be saved "apart from God's free grace"; it cannot "achieve any good" outside of this grace. Barth's refocusing on humanity's sinfulness was one of the defining characteristics of his early theology, and Eliot surely would have agreed with Barth on this point. The protest against the "whittling-down of Original Sin," after all, was something that Eliot admired in others, particularly in T. E. Hulme. For Eliot, this protest was to become the very basis for a revamped classicism and the key to much of his later religious and political thinking.

Perhaps the most interesting part of Every's review comes in his characterization of Barth's thought as "living theology."[58] Every claims that Barth challenges not just professional theologians but all believers, even those who "have no certain theological anchorhold."[59] His work changes not just how we think about divinity but how we live in response to it. Barth's theology, Every writes, is not a matter of "deduction" or logic-chopping but the result of "compulsion," the felt need to think about divinity. This integration of feeling and thinking echoes Eliot's own literary-critical ideals. In his famous 1921 essay, Eliot claimed that the metaphysical poets were able to "feel their thought as immediately as the odour of a rose. A thought to Donne was an experience; it modified his sensibility."[60]

For Every, "living theology" is not just theology that affects, and is affected by, lived experience. It is also theology that acknowledges its own provisional nature. After describing the practical effects of Barth's theology, Every quotes Barth on the necessary conditionality of all theological language: "I profoundly hope that in five or ten years' time I shall be able to speak yet another language than I do to-day, and that then also I shall be compelled to speak it."[61] Barth's work had already reflected this tendency towards self-revision. After all, the 1922 revised edition of *Epistle to the Romans*, the one that was translated into English and that shifted the century's theological grounds, was a radically different text from the original 1919 edition. Every acknowledges that there may be "obscurity and inconsistency" in Barth's writing, but this is the price one pays for a theology that is compelled to constant self-negation. (In this way, Barth's theology fits within a long apophatic tradition that includes St. John of the Cross—a central source for Eliot's later *Four Quartets*.)

While the reviews by Porteous and Every are the most sustained examinations of Barthian theology in the *Criterion*, they are by no means the only places in which Barth's presence can be felt. First, he appears as a regular reference point in essays on other theologians. Between 1934, the year in which Barth's *Epistle* was reviewed in the *Criterion*, and 1939, the year in which the *Criterion* ceased publication, Barth's name was mentioned in ten separate book reviews. Several reviewers use Barth to better place the reviewed author in the contemporary theological landscape and, often, to criticize him for not taking up the challenges that Barth has provided. For example, in one review Charles Smyth chides H. G. Wood for paying more attention to historiography than history, suggesting that "if Mr. Wood had set himself to investigate the nature of history, Karl Barth and Emil Brunner would certainly have figured more prominently in his pages," since the work of Barth and Brunner sheds light on "the Crucifixion-Resurrection; that is, [on] something that cuts right across our whole conception of the time process."[62] (Smyth's imagery echoes Barth's famous description in *Epistle to the Romans* of Jesus as "the point where the unknown world cuts the known world.")[63] Similarly, Michael de la Bédoyère, in a review of Karl Heim's *God Transcendent*, argues that Heim's negative theology "is in keeping with the common teaching of German Evangelicalism at the present day and has been pithily expressed by Barth in the phrase *Senkrecht von oben*, that God falls on us 'plumb down from above.' "[64] In another review, Barth is described as the worthy heir of Augustine and Kierkegaard.[65] In still another, Barth's dialectical vision provides a context by which to understand Reinhold Niebuhr: reviewing Niebuhr's *An Interpretation of Christian Ethics*, Cyril Hudson cites Barth's contention that Christ's prophetic commandment is "relevant" but not "applicable" to human ethical conduct.[66]

Beyond his use as a theological interlocutor, Barth was also celebrated as an opponent of Nazism and a defender of the rights of religion against statism. In the October 1934 article "Religion and the Totalitarian State," Christopher

Dawson discusses the ever-increasing encroachment of the state on all aspects of life, from the economic to the social to the religious: "The movement towards state control in every department of life is a universal one and is not to be confused with the political tenets of a party, whether Communist or Fascist."[67] Given this seemingly inevitable trajectory, Dawson asks, "Should the Church ally itself with the political and social forces that are hostile to the new state? Or should it limit its resistance to cases of state interference in ecclesiastical matters or in theological questions?"[68] The answer, it turns out, can be found in Barth: "As Karl Barth has said in his remarkable reply to the German Christians, this is not a time for political or ecclesiastical-political movements, but for the creation of a spiritual centre of resistance, a return to the real sources of spiritual vitality."[69] Dawson, an advocate of corporativism and a fierce critic of statewide socialism, saw organic communities and associations as the only solution to the twin evils of "suicidal nationalism" and a "cosmopolitanism which ignores historic realities."[70] For Dawson, Barthian theology, like the guild or the university, is valuable precisely in its unwillingness to be co-opted by the state—in its forming a "centre of resistance."

There can never be, Dawson claims, a return to liberalism's "identification of Christianity with social ethics."[71] In criticizing such liberal pieties, Dawson again looks to Barth, here quoting him directly: "As Karl Barth has written: 'All that was called Liberty, Justice, Spirit, only a year ago and for a hundred years farther back, where has it all gone? Now these are all temporal, material, earthly goods. All flesh is as grass.'"[72] In the new era of totalitarianism, religion must play a prophetic role, using the Word of God to startle humanity out of conformity and form the ground from which an opposition to the state's policies can be launched: "The state is steadily annexing all that territory that was formerly the domain of individual freedom . . . But there is one thing it can never take, because to quote Karl Barth once more, 'Theology and the Church are the natural frontiers of everything—even of the Totalitarian State.'"[73] E. W. F. Tomlin repeats these same words in the October 1935 issue, where he points to theology as the point past which the state cannot intrude: "Indeed, as Mr. Dawson observes elsewhere, the rise of the Totalitarian State is merely an indication that religion has not been totalitarian enough. For as Karl Barth has said: 'Theology and the Church are the natural frontiers of everything—even of the Totalitarian State.'"[74]

Barth would have been surprised to see Dawson, a Catholic who was criticized for his sympathies towards General Franco, find support for corporativism in Barth's own words. But it is telling that Dawson cites Barth as an example of the wedge that must be driven between God and politics. In the 1920s, the *Criterion* admired and defended Charles Maurras, a reactionary political thinker whose Action française movement looked to Catholic theology as a means to deify the state. By the 1930s, figures like Dawson instead lionized Barth and his vision of theology as a prophetic, antagonistic witness to the state.[75] In the October 1934 issue, Alec Randall reiterates this point, praising *Gral*, a German Catholic periodical that opposed Nazism and whose December issue included "a remarkable pamphlet by the Protestant theologian Karl Barth . . . paying tribute, with something of an apology, to this emphatic and challenging assertion of the Christian's right to spiritual independence of the State."[76] Barth's example seemed to show the *Criterion's* writers that, in speaking theologically, writers necessarily speak politically. That is to say, theology as a discourse is in part defined by its ability, in talking about God, to also talk about, and challenge, other realms of experience.

The *Criterion's* contributors saw Barth's neo-Orthodoxy affecting not just the field of theology or even the field of politics. They also saw it as signaling a shift in modernity's relationship to transcendence. In "Dialectics and Prophecy," V. A. Demant, an Anglican theologian and director of research at the Christian Social Council, examines "the revival of dialectical thinking in many quarters besides those in which there is direct interest in the philosophy of Communism."[77] Marxist dialectics, he argues, is naturalistic in positing that the "temporal order" contains "within itself all the terms of its dialectical movements."[78] This "sub-lunar naturalism," though, is nearing its end, as it "will be negated before long by a return in a new form of the old problem of the relation between the eternal and the temporal, God and the World."

What is the movement that will negate Communism? It is, of course, Barth's dialectical theology. (One wonders if there is anything Barth's name could not be marshaled in favor of.) Demant's concluding paragraph is worth quoting in full:

> The next dialectical movement to be expected will be in the vertical dimension represented by biology, personality and spirit. The antithesis to a biological and historical expression of religion has already appeared in the momentous appearance of the Barthian Theology. The Spirit acts not in history, but meets it. Biblical history (which for Barth gives the mode of divine revelation) "is not really history at all, but seen from above is a series of free divine acts and seen from below a series of fruitless attempts to undertake something in itself impossible." Human history in no way expresses the divine will, God decides all things in Eternity. Truth speaks in timeless acts breaking in upon man and by his response he is lifted out of history. This utter break between the eternal and the temporal order is the dialectical opposite of the humanism it supersedes. But humanism and deism are the respective ends of movements which proceed from the falling apart of positions held in balanced tension in traditional

Catholicism. Out of the clash of these positions we may expect a reaffirmation by a spirit-centered organic philosophy of life.[79]

Demant here paints a caricatured portrait of Barth. He accuses Barth of dualism, of imagining an unbridgeable, irreconcilable gap between Creator and creation. In fact, Barth claims that the break would be "utter" were it not for God's unmerited election of humanity. Through Christ's birth, death, and resurrection, Barth argues contrary to Demant, God is *in* history, just not *of* it.[80] Regardless of the theological accuracy with which Barth is treated, though, we again see how a *Criterion* contributor is both cognizant of, and indebted to, Barth. After all, Demant is not repudiating Barth's dialectical method, just relocating it within a Catholic context. Moreover, Demant signals the crucial role Barth plays not just in the field of theology but also within contemporary culture more broadly. By tracing the violent incursions of "Eternity" and the "divine will" into human history, Barth has allowed transcendence back into the modern worldview.

"An exclusive Thomist club"

If scholars associate the *Criterion* with a particular theological movement, though, it is of course not with Barth's neo-Orthodoxy but with the neo-Thomism of Maritain, D'Arcy, and others. Eliot's contemporaries made this same association between magazine and theological movement, and there was something to the connection. In 1926, while relaunching his magazine as the *New Criterion*—it would return to the simpler, more august *Criterion* by 1928—Eliot recommended a series of "classical" texts that might be said to encapsulate his magazine's "tendency."[81] One was Jacques Maritain's *Réflexions sur l'intelligence*, a book outlining the neo-Thomist philosophy of intelligence and its relationship to intuition (a book, it should be noted, that proved a crucial resource for the Murry-Eliot-D'Arcy debate over romanticism, classicism, and Thomism a year later). In this same 1926 issue, Herbert Read, a regular contributor to the magazine who was involved in many of its editorial decisions, writes, "If we were required to point to a philosophy worked out in the terms of Western reality and consonant with our deepest instincts, we should turn to medieval philosophy and particularly to the thought of St. Thomas Aquinas."[82] Two years later, Eliot himself addressed the charge that his magazine was essentially a neo-Thomist club.

What exactly was neo-Thomism, though, and who were its modern proponents? Critics who have examined the attractiveness of neo-Thomism to literary figures of the 1920s and 1930s have emphasized the movement's confident assertions of completeness and order. Douglas Patey, for instance, describes the

Scholastic revival that Evelyn Waugh so admired as "triumphantly sure in its possession of a finished, complete, systematic account of matters of faith and morals."[83] David Goldie similarly describes neo-Thomism as "emphasizing the positivistic, rational arguments for the existence of God, incorporating a rigid causality that too easily lent itself to a simple quantification of belief."[84] This characterization finds a perfect fit between the theology, aesthetics, and politics of Waugh and Eliot: all three emphasize order, authority, and tradition over the chaos and fragmentation of modernity.

The link between order in religion and order in politics and art can be seen most clearly in Eliot's relationship to Action française and the monarchist Charles Maurras. A nasty person but a skilled polemicist, Maurras, himself an atheist, believed that neo-Thomism could be marshaled as an intellectual defense for his antidemocratic, anti-Semitic positions. Eliot was attracted to certain tendencies of Maurras's thought, particularly his criticisms of the romantic mindset. Indeed, Eliot's friend Paul Elmer More went so far as to claim that Eliot's conversion to Christianity was "due largely I believe to the influence of Maurras and the Action Française."[85] Maurras's enlistment of neo-Thomist arguments for his own purposes was not well received by the Roman Catholic Church. In 1926, Pope Pius XI condemned Action française's instrumental vision of religion. In 1927, the movement's magazine became the first periodical placed on the church's list of banned books—and Eliot eventually distanced himself from Maurras's more extreme positions.[86] But the legacy of Eliot's flirtation with the movement lives on, at least for scholars, who still tend to read "neo-Thomism" as "reactionary and authoritarian."

As mentioned earlier, there are certain key characteristics that unite all neo-Thomists—most notably a belief in the project of natural theology (the provisional inquiry into the nature of God without reference to divine revelation) and a commitment to a realist epistemology. Despite this overarching unity, though, twentieth-century neo-Thomism was, as Gerald McCool writes, a movement of "diverse and distinctive forms," ranging from the transcendentalism of Joseph Maréchal to the existentialism of Maritain to the historicism of Gilson.[87] The *Criterion*'s treatment of neo-Thomism reflected this diversity of approaches. The *Criterion* printed, praised, and criticized philosophical Thomism and cultural Thomism and historical Thomism and theological Thomism and mystical Thomism. It printed, praised, and criticized Thomisms, in other words, and not Thomism.

Neo-Thomisms

The best place to look for neo-Thomism's place within the *Criterion* is, once again, the "Books of the Quarter" section. Taking the October 1933 issue as a test case, we can see how the *Criterion* displayed a thoughtful, oftentimes supportive, sometimes critical attitude towards neo-Thomism. I choose this issue for several reasons. First, because it was published after the *Criterion* had made its supposed transition into being a neo-Thomist organ; second, because it includes reviews both by and about neo-Thomists; and third, because it crystallizes the varied styles of neo-Thomism, from the philosophical investigations of D'Arcy to the historicizing of Gilson to the cultural criticism of Dawson. Almost any issue from roughly 1930 onwards, however, could serve the same analytical purpose.

This particular issue's impressive roster of reviewers includes Eliot himself, Auden, Stephen Spender, and Geoffrey Grigson. Only two of the reviewed authors are named explicitly on the cover: A. E. Housman, whose *The Name and Nature of Poetry* is listed as "Housman on Poetry," and Etienne Gilson, whose *L'Espirit de la philosophie médiévale* is listed as "Etienne Gilson." (Again, a theologian gets the rare privilege of having his name, rather than his work, on the cover.) Moving into the content of the issue, neo-Thomism provides a guiding thread from the first review, in which Martin D'Arcy reads Alfred North Whitehead's *The Adventure of Ideas* through a Thomist lens, to the last, in which Algar Thorold reviews Gilson.

D'Arcy, the *Criterion*'s most frequent neo-Thomist contributor, was arguably more a philosopher than a theologian. His reviews rarely mention religious doctrine, instead focusing on how the Catholic intellectual tradition can shed light on modern humanism, phenomenology, and psychology.[88] In this particular issue and elsewhere, D'Arcy criticizes other philosophers from a stylistic perspective, in large part because he sees clarity as the chief virtue of philosophical thinking. A favorite rhetorical trick is to quote a particularly obscure sentence, then throw his hands up at the linguistic (and philosophical) confusion that could lead to such a formulation. Describing Whitehead, for instance, D'Arcy writes: "Perhaps the brightness of [his] interpretations is enhanced by the surrounding obscurity. Towards the end of the book the sentence occurs: 'But after all, it is the blunt truth that we want.' This Sordello remark may make the reader wonder what complicated truth must be like, unless the word 'blunt' stand for blunted, abstract words in place of personal and direct ones."[89] In his review of Harold Osborne's *Foundations of the Philosophy of Value* from the same issue, D'Arcy begins by stating that the book "has the rare virtue of combining clear thought and clear expression. Even those who have no special training in philosophy and cannot boast a wide acquaintance with the current literature on ethical problems will be able to follow the argument."[90] Coming from D'Arcy, this is high praise.[91] D'Arcy's own books were also praised in the *Criterion* for a "style so limpidly clear that it is a joy to read even for that alone."[92] Here, we can see neo-Thomism associated with a no-nonsense, lucid, commonsensical approach to the world that largely brackets mystical concerns and instead relies upon a clear, rigorous, ordered mind.

D'Arcy's particular brand of neo-Thomism, however, which valued order and philosophical clarity above all else, was also the subject of intense criticism by other reviewers in the *Criterion*. In this same October 1933 issue, we find Montgomery Belgion, an even more visible, regular presence in the *Criterion* than D'Arcy, criticizing neo-Thomism's tendency to idealize order in his review of a book by Christopher Dawson. Eliot cultivated Belgion's caustic tone and incendiary reviewing style, using his screeds both to ratchet up interest in the magazine and to head off charges of the *Criterion's* hidebound nature.[93] Belgion had elsewhere criticized Maritain's *Art and Scholasticism*, a touchstone of neo-Thomist aesthetics, claiming that "Mr. Maritain's theory being false, it is imperative that its falsity should be clearly exhibited by someone."[94] In choosing Belgion to review Dawson's book, then, Eliot all but guaranteed that another prominent neo-Thomist—and a close personal friend towards whom Eliot felt intellectual sympathy—would receive a public dressing-down.

Belgion did not disappoint. He harshly criticized Dawson, who was described later as England's "leading neo-Thomist," for envisioning Christianity as a means towards order and culture rather than the one path to salvation.[95] According to Belgion, Dawson believes that "Comte was quite right in stressing the importance of the social benefits conferred by a common body of beliefs," but that these benefits will only be had "if the common faith is in our traditional 'culture,' namely, Roman Catholicism. Hence we should all be Catholics for the sake of civilization and progress."[96] Belgion disagreed with this pragmatic approach to religion: "If anyone ought to become a Christian . . . surely the only reasons remain still to-day what they were when Saul of Tarsus took the road to Damascus—first, that he individually needs to be saved; and, secondly, that only through Jesus Christ can he win salvation."[97] Dawson's problem, Belgion suggests, is that he tries to combine "anthropology" with "apologetic," and in the process compromises both. His conception of culture does not do justice to historical fact ("the first Christians numbered only thirteen, and they bothered neither with tradition nor 'cultures'") nor to authentic religion (which should concern itself with salvation rather than sociology).[98] Belgion accuses D'Arcy of the same mistake that others have accused Eliot of: seeing religion simply as a means to civilizing order.

As Robert Scholes and Clifford Wulfman note, in little magazines like the *Criterion* "it is the editor(s) and the staff of regular contributors who dominate. What the author is to a book, the editor(s) and staff are to a periodical—the major influence on the contents of the object."[99] It is telling, then, that the figure who replaced Belgion in the late 1930s as the most frequent reviewer at the *Criterion*, Michael Roberts, was also a critic of neo-Thomism.[100] In a long January 1937 review, for instance, Roberts points to the inadequacies of philosophical Thomism: "To some minds the deity which emerges from the celebrated Thomist proofs is simply a verbal concept invented to round off the limitations of a particular logic"; "to some readers [Thomism] will seem to have no vital spiritual, aesthetic, or moral consequences," since the "Thomist God may be a necessity of Thomist logic but the criterion of logical coherence is not the only criterion."[101] Roberts counted himself among those who found Thomism unsatisfying. In his 1937 *Modern Mind,* he wrote that "rational theologians may erect a transcendent concept and call it God; but such a step will not of itself bring strength and comfort to humanity, and it does not serve to express the quality of religious experience."[102] Yet despite this hostility to Thomism, Roberts continued to play a crucial role at the magazine. In a 1949 obituary for Roberts, Eliot claimed that, if the *Criterion* had lived on, Roberts likely would have succeeded Eliot as editor.[103] Even without the formal title of editor, the anti-Scholastic Roberts found a home in this supposedly Scholastic organ.

Yet D'Arcy's philosophical Thomism and Dawson's cultural Thomism were only two forms that the movement took within the pages of the *Criterion.* Another prominent strand was the Thomism of Etienne Gilson. Gilson's thinking and writing displayed a sharp historicist sense, arguing that Thomism must be understood as theology first and philosophy second. In the October 1933 issue, Algar Thorold reviews Gilson's *L'Espirit de la philosophie médiévale.* This book argued that the conceptual terms of neo-Thomism—the subject, the object, *esse*—could only be understood properly by recovering what they meant in their original, medieval context; you had to look at the medieval spirit before you could understand medieval philosophy. If Belgion criticizes Dawson for conflating religion with culture and advocating an ahistorical return to tradition, then Thorold praises Gilson for his historical rigor and his treatment of the medieval period as a topic to be studied rather than emulated. Thorold describes Gilson as a "scholar" and a "philosopher of the authentic breed," drawing attention to the "ample notes and bibliography [which] are of the greatest importance and increase tenfold the value of the book."[104]

Elsewhere, Gilson's own review of a new translation of Guido Cavalcanti's poetry (the translator, anonymous at the time, turned out to be Ezra Pound) shows the historical specificity necessary in any discussion of medieval philosophy. Gilson disagrees with the translation of *"possibile intelletto"* as "latent intellect," since, as he writes, "the *passive* intellect belongs to Aristotle and Alexander, the *possible* intellect to Albertus Magnus and Thomas Aquinas, *passive* implying the materiality, *possible,* on the contrary, the immateriality of the intellect."[105] This is a far cry from D'Arcy and Dawson. Just as importantly, Gilson emphasized that, if we actually looked at the medieval context, we would recognize that Thomism's force as a philosophical system derived from its theological origins. You could not, as Maurras and D'Arcy seemed to suggest, accept Thomistic philosophical arguments if you did not first accept

Thomism's theological first principles. As Brian Shanley writes, "Because Aquinas's deepest philosophical insights are embedded in his theological works, Gilson insisted that Thomistic philosophy always be presented according to an explicitly theological order that begins with God and then moves to creatures."[106] (In this, Gilson agreed with J. Middleton Murry: Thomist epistemology depends upon a Christian metaphysics.)

The *Criterion*'s reviewers also focused on what might seem a contradiction in terms: mystical Thomism. In another review of Gilson, this time of his *La Théologie mystique de Saint Bernard*, Evelyn Underhill describes how mysticism does not, and indeed cannot, involve an absorption of the human into the divine. Gilson, Underhill writes, realizes that "the distinction between Creator and creature is radical for Christianity. The ultimate problem for the Christian mystic is, 'How can I, who am not-being, attain God, who is Being?'" Gilson is able to show that the mystic and the intellectual cannot exist one without the other. As Underhill writes, Gilson is concerned with "mystical theology; that is to say, the intellectual aspect of his doctrine of the spiritual life."[107] In a 1931 review of several books on St. John of the Cross—one of which contains a preface by "the fierce protagonist of scholastic philosophy," Jacques Maritain— Robert Sencourt emphasizes that the Spanish saint's mysticism weds "metaphysics" to "aesthetics," showing that art, affect, and philosophy are all necessary components of the true mystical state.[108] That one of Maritain's books, reviewed by Eliot in the *TLS*, was entitled *Prayer and Intelligence*, hints once again that, for Eliot as well as for Maritain, neo-Thomism was not a repudiation of affect so much as a means of integrating it into a more capacious, reasoned, and philosophically rigorous sense of religious truth. In a review of Maritain's *Three Reformers* appearing in the *TLS*, Eliot surprisingly described Maritain as "an emotional rather than an intellectual Catholic." While this surely overstates matters, it does show that neo-Thomism, as Eliot himself wrote in this same review, "may be taken with more than one meaning."[109]

Neo-Thomism, then, was not a source of intellectual excitement for Eliot and others because it offered definitive answers to the central questions of theology. Rather, like Barthian theology, it was exciting because its different approaches—philosophical, cultural, historical, and mystical—all addressed a common problem: how to articulate propositions about a transcendent God using the fallible gift of earthly reason.

Beyond the *Criterion*

This reconciling of revelation with reason was, as we will see in the work of Eliot and Jones specifically, one of the central problems for the poets of theological modernism. It was also a problem taken up by interwar magazines other than the *Criterion*.

The *Criterion* always was written, as Denys Thompson said, for an "intellectual minority."[110] The magazine's cultural impact was disproportionate to (and, in the modernist, antipopulist calculus, enhanced by) its low circulation. The *Criterion*'s book reviews, Eliot claimed, existed to "criticize and correct at more leisure" the "daily and weekly journals" that did not have the luxury of a quarterly (or even monthly) publication schedule.[111] One of the weekly journals that Eliot simultaneously admired and sought to correct was the *Times Literary Supplement*, which Eliot called the "top rung of the ladder of literary journalism" and which consistently had around 24,000 subscribers throughout the 1930s.[112] From 1902 to 1937, Bruce Richmond served as its editor, establishing the standard by which Eliot judged his own stewardship of the *Criterion*.[113] And, though not a believer like Eliot, Richmond regularly solicited and printed reviews of theological works.

Brief reviews of several of Niebuhr's early works, for instance, appeared throughout the 1930s, while *The Nature and Destiny of Man*, his magnum opus, received two long, positive reviews, in 1942 and 1943.[114] In one of these reviews, the conservative journalist Ivor Thomas called Niebuhr's earlier *Beyond Tragedy* "a portent in the theological sky" and claimed that Niebuhr's new book, *The Nature and Destiny of Man*, demanded "the earnest consideration of all moral theologians and students of ethics."[115] Thomas was also Richmond's regular choice to review Karl Barth. The curmudgeonly, conservative Anglo-Catholic never gave the Protestant Swiss a fair reading, helping to contribute to a misunderstanding of Barth as a dualist who believed man was "wholly bad."[116] Still, the *TLS* was one of the first literary periodicals to examine Barthian thought in depth (1936 alone saw three full-length reviews of Barth's work), and Thomas himself grudgingly came to respect if not admire Barth, calling his 1938 Gifford Lectures "a stimulating challenge to natural theology."[117]

The most interesting point of comparison between the *TLS* and the *Criterion*, however, comes in their treatment of Maritain. Maritain was reviewed more than twenty times in the *TLS* between 1923 and 1940, several times by Eliot himself, and while Eliot's editorial decisions at the *Criterion* shed some light on his complex relationship with the French neo-Thomist, his writing for the *TLS* offers an even more illuminating view. Take, for instance, his June 21, 1928, review of Maritain's *Prayer and Intelligence*. There, Eliot writes that this book is "for those who approach [religion] intellectually," yet it "is itself a corrective to the authors' intellectualism."[118] By balancing prayer and intelligence, emotion and reason, Maritain reminds his readers that genuine Thomism can never be "solely a mental feat," but instead must illustrate "that the development of the mind and the development of the emotions [in religion] must proceed together."[119] In this same year, Eliot offered a more measured evaluation of Maritain's *Three Reformers*. The book, he writes, is "brilliant, delightful and easy to read," yet sometimes its "appeal is to the heart rather than the head"—a seemingly minor criticism, but, in Eliot's lexicon, quite cutting. Eliot lamented that Maritain, while "a brilliant and accomplished scholar, is more important as a popularizer of ideas than as an original thinker."[120]

Most of the *TLS*'s theological reviews were written not by trained theologians but by literary figures. J. Middleton Murry reviewed Maritain six times for the *TLS*, for instance, and Ernest de Selincourt, editor of Spenser and Words-worth, reviewed Maritain's *Art and Scholasticism*.[121] Two American magazines, the *Nation* and the *New Republic*, followed the lead of the *TLS* in regularly pairing theological texts with a literary reviewer—in their case, W. H. Auden. Between 1938 and 1944, Auden wrote extensive, sophisticated reviews of theo-logical texts, including John Macmurray's *The Clue to History* (1939), Reinhold Niebuhr's *Christianity and Power Politics* (1941) and *The Nature and Destiny of Man* (1941), and Kierkegaard's *Either/Or* (1944). Throughout these reviews, Auden displays an awareness of the theological landscape, both contemporary and traditional, discussing Barth and Augustine, Niebuhr and Pascal. Again and again, Auden argues for the contemporary importance of theology. As he writes, "Cultured people, to whom, until recently, theological terms were far more shocking than any of the four-letter words," were now "overcom[ing] this final prudery."[122] Elsewhere, he writes that "recent history is showing . . . that man cannot live without a sense of the Unconditional," a "fear of the Lord" that contemporary theologians sought to explore.[123]

In the 1930s and 1940s, then, it wasn't just the *Criterion*'s writers and editor who saw contemporary theology as having something important to say to con-temporary literature. As Auden, Murry, and others make clear, interwar liter-ary culture more generally believed that "a sense of the Unconditional" needed to be interrogated. For them, figures like Barth, Maritain, and Niebuhr offered the hope that a "fear of the Lord" could lead to religious thinking that was rigorous and philosophical in nature. To see how this "fear of the Lord" influ-enced modern poetry, though, we must go to the poetry itself—to the works of "theological modernism" that grew, in part, out of this periodical culture.

CHAPTER THREE

T. S. Eliot, Karl Barth, and Christian Revelation

What Lucretius and Dante teach you, in fact, is *what it feels like* to hold certain beliefs. —T. S. ELIOT, "The Social Function of Poetry"

In "Types of English Religious Verse," a lecture written in 1939, T. S. Eliot forecast an increase in the creation and consumption of religious poetry.[1] This new verse, Eliot claimed, would take Christian revelation—"the central mysteries of the Incarnation and the Eucharist"—as its subject.[2] It would reject the easy optimism of nineteenth-century religious liberalism, instead approaching the problem of human sin and the possibility of divine transcendence with theological rigor: "The probable direction of religious poetry in the immediate future is towards something more impersonal . . . It will be much more interested in the dogma and the doctrine; in religious thought, rather than purely personal religious feeling." If romanticism rerouted subjective religious feeling into poetic expression (resulting in what T. E. Hulme called "spilt religion"), then this new classicism would be disciplined and philosophical.[3] It would concern itself with "giving poetic form to theological thought," receiving intellectual ballast from the theology of the recent past—more specifically, Eliot wrote, from "Thomism, and to some extent also . . . Karl Barth and Kierkegaard."[4]

Much of this sounds like a summary of Eliot's regular critical positions. We should recognize his usual binaries. He praises thought over feeling, classicism over romanticism, firm religious doctrine over vague religious sentiment. And as is so often the case with Eliot, we cannot help but notice the self-serving nature of his supposedly impartial analysis. After all, by 1939, Eliot had already written and published "Burnt Norton," which opens with this impersonal, theological-sounding pronouncement: "Time present and time past / Are both perhaps present in time future, / And time future contained in time past."[5] It seems that Eliot's description of "religious poetry in the immediate future" is really a description of the religious poetry that *he* would be working on in the immediate future: *Four Quartets*. Eliot is once again using his criticism to create the kind of reader his poetry demands.[6]

Yet, despite the words of this lecture and despite Barth's regular presence within the pages of the *Criterion*, very few critics have offered readings of Eliot's poetry with Barth's theology in mind. Even those scholars who have drawn such connections have done so in a cursory manner. Steve Ellis is typical in this regard. In *The English Eliot*, he expresses "surprise that Eliot's source-hunters seem to have passed Barth over in silence," offers several points of potential comparison, and concludes by calling for a more "extensive treatment of the relationship."[7] Similarly, in an introductory essay on religion and modernism, Pericles Lewis tells us that Barth's "reaction against theological liberalism" was, in many ways, "intellectually in tune with literary modernism," but he does not engage with the specifics of Barth's theological vision or with how knowledge of Barth's critique of religious liberalism might change our reading of Eliot's poetry.[8] W. David Soud has recently taken up this challenge, arguing that Barth's "anti-mystical stance"—that is, his sense of "the unreality of the earthly in relation to the eternal"—makes for a useful point of comparison with Eliot's most mystical work, *Four Quartets*. But he largely focuses upon the poem's experiential dimensions, paying less attention to theology as theology and its influence on Eliot's thinking about the Incarnation.[9]

This chapter, then, attempts to recover the Barthian context not for Eliot the editor but for Eliot the poet, specifically reading *Four Quartets* as a Barthian poem at heart. It is a truism that while Eliot the critic was a classicist, Eliot the poet was a romantic.[10] A similar disjuncture exists between Eliot the religious critic and Eliot the religious poet. As a critic, Eliot was associated with French neo-Thomism, a theological movement that emphasized the *analogia entis,* stressing that nature was not destroyed but perfected by grace and that Creator and creation could live in harmonious order.[11] As a poet, however, Eliot was more aligned with the Barthian position, which focused not on the analogy between Creator and creation but on the absolute gap between them. In Eliot's poetry, as in Barth's theology, the pain of temporal existence arises from the seemingly irreconcilable conflict between nature and grace, between "the waste sad time" of our earthly existence and the beatific vision in which "the fire and the rose are one."[12] Eliot's poetry generally, and *Four Quartets* specifically, explores not a world charged with the grandeur of God, but a fallen world only occasionally and violently intersected by transcendence.

Reading *Four Quartets* with Barth's theology in mind, we can see the sharp contrast between what Eliot's poetry asserts and what it enacts. In "The Dry Salvages," Eliot writes that our earthly moments of transcendence are analogous to the moment when Christ entered history: in these epiphanic moments, "The hint half guessed, the gift half understood, is Incarnation."[13] In tension with these analogical, sacramental assertions, however, is the sequence's overwhelmingly dialectical sense that this world and the next are not so closely connected, that the Incarnation is a singular rather than a sustained event, and that nature must be violently changed, even obliterated, rather than perfected or enriched. Part of the power of *Four Quartets* comes from this tension between the analogical and dialectical modes. We might say that Eliot is a Barthian poet who wants to become something very different.

In 1937, Faber and Faber published *Revelation*, a collection to which Barth contributed an essay and for which Eliot wrote the introduction. We know that Eliot would have read Barth's essay and that Barth's theology—in particular, the dialectical theology of Barth's second edition to *Epistle to the Romans*—would have been in his mind when he wrote his introduction to the volume. We also know that Eliot was familiar with the broad contours of Barth's theology, both from his work as editor of the *Criterion* (see Chapter 2) and from his work at Faber and Faber, where, as William Blissett writes, "Eliot was responsible not only for the poetry list but for books on religion in its wider definition."[14] We do not know, however, and probably never can know, what specific texts of Barth's Eliot read, or whether he read them in German or English. Eliot's public comments on Barth are few and far between—perhaps because admitting his appreciation for a radical Protestant theologian would have compromised his public image as an Anglo-Catholic committed to doctrinal orthodoxy. As a result, this chapter is as much an essay in theological and stylistic affinities as it is an essay in influence. I do not argue that Eliot borrows specific images from Barth (though there are provocative parallels, particularly in Eliot's description of the Incarnation), and I do not claim that Barth is *the* major theological source for Eliot in *Four Quartets* (Augustine and Julian of Norwich, to name but two, are more obvious resources), or that the sequence's dialectical form arises solely from Eliot's reading of Barth rather than from his reading of, for instance, St. John of the Cross.

My goal, in short, is not to reject previous readings of Eliot's work but rather to enrich these readings by showing how *Four Quartets* engages with yet another theological context, this time a contemporary one. Barth's interwar work refocused theological inquiry on several issues—the relationship between reason and revelation, nature and grace, unredeemed history and the Incarnation—that were crucial to Eliot's own later poetry. Eliot, as editor of a literary magazine that often seemed to double as a theological review, was aware of the shifts that Barth had helped bring about in interwar theology, and his poetry could not help but reflect upon and react to these changes. Reading *Four Quartets* in light of Barthian theology yields a religious vision that is, as David Tracy has written, "something richer, stronger, indeed altogether more unsettling" than we might have imagined.[15]

A small methodological note: throughout this chapter, when I write "Barth's theology," I mean Barth's theology of the 1930s and 1940s—and, even more specifically, I mean the theology of *Epistle to the Romans* and, somewhat less regularly, *The Word of God and the Word of Man*. These are the texts that Eliot most likely would have been familiar with, and they offer a very different Barth from that of the later *Church Dogmatics*.

Theology of Crisis, Poetry of Crisis

Willa Cather once claimed that "the world broke in two in 1922 or thereabouts."[16] Cather had good reason to make such a pronouncement, as this single year saw the publication of *Jacob's Room*, *Ulysses*, and *The Waste Land*, all works that seemed to signal a turning point in literary history. As Michael North has shown, many other fields, including anthropology and philosophy, saw discipline-shifting works appear in or around this *annus mirabilis*, leading to a feeling of "open generational conflict" in which the old traditions seemed to be giving way to "a new social and cultural world of which the new works were merely a part."[17] In each of these fields, there was the Yeatsian sense that all was changed, changed utterly.[18]

One discipline that North does not examine is Christian theology.[19] If 1922 seemed a literary turning point due to the blossoming of a common aesthetic project in several different works by several different writers, then the year's importance for theology arose primarily from the publication of a single book: the heavily revised, much acclaimed, much criticized second edition of Karl Barth's *Epistle to the Romans*. In 1939, John Baillie wrote of Barth that "nobody seems to be able to talk theology these days without mentioning him."[20] More recently, Mark C. Taylor has described Barth's achievement in this way: "Rereading Paul amid the smoldering ruins of World War I, Barth pronounced a resounding '*Nein!*' to every form of theological liberalism," as his work "echoed Luther's world-transforming proclamation at the Diet of Worms: 'Here I stand, I can do no other.'"[21]

In his revolutionary text, Barth attacked proponents of religious liberalism, reserving his most withering criticism for Friedrich Schleiermacher. Schleiermacher was a theologian of immanence, claiming that "'Miracle' is merely the religious name for event, every one of which, even the most natural and usual, is a miracle as soon as it adapts itself to the fact that the religious view of it can be the dominant one. To me everything is miracle."[22] For Schleiermacher, Creator and creation live in a harmonious relationship that is all the more wonderful for its being constant. Barth, contrarily, argued in his *Epistle to the Romans* that "only when the all-embracing contrast between God and men is perceived can there emerge the knowledge of God, a new communion with Him, and a new worship."[23] He asserted that Schleiermacher, by focusing on the emotions and experiences of believers rather than on the absolute transcendence of God, had obscured the proper project of theology.

What was the proper project of theology? It was to remind humanity, with relentlessness and with violence if necessary, that humanity was not God. Theologians, Barth wrote, must grapple with the fact that God does not reside in the human breast but is "above him—unapproachably distant and unutterably strange."[24] To live in this knowledge is to live under constant judgment of the eternal; it is to reside in the crisis that comes from being radically separated from one's Creator. Barth's theology of crisis would focus on original sin. Humanity would no longer be seen as progressing towards perfection but as a sinful creation in need of God's shattering grace. It would be dialectical not only in its emphasis on the antithesis between God and humanity but also in its methodology. True theology, Barth argued, should be characterized by self-negation. Indeed, the truest theology, the theology most attuned to the divine source that it attempts to describe, would end in silence. Barth's was a "theology of crisis" in several senses, then: first, in its articulating a sense of historical crisis in the wake of World War I; second, in its depiction of the existential crisis of a sinful world always and everywhere living under the judgment of God; third, in its representation of what we might call the ontological crisis brought about through the Incarnation, the intersection of eternal Being with earthly being in the form of Jesus Christ; and fourth, in its foregrounding of the methodological crisis of theology, the continual self-negation under which all theological language must stand.

It did not take contemporary critics long to point to the similarities between the sense of crisis animating Barth's theology and the sense of crisis animating interwar literature. In a 1936 essay in the *Hibbert Journal*, M. Chaning-Pearce analyzed the relationship between Barth and the postwar cultural moment, tracing the shared thematic concerns of Barth and a sizable and varied group of modern poets (Eliot, Yeats, Breton, and others), identifying several contemporary writers who, like Barth, "betray a catastrophic or cacophonic strain."[25] Indeed, it seemed to Chaning-Pearce that modern literature was defined by this catastrophic strain—by the formal strain involved in making it new, by the historical strain of living in a time of intense change. In particular, Chaning-Pearce argues that the publication of Eliot's *Murder in the Cathedral* can be seen as the specific moment at which "the Barthian denunciation of the worship of the 'Man-God' passes from prophecy to poetry."[26]

While Chaning-Pearce does not make the case that Barth directly influenced Eliot, he does argue that both theologian and poet disclose "catastrophe, a transcendental reality breaking in upon, running counter to, the rhythm of our life, a 'Waste-Land' which is yet pregnant and lit with a light 'that never was on land or sea.' "[27] For Chaning-Pearce, both Barth and Eliot are what he calls "minor prophets," those who most clearly articulate "the tide of thought and . . . the contemporary mood": "For the chief causes of this consensus of feeling are not far to seek. The war, for those who passed in person through those fires of Moloch, and for those of the next generation who have received the baptism of their spirit, brought universally the sense of imminent catastrophe and, occasionally, catharsis. Such spirits . . . as these are well accustomed to catastrophe; they were born in a light of eclipse. The rhythm of their blood is the rhythm of catastrophe, a counter-rhythm striking from lightning skies across the familiar rhythms of natural life."[28] Again, this "consensus of feeling" is seen as characterizing not just the work of Barth and Eliot but the entire postwar cultural moment. An entire generation of writers and thinkers has felt itself and its world made new through a terrible violence, which is imagined here in striking terms: as the war or an eclipse or a lightning strike. Chaning-Pearce refers to the crisis-ridden world as a "Waste Land" on several occasions, and his point is clear: Barth is the theologian of the "Waste Land" just as Eliot is its poet.[29]

Barth and Eliot, however, shared not just a sense of the gap separating God from humanity—a sense that Eliot also received from Hulme and Pascal, among others—or a general feeling of historical crisis.[30] For both poet and theologian, historical fracture demanded formal fracture. The Catholic theologian Hans Urs Balthasar has noted that Barth, by demanding that theology concern itself primarily with the gap separating God from humanity, revolutionized not just the content of modern theology but also its style: "For Barth, Revelation raised the elementary question of style and form in theology. He wanted not only to say something proper about the content of Revelation, but also to convey the stupendousness of the dramatic event being unfolded. Here the style is a necessary ingredient of the truth of what is being said."[31]

Here, Balthasar makes a claim about the relation of form to content in Barth's theology, and perhaps in all theology. If, as Barth believed, theology is concerned with reorienting our attention towards the crisis under which we always live—namely, we live in this world under judgment by eternity—then theology must not just describe this crisis but make it felt. As we will see, this sense that a work, whether literary or theological, should not mimetically represent but expressively enact will be crucial for David Jones and other modernists. What is worth noting here, however, is that Balthasar describes Barth's new, dramatic style of argumentation as "theological expressionism," thus explicitly connecting Barth's theology with the most influential German avant-garde literary movement of the early twentieth century.[32]

To exemplify Barth's expressionist theology, Balthasar offers this quotation from *Epistle to the Romans*: "Is any word of mine *the* Word, the one I am looking for, the one which I, in my distress and longing, would like to utter? Can I speak without having one word cancel out the other?"[33] How, in short, can the individual, temporal word express the divine, eternal Word?[34] These sentences, Balthasar suggests, do not just *claim* that all human language must fail when trying to describe God. The second sentence actually *exhibits* this failure. If the first question worries over whether any word can express the Word, thus holding out hope that some word might be found, the second question cancels the possibility—indeed, the very question that has just been asked.

A more telling stylistic example of Barth's expressionist theology, though, comes in Barth's commentary on Romans 2:14:

> *Gentiles, which have not the law, do the things of the law.* The law is the revelation once given by God, given in its completeness. The law is the impression of divine revelation left behind in time, in history, and in the lives of men; it is a heap of clinkers marking a fiery miracle which has taken place, a burnt-out crater disclosing the place where God has spoken, a solemn reminder of the humiliation through which some men had been compelled to pass, a dry canal which in a past generation and under different conditions had been filled with the living water of faith and of clear perception, a canal formed out of ideas and conceptions and commandments, all of which call to mind the behaviour of certain other men, and demand that their conduct should be maintained.[35]

The imagery of a bombed-out earth, the refusal to settle into one metaphorical description of the law, the yoking of God and violence—all are typical of the Barthian style (and, it hardly needs to be said, of modernist style as well). Barth's *Epistle to the Romans* provides an array of apocalyptic, often militaristic images: the word of God is figured as "dynamite [that] is prepared and ready to explode," revelation as a stroke of lightning that "purifies . . . carbonizes . . . consumes and destroys," the gap between God and man as "the crevasse, the polar zone, the desert barrier."[36]

Barth's *Epistle to the Romans* derives much of its force (and difficulty) from its sharp juxtapositions. Barth proceeds by paradox, placing opposites beside each other without causal explanation. Humankind is sinful, and it is also saved; Christ is God, but he is also man; God's grace is shattering, and it is also creative. Of course, Christianity is built out of such paradoxes, but Barth forces his reader to face these paradoxes without hiding from them.[37] In describing the seemingly pious "man of religion," for instance, Barth writes, "He is Moses AND Aaron, Paul AND Saul, enthusiast AND obscurantist, prophet AND pharisee, priest AND blatant sacerdotalist. . . . He is always both positive and negative, and he is the first because he is the second."[38] Barth is a theologian of the nevertheless. For all believers, he writes, faith is "a scandal, a hazard, a 'Nevertheless'; to all it presents the same embarrassment and the same promise; for all it is a leap into the void. And it is possible for all, only because for all it is equally impossible."[39]

The prose of *Epistle to the Romans* is marked everywhere by dynamism and fragmentation. Indeed, David Tracy's description of Kierkegaard as the great fragmentary theologian could apply equally well to Barth, whose early fragmentary style also "expos[es] the bizarre drive to totality of all modern rationalist idealist systems and of Christendom alike."[40] In *Epistle to the Romans*, images cancel each other out and sentences move feverishly forward only to circle back to their beginnings. As Stephen Webb writes, "It is an attempt to fly without landing, a movement without rest."[41] To a striking degree, the theological force of Barth's argument depends upon its poetic, expressive force. At times, *Epistle to the Romans* seems as much an expressionist poem as a work of theology; or, perhaps more accurately, it seems a work that does theology through the creation of expressionist imagery.[42]

Movement without rest and fragmentation also characterize Eliot's early verse. His poems of the 1910s are dominated by a twin obsession: first, an obsession with capturing the slightest shifts in mood and emotion; and second, an obsession with precisely capturing physical detail. Combining these Expressionist and Imagist inclinations resulted in Eliot's great urban landscape poems, "Preludes" and "Rhapsody on a Windy Night." In "Rhapsody on a Windy Night," the speaker describes his mind as he wanders through a scene of urban desolation:

> The memory throws up high and dry
> A crowd of twisted things;
> A twisted branch upon the beach
> Eaten smooth, and polished
> As if the world gave up
> The secret of its skeleton,
> Stiff and white.
> A broken spring in a factory yard,
> Rust that clings to the form that the strength has left
> Hard and curled and ready to snap.[43]

Poetic creation is envisioned as a kind of physical expulsion; violent poetic images are the result of a violent poetic process. The break between the first two lines leads the reader to imagine the memory not so much bringing forth images as throwing them up. The poem gives us the act of vomiting and only then, once we get to the second line, does it focus on what has been thrown up, what are the contents of this memorial activity. The poem is not a careful exploration of an individual consciousness—throughout, the speaker refers to "the memory" rather than "my memory"—but an attempt to embody the affective memory of any person encountering this urban scene. There is the feeling that some "secret" exists deep within things, if only it would give itself up.

Above all else, however, this is a poetry of fragments. The speaker obsessively seeks out objects—the rusted spring, the twisted branch—that are left over and broken off, objects that express some relationship to an unknown (and perhaps unknowable) whole. Throughout *Prufrock and Other Observations* (1917), Eliot searches for the "thousand sordid images / Of which your soul was constituted," and it is as an image-maker that Eliot is most notable in this early work.[44] We remember the metonymic "hands / That are raising dingy shades / In a thousand furnished rooms" in "Preludes," the cat that "devours a morsel of rancid butter" in "Rhapsody on a Windy Night."[45] We remember, in short, fragments, and this poetry-as-fragmentation prepares us for *The Waste Land*, modernism's great poem of fragmentation.

The Waste Land, like "Preludes" and "Rhapsody on a Windy Night," appears to be "a heap of broken images," a concatenation of images connected only by their common mood of despair and disillusionment.[46] Yet what is arguably most distinctive about *The Waste Land* is not the precision with which Eliot renders these images, but the force with which he breaks them. "The Burial of the Dead," for instance, opens quite undramatically, with its revision of Chaucer's *General Prologue* ("April is the cruellest month") and its depiction of a leisurely day spent near the Starnbergersee in southern Bavaria.[47] The poem begins to fracture most obviously with the inclusion of untranslated German: "Bin gar keine Russin, stamm' aus Litauen, echt deutsch." The speaker (or speakers) then immediately switches back to English: "And when we were children, staying at the arch-duke's, / My cousin's, he took me out on a sled, / And I was frightened." The lines proceed by juxtaposition. The governing syntactical device is parataxis: we leap backwards in time and move from a plural to a singular speaker, with no preparation and no explanation beyond the connective "and." The first stanza contains within it much of the poem's larger governing strategies of disjuncture, including fragments of language jostling against one another, unexplained temporal shifts, and ambiguity as to the speaker's position in time, space, and language.

As critics and undergraduates alike know, to read *The Waste Land* is to be confronted by difficulty. The same could be said of the experience of reading Barth's *Epistle to the Romans*, and both Eliot and Barth argued that what might have seemed like obscurantism was in fact the intellectual and stylistic complexity required of their respective projects. Here is Barth in the preface to the second edition of his *Epistle to the Romans*: "For us neither the Epistle to the Romans, nor the present theological position, nor the present state of the world, nor the relation between God and the world, is simple. And he who is now concerned with truth must boldly acknowledge that he cannot be simple . . . Those who claim to speak simply seem to me to be—simply speaking about something else. By such simplicity I remain unconvinced."[48] And here is Eliot in his 1921 essay "The Metaphysical Poets": "We can only say that it appears likely that poets in our civilization, as it exists at present, must be *difficult*. Our civilization comprehends great variety and complexity, and this variety and complexity, playing upon a refined sensibility, must produce various and complex results. The poet must become more and more comprehensive, more allusive, more indirect, in order to force, to dislocate if necessary, language into his meaning."[49] Both theologian and poet see the world as complex, and both theologian and poet imagine that language must be dislocated in order to do justice to this complexity. At one point in his *Epistle to the Romans*, Barth claims that theological discourse is "twice-broken."[50] Stephen Webb glosses this phrase thus: "It is about a reality broken by God, and it is itself broken, a shattered mirror reflecting a shattered world."[51] Eliot's poetry is likewise twice-broken; it is both about a fractured world and an example of the fracturing this world has brought about. For Eliot and for Barth, difficulty is largely the result of stylistic fragmentation, and stylistic fragmentation is the only honest way to write in a broken world.

Barth, like Eliot, tries to create unity amidst his formal and thematic disintegration. Where Eliot in *The Waste Land* finds recourse in the mythic method, which, in Franco Moretti's words, tries to "tame polyphony" and give chaos "a form and meaning," Barth asserts that all of his text's paradoxes are united under the larger, determining contradiction between God and humankind.[52] Still, both writers, at least in these early works, leave us more with a sense of brokenness than with a sense of harmony. Terry Eagleton has described Wittgenstein's *Tractatus Logico-Philosophicus* as "the first great work of philosophical modernism—not a theoretical reflection on that avant-garde cultural experiment, but an example of it in its own right."[53] We could make a similar claim about Barth's second edition of *Epistle to the Romans* as the first great work of theological modernism (understanding "modernism" as the artistic, and not the religious, movement).[54]

Now, I want to move beyond a stylistic comparison of Barth and Eliot and ask something different: What are the theological affinities between Barth's work and Eliot's most sustained poetic examination of the Christian faith, *Four Quartets*?[55] How can we relate Barth's theology, which was obsessed with the chasm separating God from humanity, to Eliot's late sequence, which asserts that its central subject is the event that bridges this gap, the Incarnation? To begin to answer these questions—and to distinguish more clearly between Barthian and neo-Thomist conceptions of revelation—it will be useful to look at two essays from Faber and Faber's 1937 collection *Revelation*: the opening essay by Barth and the later essay by the neo-Thomist philosopher Martin D'Arcy, Eliot's friend and a regular contributor to the *Criterion*.

"The crater made at the percussion point of an exploding shell"

One of Karl Barth's best expositors, George Hunsinger, has written that the "creaturely sphere" for Barth means "the sphere of that which is not God."[56] How, then, does God come to reveal himself within this sphere? What is the nature of Christian revelation? Barth's incessant and urgent posing of these questions forced his contemporaries to offer their own answers. In 1937, Faber and Faber decided to intervene in this conversation, publishing a collection of essays on the subject of revelation—a subject that John Baillie, the book's editor, described as currently "the most frequented hunting ground of the theologians."[57] This state of affairs, Baillie writes in his preface to the volume, is a "remarkable contrast to the situation obtaining in, say, the years immediately prior to the Great War" (which are, of course, also the years immediately prior to Barth's *Epistle to the Romans*).[58] The Faber and Faber collection was an ecumenical effort, with contributions from Catholic, Anglican, Russian Orthodox, and Baptist theologians. But Barth's shadow looms everywhere.

Eliot wrote the introduction to *Revelation*, and his contribution to the book is a strange one. He begins by disavowing any expertise in theological matters: "What I have to write is not an introduction to the essays in this book, but an introduction to the subject; and it is because I am not a theologian that I have been asked to contribute . . . My qualification is the eye of the owl, not that of the eagle."[59] This self-deprecating pose was one that Eliot often struck when writing on theological matters. For example, in the midst of the romanticism versus classicism debate in the *Criterion* in 1927, Eliot admitted that his "knowledge of Aquinas is slight: it is limited to the accounts of Gilson and de Wulf, to two volumes of extracts . . . to two or three books by M. Maritain and modern Dominicans, and to the new edition of the *Summa* published by Desclée."[60] Four to five commentaries, plus the primary text itself: a strange description of "slight knowledge." After apologizing for his own supposed lack of theological sophistication, Eliot immediately launches attacks against, among other targets, humanism, Buddhism, and Bertrand Russell. Eliot's introduction does have occasional moments of interest, as when he writes, "The division between those who accept, and those who deny, Christian revelation I take to be the most profound division between human beings."[61] Still, Eliot admits that his musings have little bearing on the essays that follow. The piece reveals a good deal about Eliot's own regular polemical style—calm on the surface, angry underneath—but it does not truly serve as an introduction to the volume at hand.

Baillie's preface, however, clearly delineates the theological issues at stake. More specifically, Baillie uses Barth to frame the two debates animating *Revelation*:

first, "the old distinction of natural and revealed knowledge of God"; and second, "the new distinction between a general and a special revelation."[62] The first debate, over natural and revealed knowledge of God, involves dialectical theology's critique of nineteenth-century religious liberalism. Echoing Barth's disparagement of figures like Schleiermacher, Baillie argues that nineteenth-century religious writing had begun "to speak of our Christian knowledge in terms of human discovery, and to make less and less use of the terminology of revelation."[63] According to this view, knowledge of God arises less from God's self-revelation and more from humanity's own inquiries. In contrast, Baillie holds up Barth as symptomatic of the modern theologian who believes that "our religion, if we are to have one at all, must be something given to us by God rather than provided by ourselves."[64] For Barth, Baillie writes, "only in Christ have we any true knowledge of God at all; there is no natural knowledge of God, and only in 'a perverted, invalid and loose sense' of the concept can there be said to exist any revelation apart from Christ."[65] Without Christ, God is hidden; no matter how hard humanity may try to reason towards him, it will fail. With Christ, though, God enters humanity and makes himself known. The second debate—between "a general and a special revelation"—asks primarily whether God reveals himself only through Christ or also through other, non-Christian religious traditions.[66] This debate also asks whether revelation should be limited to the Incarnation (the Word made flesh) or whether it is present in other aspects of the church and its life: the communion of saints, the Eucharist, sacred dogma, and church tradition.

Barth's essay, which opens the volume proper, exhibits his usual theological and stylistic vigor. He begins by offering a lucid, limited definition of revelation: "The Christian apprehension of revelation is the response of man to the Word of God whose name is Jesus Christ. It is the Word of God who creates the Christian apprehension of revelation."[67] For Barth, "apprehension," human understanding of the divine presence, is really a matter of "response," of human reaction to the divine presence. Man must "bring himself to an attitude of attention, of awe, of trust, of obedience"—an attitudinal change that is itself created by God—in order to hear God's Word.[68] Response, in short, creates the grounds upon which revelation can be understood, and the ability to respond is itself created by God. Barth sees epistemology (how we understand revelation) as secondary to, and dependent upon, ontology (how our being is transformed by the Being revealed in and through the Word of God).

For Barth, Christ's Incarnation *is* revelation, full stop, and this singular, shattering incursion of the eternal into the temporal is not to be confused with what he calls "tokens" of God's revelation, such as the sacraments and the institutional church. As he exclaims, "There are no multiplications of the Incarnation!"[69] Christ is the object, subject, and medium of revelation: "From Him it gains its content, its form and its limit."[70] ("Token," we might note, is also the word used by Eliot in "Ash-Wednesday" to describe God's call to sinful humanity: "The token of the word unheard, unspoken."[71] Like Barth, Eliot believes that the tokens of God's revelation do not reveal humanity's proximity but its distance from God's presence. The word is unheard, unspoken.)

Barth focuses very little on the ways in which this world expresses God's presence: "The conception of an indirect revelation in nature, in history and in our self-consciousness is destroyed by the recognition of grace, by the recognition of Jesus Christ as the eternal Word who was made flesh."[72] In *Epistle to the Romans*, Barth writes that, in the Incarnation, "two worlds meet and go apart, two planes intersect," as "the hidden line, intersecting time and eternity, concrete occurrence and primal origin, men and God, becomes visible."[73] For Barth, revelation is a sudden moment of rupture that reverberates outward, and theology's job is to examine this intersection of time and eternity, to explore "the crater made at the percussion point of an exploding shell."[74]

The contribution of *Criterion* regular and Catholic neo-Thomist Martin D'Arcy provides a sharp contrast to Barth's theology of revelation. Where Barth begins by radically limiting the scope and meaning of revelation, D'Arcy opens by acknowledging the concept's definitional vagueness. Revelation, D'Arcy writes, "can be used in a strict, and in a general or loose sense."[75] The strict sense denotes that which "is directly communicated by God Himself and is called by the Apostle Paul the gospel of Jesus Christ"; the general or loose sense includes all that is revealed through the church and its tradition—the communion of saints and church dogma, for instance.[76]

D'Arcy's more expansive view of revelation proceeds from two core principles. First, he trusts in the Thomist *analogia entis*, the idea that there is a deep and abiding link between Creator and creation, and that we can move, always imperfectly but still productively, from one to the other. Barth, by contrast, loathed this typically Catholic theological position, going so far as to describe "the analogy of being as the artifact of the anti-Christ. It is precisely because of this that one cannot be a Catholic."[77] Second, D'Arcy trusts in the mind's ability to understand, however incompletely, God's revelation. It is "false," D'Arcy argues, "to separate off the Word of God from all that man discovers by the light of his natural reason."[78] In a dry, abstract style—a striking departure from Barth's tendency towards prophetic exclamation—D'Arcy carefully lays out his argument that "there is . . . a sphere of the suprasensible which is attainable by the human mind, and this fact once and for all guarantees reason in its search for ultimate causes and for God."[79]

The word "attainable" would have been anathema to Barth. The crisis under which we live, Barth believed, resides precisely in the fact that God remains unattainable except through his sudden, loving grace. Note the shift in emphasis. If Barth's theology of revelation asks how the eternal, perfect God can descend into our fallen world, then D'Arcy asks how humanity, through reason and the church, can come to understand God. Midway through his essay, D'Arcy writes, "The Incarnation and the Redemption being living facts, and the evidence of the divine authority and truth being ever externally present in the Church, the soul 'comes and sees.' This act of assimilation or response, call it what one may, is made possible by grace."[80] One can only imagine how Barth would have responded to the idea that "assimilation" and "response" are equally valid words to describe the relationship of humanity to divinity.

At one point, after criticizing the humanist who trains his eye solely on human experience and discounts transcendence, D'Arcy acknowledges the corrective purpose of Barth's theology: "It is no wonder that religious minds sensible of the awful distance of God from man . . . should fence off revelation from all human interference."[81] And yet, D'Arcy ultimately finds this theological purity "defective through [its] ignorance of the bounty of God." In D'Arcy's reading, to see God as "unapproachably distant and unutterably strange," to emphasize the qualitative distinction between Creator and creation as opposed to the Creator's sacramental presence within the world, is to have an impoverished vision of humanity and also of God and the love that he has lavished on the world. A more perfect encapsulation of the Barthian-Thomist divide would be hard to find.

Analogy and Dialectic, Hopkins and Eliot

The specific contrast I have drawn between Barth and D'Arcy conforms to a more general division offered by David Tracy in his influential work, *The Analogical Imagination: Christian Theology and the Culture of Pluralism*. In this book, Tracy argues that theology has "two major conceptual languages": the dialectical imagination, which emphasizes the radical disjunctions between God and humanity and preaches "the negation of all poisonous dreams of establishing any easy continuities between Christianity and culture"; and the analogical imagination, which employs a "language of ordered relationships articulating similarity-in-difference" and which posits a world that is "theologically envisioned as sacrament."[82]

Though part of Tracy's project is to show that all good theology must be both dialectical and analogical, he articulates many clear distinctions between these two conceptual languages. Dialectical thinkers, generally Protestant, emphasize rupture, "the purging fire" of negative dialectics, and the prophetic proclamation of the Word of God.[83] Analogical thinkers, generally Catholic, accentuate harmony, metaphorical relationships, and the manifestation of the Word of God in this world. Where Barth, the exemplary dialectical theologian, says, "God is in heaven, and thou art on earth," the analogical thinker says, "God is in heaven, yet manifests himself on earth." Another way of describing this difference is to say that the dialectical theologian practices apophatic theology, which describes God through negation, while the analogical theologian practices cataphatic theology, which describes God through what he is (love, peace, justice, etc.).

Tracy's work has been taken up not just by theologians but also by literary scholars.[84] In fact, Tracy himself uses Eliot's poetry as a reference point in *The Analogical Imagination*, making the case that, in Eliot's development from the high modernism of *The Waste Land* to the Anglo-Catholicism of *Four Quartets*, we can see a shift from the dialectical to the analogical imagination: "In contemporary poetry, the *Four Quartets* of T. S. Eliot are representative of this 'Johannine' (and Anglican) tradition, in contrast to the more negation-oriented (and, in that limited sense, more Pauline) character of Eliot's *The Waste-Land*."[85]

Tracy is correct in arguing that the early Eliot is more obviously Pauline— using the categories of modern theology, we might say more obviously Barthian— than the late Eliot. Barth's vision of the Incarnation is presaged in Eliot's 1920 "Gerontion," in which "Christ the tiger" suddenly, violently comes into the "depraved May" of this world, resulting in a Barthian consuming rather than a Thomist perfecting: "The tiger springs in the new year. Us he devours."[86] But, as Tracy himself has acknowledged, this easy division between dialectical-modernist Eliot and analogical-Anglican Eliot doesn't quite hold. The fragment, Tracy claims, is arguably more important to *Four Quartets* than it is to *The Waste Land*, and its appearance in the former has a serious theological purpose: "In the *Quartets*, Christianity does not provide a restored unity to our contemporary culture (as [Eliot's] essays had promised) but rather a renewed sense of the saturated fragments of gift, promise, body, and faith as a new kind of knowledge born of love."[87]

So where can we locate *Four Quartets* within the analogical-dialectical typology, and how does this relate to Barth's theology of revelation? Before answering these questions, it will be useful to establish a brief contrast by examining another poet interested in turning theological thought into poetic form: Gerard Manley Hopkins. In an essay on Catholicism and the sacraments, Susan K. Wood writes, "Catholicism is not sacramental simply because it celebrates seven sacraments, but because it views the world through the lens of sacramentality. In this view creation becomes diaphanous of the divine."[88] To illustrate Catholicism's sacramental worldview, Wood quotes from one of the most strikingly analogical, sacramental poems in the English language, Hopkins's "God's Grandeur."[89]

The poem opens with a bold assertion of God's immanence:

The world is charged with the grandeur of God.
It will flame out, like shining from shook foil;

It gathers to a greatness, like the ooze of oil
Crushed. Why do men then now not reck his rod?[90]

Hopkins retains the startling nature of revelation. God's grandeur "flame[s] out," and we are shocked by the percussive repetitions of "flame," "like," "shook," and "foil." Even when the language becomes gentler (the nice play of "o" in "ooze of oil"), the next line startles us anew, with the stress falling on the hard "c" of "Crushed." But the truly startling aspect of revelation here is how it is always and everywhere around us. The world does not *intersect* with the grandeur of God; it *is charged* with the grandeur of God. The participle hints that this charging is a continuous action: the world holds within itself, like a charged battery, the shock of God's beauty and grace. (The poem would read very differently if it claimed that God's grandeur "charges" the world.) Hopkins shifts verb tenses, from the future tense of "will flame out" to the present tense of "gathers to a greatness," since God has been present, is present, and will be present, flaming and shining and gathering, in his creation.

Hopkins mirrors the sheer profusion of God's presence in this world with the formal profusion of his verse. Every line is charged, almost to the breaking point, with the compressed, sacramental intensity of sensory experience. Dense alliteration ("gathers to a greatness," "flame out like shining from shook foil"), the piling up of stressed syllables ("flame out"; "shook foil"), incessant repetition ("have trod, have trod, have trod"): all serve to show the world overflowing with divine presence. Hopkins acknowledges the fallen nature of worldly existence—as he says, "all is seared with trade; bleared, smeared with toil"—and yet, "for all this, nature is never spent; / There lives the dearest freshness deep down things." The dearest freshness of all things—we might say, their holiness— doesn't just appear in the world, it lives there; and it doesn't just live on the surface of things, it lives "deep down," in the world's very pith and marrow.

For Hopkins, there is a mysterious but continuous connection between "nature" and "God's grandeur," between a particular thing's being (following the medieval theologian Duns Scotus, Hopkins calls this a thing's *haecceitas*) and the Creator who authorizes this particular thing's being. Moreover, for Hopkins, this connection is a direct result of the Incarnation. "God's Grandeur" concludes with an image that asserts the causal relation between the world's sacramentality and Christ's birth brought about through the Holy Spirit. Things of this world exhibit freshness and beauty, Hopkins writes, "Because the Holy Ghost over the bent / World broods with warm breast and with ah! bright wings." In "The May Magnificat," Hopkins even more directly links nature's beauty to the Incarnation. In the spring, with "All things rising, all things sizing," the Virgin Mary sees that the "magnifying of each its kind / With delight calls to mind / How she did in her stored / Magnify the Lord."[91] The poem concludes by explicitly drawing the connection between the bounty of God and the bounty of earth: "This ecstacy all through mothering earth / Tells Mary her mirth till Christ's birth / To remember and exultation / In God who was her salvation."[92]

Eliot's public pronouncements on Hopkins were often dismissive. In *After Strange Gods*, he praises Hopkins's metrical innovations but argues that these innovations, "like the mind of their author," "operate only within a narrow range." Despite being "the author of some very beautiful devotional verse," Eliot writes, Hopkins "is not a religious poet in the more important sense in which I have elsewhere maintained Baudelaire to be a religious poet."[93] The "more important sense" that Eliot alludes to can be found in his 1930 essay on the French poet, where Eliot argues that in spite of—or, more surprisingly, because of—Baudelaire's focus on perversity and suffering, his is a fundamentally religious imagination: "Such suffering as Baudelaire's implies the possibility of a positive state of beatitude. Indeed, in his way of suffering is already a kind of presence of the supernatural and of the superhuman. He rejects always the purely natural and the purely human."[94] Eliot, in other words, defines Baudelaire as a religious poet precisely because of his dialectical imagination. The poet who descends into hellishness and despair suggests, by the very descent, a state of beatitude and plenty; the poet who resides within creation, who describes how this world manifests God's presence, offers no such suggestion. Eliot's attitude towards Hopkins would shift over the years. Indeed, in "Types of English Religious Verse," the lecture with which this chapter begins, Eliot planned to reverse his earlier position, arguing that Hopkins was "the greatest religious poet of his own century," the one poet in whom "the nature-worship of the Romantics is taken up into something higher, and reaches its consummation by being re-integrated into an orthodox Christian view of life."[95] Still, it is worth remembering that, for Eliot, "religious poets" were those poets who most powerfully exhibited Tracy's dialectical imagination—not those who, like Hopkins, most powerfully exhibited Tracy's analogical, sacramental imagination.

Four Quartets, like "God's Grandeur," takes as its central subject the Incarnation. As Eliot writes in "The Dry Salvages," "The hint half guessed, the gift half understood, is Incarnation."[96] Yet Eliot's poetry could not be further from the formal compression and bold analogical thinking of Hopkins. Consider, for instance, the opening of "The Dry Salvages," the poem that contains Eliot's most direct, sustained examination of the Incarnation. The first lines establish the poem's finicky scrupulousness: "I do not know much about gods; but I think that the river / Is a strong brown god—sullen, untamed and intractable."[97] While this metaphorical description of the Mississippi hearkens back to Mark Twain and Walt Whitman, the speaker lacks the confidence that such allusive authority might be expected to give him. The claim is couched by apology and qualification; we are left with what the speaker "thinks" rather than with what "is." (Imagine Hopkins writing, "I do not know much about God; but I think that the world / Is charged with His grandeur.")

In the second stanza, Eliot moves away from such hedging and towards a more confident lyricism with his Whitmanian list of the sea's flotsam, "Its hints of earlier and other creation: // The starfish, the hermit crab, the whale's back-bone; / The pools where it offers to our curiosity / The more delicate algae and the sea anemone."[98] Here, Eliot first brings up the question of analogy: what exactly are these objects hints of? Crucially, they are hints not of a Creator but of impersonal, elemental creation, intimations not of eternity but of primitive history, "a time / Older than the time of chronometers."[99] A. David Moody writes that the opening of section 1 of "The Dry Salvages" seems a "study in an unsatisfactory way of putting man's relation to nature"; it "connects the elemental rhythm of the ocean with instinctive fear and terror, and the sense of man's helpless subjection to fate."[100] To use Charles Taylor's term, nature here seems to lack an "ontic logos," a meaningful order that is, in the Christian vision, the result of divine, loving creation: "the whole exhibit[ing] its own kind of goodness: plenitude, reason, or the benevolence of the Creator."[101] If the world provides humanity with any gifts here, they are simply the images of inhuman nature. We are far from Hopkins's assertions of a benevolent, personal Creator.

Section 3 of "The Dry Salvages" opens in a similar manner, once again surrounding and interrupting traditional lyrical material with self-correction:

> I sometimes wonder if that is what Krishna meant—
> Among other things—or one way of putting the same thing:
> That the future is a faded song, a Royal Rose or a lavender spray
> Of wistful regret for those who are not yet here to regret,
> Pressed between yellow leaves of a book that has never been opened.[102]

Like Hopkins, Eliot stretches his lines to the breaking point. Eliot does this, however, not because God's grandeur overwhelms the limits of the poetic line, but because the speaker cannot rein in his own ruminations. The entire sequence is filled with chatty asides, even apparent banalities: "You say that I am repeating / Something I have said before. I shall say it again"; "There is, it seems to us, / At best, only a limited value / In the knowledge derived from experience."[103] Eliot himself recognized this lyric dullness in a 1947 letter to H. W. Heckstall-Smith, where he describes "passages in the poems which are deliberately intended to give an effect of flatness."[104]

But what Donald Davie has described as "stumbling trundling rhythms" and "inarticulate ejaculations of reach-me-down phrases" serve mainly as a contrast to the sequence's moments of intense lyricism.[105] Indeed, in his letter to Heckstall-Smith, Eliot goes on to claim that the flat passages are included "for purposes of contrast."[106] That is to say, the passages that are flat are flat because they stand in juxtaposition to passages that are heightened, and the passages that are heightened are only experienced as such because they stand in juxtaposition to the passages that are flat. *The Waste Land* has long been recognized as Eliot's masterpiece of juxtaposition, but *Four Quartets* is just as startling in its use of formal and thematic contrasts. It is certainly a different kind of juxtaposition than that exhibited in *The Waste Land*. Rather than placing poetic fragments alongside one another, Eliot shifts verse forms (terza rima, blank verse), offers statement followed by counterstatement (the opening of "Burnt Norton"), and, most importantly, abruptly shifts the lyrical intensity of his verse. Eliot shuttles back and forth between moments of dramatic anguish—"So I assumed a double part, and cried / And heard another's voice cry: 'What! are *you* here?'"—and periods of boredom that are represented by the flattest style imaginable.[107]

Eliot theorized the necessity of lyrical contrast in his essay "The Music of Poetry," where he writes, "I do not believe that any word well-established in its own language is either beautiful or ugly. The music of a word is, so to speak, at a point of intersection: it arises from its relation first to the words immediately preceding and following it, and indefinitely to the rest of its context."[108] *Four Quartets* is structured around a series of epiphanies—the moment in the rose garden, the flashing of "winter lightning," the "Midwinter spring" when "the short day is brightest, with frost and fire"—that derive their intensity from all the nonepiphanic time and language that precede and follow them.[109] It is in part because they are hemmed in by flatness that these moments soar so high; the "boring" poetry creates the conditions by which the lyrical moments can be most revelatory.

I use the word "revelatory" intentionally, since the most lyrical moments in *Four Quartets* are, in a deep sense, also the most theological. They concern what Eliot took to be the central mystery of religious experience—the brief moments when the eternal and the temporal meet before moving apart once again. In "The Dry Salvages," Eliot describes these moments of transcendence:

> For most of us, there is only the unattended
> Moment, the moment in and out of time,
> The distraction fit, lost in a shaft of sunlight,
> The wild thyme unseen, or the winter lightning
> Or the waterfall, or music heard so deeply
> That it is not heard at all, but you are the music
> While the music lasts.[110]

These experiences of transcendence present themselves in different settings. Sometimes, they come from the pure perception of nature, as when one sees the flashing of winter lightning; at other times, they come from the pure perception of art, as when one listens to a beautiful piece of music. In either case, though, the moments are both transient (the musical reverie lasts "While the music lasts"; the lightning flashes and then is gone) and eternal. They are the self's most intense experiences precisely because they allow an escape from the self. Or, not exactly an escape from the self, but a revelation of the self's deep connection to, even submersion within, something beyond the self. The perceiver becomes part of what is perceived; the medium is all.

Shortly after this listing of the different types of revelatory experience, Eliot claims that these are "only hints and guesses, / Hints followed by guesses," and that the "hint half guessed, the gift half understood, is Incarnation." Like the Incarnation, these moments wed the temporal and the eternal. Like the Incarnation, they allow nature to shine through with grace's glory. But, of course, they are not the Incarnation itself; they are only hints at it. What they reveal is a feeling of oneness, a sense that the temporal and concrete can manifest the eternal and transcendent. But they lack any real content: again, the medium, rather than the message, is all. We can speculate about the knowledge and truth that lie behind these moments, we can guess at the gift they offer and the giver who offers them, but that is it.

In short, these hints and guesses are what Barth calls "tokens." They remind us of revelation, but they are decidedly not revelation itself. In the chorus from *The Rock,* Eliot tests out many of the theological ideas that he will develop in *Four Quartets.* In the seventh chorus, we hear of the singular nature of the Incarnation:

> Then came, at a predetermined moment, a moment in time and of time,
> A moment not out of time, but in time, in what we call history: transecting,
>   bisecting the world of time, a moment in time but not like a moment of time,
> A moment in time but time was made through that moment: for without the
>   meaning there is no time, and that moment of time gave the meaning.[111]

Eliot foregrounds the Incarnation's relationship to human history. God's self-revelation cuts through and makes time, turns mere sequence into meaningful narrative, and makes possible the halting journey of humanity towards faith: "Yet always struggling, always reaffirming, always resuming their march on the way that was lit by the light; / Often halting, loitering, straying, delaying, returning, yet following no other way."[112] Yet just as important is the Incarnation's suddenness ("Then came") and, crucially, its singularity. In the stanza before the description of Christ's Incarnation, the unredeemed world is characterized as "Waste and void. Waste and void. And darkness on the face of the deep"; in the stanza after the description of man's faithful struggle, we hear that "Men have left GOD not for other gods, they say, but for no god."[113] The seventh chorus ends with the repeated intonation of "Waste and void. Waste and void. And darkness on the face of the deep," with men forgetting "All gods except Usury, Lust and Power."[114] If Christ's entrance into the world gives that world meaning ("that moment of time gave the meaning"), then what is remarkable is how meaningless the world still seems afterwards. Revelation is surrounded by waste and void on both sides. Christ's revelation bisects and illuminates history, but the continued signs of this revelation are hard to find.

Eliot ends "Burnt Norton" with the memorable lament: "Ridiculous the waste sad time / Stretching before and after."[115] *Four Quartets* is Eliot's poem of the "waste sad time." If Hopkins is the great poet of revelation's profusion— the lyrical speaker in "God's Grandeur" almost feels assaulted by God's presence—then Eliot is the great poet of revelation's retreat. Barth described revelation as an exploding shell that left a crater in its wake, and Eliot's *Four Quartets* moves ceaselessly between shell and crater, revelation and its withdrawal. Eliot wants to dwell in a world suffused with the grandeur of God; he wants to see God's presence gather to a greatness; he wants to be a sacramental poet. Yet what we are left with is the sharp Barthian contrast between the "intersection of the timeless with time" and the "waste sad time." As Lee Oser puts it, "We are met with a sensibility that explores a middle way between Aristotle and Luther. The result is not so much a field of gray as it is darkness alternating with radiances of light along the path of experience."[116]

And what is more, and what links Eliot's poetic vision even more closely to Barth's theological vision, is the way in which, even in these moments of intersection, we are left less with a loving appreciation of time and its processes than with a longing for pure timelessness. Steve Ellis, in a brief discussion of Barthian echoes in Eliot's poetry, points to a particular passage in *Revelation*, one in which Barth offers a shocking dismissal of the things of this world: ". . . the voice of earth and of animal life; the voice of the apparently infinite heavens and, sounding through this voice, the voice of the heavens' apparently inescapable fate; the voice of his own blood and of the blood of his parents and of his ancestors flowing in his veins; the voice of the genius and of the hero in his own breast: voices all falsely endowed with divine dignity and authority, and for that very reason, not the eternal Word of God!"[117] Barth has been accused of being a dualist, and, at least in his early work, there are good reasons for such accusations. He does not say, with Hopkins, "Glory be to God for dappled things"; he says, "Woe be to creation for its sinful ways."[118]

Similarly, Eliot's revelatory moments do not really embody God's presence, nor do they offer a sacramental vision of creation. Eliot may claim that he seeks out "the intersection of the timeless with time," yet almost every instance of this dramatic meeting results in an ecstatic removal from time and the senses. Here is the setting for the first such epiphany in the rose garden of "Burnt Norton":

> There they were, dignified, invisible,
> Moving without pressure, over the dead leaves,
> In the autumn heat, through the vibrant air,
> And the bird called, in response to
> The unheard music hidden in the shrubbery,
> And the unseen eyebeam crossed, for the roses
> Had the look of flowers that are looked at.[119]

The world seems awash in revelation—"over," "in," and "through" the world, the presence of some great glory echoes. But this sense, Eliot tells us, is "the deception of the thrush." Moreover, this epiphanic presence is felt through physical absence. Everything is defined negatively: the presiding spirits are "invisible," the music "unheard," the eyebeam "unseen."

This negation of physical presence continues as the speaker walks down "the empty alley" towards "the drained pool." Then, suddenly, the dry pool undergoes a transformation:

> And the pool was filled with water out of sunlight,
> And the lotos rose, quietly, quietly,
> The surface glittered out of heart of light,
> And they were behind us, reflected in the pool.
> Then a cloud passed, and the pool was empty.
> Go, said the bird, for the leaves were full of children,
> Hidden excitedly, containing laughter.
> Go, go, go, said the bird: human kind
> Cannot bear very much reality.[120]

Apparently human kind cannot bear very much eternity, either; eternity makes itself felt in the sunlit pool only to shatter of its own perfection. The cloud must pass and the pool must become empty once again. The quiet must give way to the bird's chattering.[121]

Eliot says that this is the moment "in and out of time," but it is far more out than in. (It is also arguably more Buddhist than Christian, particularly in its image of the lotus.) As Mutlu Blasing has argued, the "association of sin with the flesh thematically pervades Eliot's work in general"—not just in the early, romantic verse but also in the orthodox, Christian verse of the 1940s.[122] For Eliot, this world may be cut through with eternity, but we are ultimately left with a desire for pure transcendence rather than with an appreciation of divine manifestation. In 1945, Eliot argued that the greatest philosophical poems, like

Lucretius's *On the Nature of Things* or Dante's *Divine Comedy*, "were not designed to persuade the readers to an intellectual assent, but to convey an emotional equivalent of the ideas. What Lucretius and Dante teach you, in fact, is *what it feels like* to hold certain beliefs."[123] What Eliot's poetry teaches us, surprisingly, is *what it feels like* to hold Barthian views on revelation.

But this is not quite accurate, either. One of the challenges of *Four Quartets* is that it is a dialectical poem that wants to be an analogical poem. Eliot sees the world as a brutal shuttling between pure presence and complete absence, between transcendence and banality. Yet he wants to move beyond this oscillation towards a more consistent, harmonious relationship between temporality and eternity. F. R. Leavis, dissatisfied with Eliot's theological turn in "Little Gidding," argued that Eliot's treatment of the sacred in this last poem was "in essence one of mere statement—statement so insistent as fairly to be called emphatic assertion."[124] But this is the brilliance (and the complexity) of Eliot's achievement. He balances this emphatic statement with formal enactment, and form and content, embodiment and assertion, often exist in productive tension with one another. Formally, Eliot's work is a poetic enactment of Barth's theology, illustrating the sudden ruptures brought about by God's presence. Yet this exists in contrast to Eliot's claim that all the "timeless moments" of transcendence are not removed from this world but are part of history, and a specific cultural history at that: "for history is a pattern / Of timeless moments. So, while the light fails / On a winter's afternoon, in a secluded chapel / History is now and England."[125] This is a decidedly Catholic sentiment. Yet even while Eliot asserts the world's sacramental nature, his poetry tells a different story, oscillating between a "periphrastic study in a worn-out poetical fashion" and an evocation of "the still point of the turning world" when God's grandeur erupts momentarily into the world.[126]

This tension between statement and enactment, analogy and dialectic, relates interestingly to Eliot's practices as editor of the *Criterion*. As we have seen, to many of its contemporary readers, and even more to its later critics, the *Criterion* appeared to be "an exclusive Thomist club."[127] But, as I argued in Chapter 2, the *Criterion*'s theological identity was much more complicated—and much more open-minded—than critics gave it credit for. Barth had a place within its pages, and so did Kierkegaard, Niebuhr, Tillich, and others. The *Criterion*, in short, could rightly be described as exhibiting a neo-Thomist bent. But this bent allowed for—and, in Eliot's conception of the ideal literary review, even demanded—the expression of the countervailing, Barthian theological position.

Eliot's poetry, then, follows his editing. In each, productive tension is favored over advocacy for a particular theological position. In *Four Quartets*, the dissonance of Eliot's dialectical vision, its discord and instability, does not quite resolve itself into the consonance of the analogical vision. The sequence ends with a vision of integration, when "the tongues of flame are in-folded / Into the crowned knot of fire / And the fire and the rose are one." Eliot hopes for the moment when "all shall be well and / All manner of thing shall be well," when the purgatorial fire and the celestial rose will be united.[128] But, in this world of "waste sad time," the hoped-for resolution is always not-yet.

CHAPTER FOUR

Sacramental Theology and
David Jones's Poetics of Torsion

This is not a representation of a mountain, it *is* 'mountain' under the form of paint. —DAVID JONES, "Art and Sacrament"

In "Distinguo," a short poem from his 1991 collection *Dog Fox Field*, the Australian poet Les Murray distinguishes poetry from prose, identifying each form with a particular religious tradition:

Prose is Protestant-agnostic,
story, discussion, significance,
but poetry is Catholic:
poetry is presence.[1]

Murray, who converted to Catholicism in his early twenties, writes with the convert's fervor. For him, there is a deep connection, even an identity, between the Catholic celebration of the sacraments ("presence" alludes to the Catholic belief in "the unique, true presence of Christ in the Eucharist under the species or appearance of bread and wine") and the lyric poem.[2] If, as Jonathan Culler has argued recently, "lyric aims to be an event, not a representation of an event"; if, as Mutlu Blasing has written, "lyric poetry is not mimesis" but something more direct and enactive, "an experience of another kind of order," then Murray's claim makes a certain amount of sense.[3] For the Catholic, the Eucharist does not represent an event—Christ's sacrifice—but rather makes that sacrifice active once again. It does not imitate; it embodies. Elsewhere, Murray makes this comparison between the Catholic Eucharist and the lyric poem even more explicit. As a poet, he writes, "I identified with the Eucharist. I thought, yes, yes, the absolute transformation of ordinary elements into the divine. I know about that."[4]

The Anglo-Welsh poet, painter, and modernist David Jones would have agreed with Murray's formulation. Like Murray, Jones was a Catholic convert who saw a commitment to the sacraments, and particularly a commitment to the Eucharist, as Catholicism's defining characteristic; and like Murray, Jones believed that it was the task of the poet to show how the stuff of this world might point towards, and make physically present, God's divine grace. In both his poetry and his prose, Jones explored how, as he put it, we can relate "sacraments with a capital 'S'" (more specifically, the Eucharist) to "sacraments with a small 's'" (Jones means all human sign-making, including especially painting and poetry).[5] In fact, Jones goes so far as to define sacramentality as the defining feature of humanity: "Angels only: no sacrament. Beasts only: no sacrament. Man: sacrament at every turn and all levels of the 'profane' and 'sacred', in the trivial and the profound, no escape from sacrament."[6] Humanity's mixed nature—neither purely angelic nor purely bestial—requires sacrament, which is that which bridges the gap between spirit and matter.

Jones opens his 1952 epic poem *The Anathemata* with this description: "We already and first of all discern him making this thing other. His groping syntax, if we attend, already shapes."[7] The lines refer to a Catholic priest saying the Prayer of Consecration, but they could just as easily describe what the poet does in writing poetry, and that is the point. Both priest and poet are concerned with making something other, allowing the material of this world to signify—and, in the process of signification, to make present something beyond this world, something transcendent and holy. This process can be awkward and tentative, a "groping" after sacramental transformation; and this sacramental transformation can be difficult to "discern," requiring our attendance and attention. But, Jones suggests, if we do attend to the priest and the poet, to the Eucharist and the work of art, then we will be rewarded, experiencing the world made new.

Given his commitment to the sacramental nature of poetry (and to the poetic nature of the sacraments), it should come as little surprise that Jones was an enthusiastic reader of contemporary theology. He was willing, even eager, to acknowledge the debts his poetry owed to modern Catholic thinking about the Eucharist. In his preface to *The Anathemata*, for instance, Jones offered a list of writers and thinkers who had helped shape his own work. The list included several contemporary theologians, including Jacques Maritain, whose *Art and Scholasticism*, we will see, had a profound impact on Jones's own thinking about the artistic act; Martin D'Arcy, *Criterion* contributor and a personal friend to Jones; and Gregory Dix, whose work helped Jones to see the similarities between literature and liturgy.[8]

In this preface and elsewhere, however, Jones singles out one theologian for particular praise: the French Jesuit Maurice de la Taille. After offering his "brief, arbitrary and very chancy list" of intellectual influences, Jones points specifically to de la Taille's 1921 *Mysterium Fidei* (translated into English in 1930 as *The Mystery of Faith*) as one of the "great and crucial works" upon which *The Anathemata*'s aesthetic and theological vision had been built. Jones lauds the book's "integration and creativity," claiming that, despite its seemingly narrow focus upon aspects of Catholic doctrine, *The Mystery of Faith* had, for him at least, a wider significance: "It seemed to illumine things outside its immediate theological context."[9] Again, we see modern poetry's interest in the comprehensiveness of Christian theology; in the fact that, in speaking about the Catholic Mass, the theologian illuminates other aspects of existence.

This was far from the only occasion on which Jones acknowledged the influence of de la Taille, whom he referred to in conversation as "my theologian."[10] Jones ends his 1955 essay "Art and Sacrament," for example, with a quotation from *The Mystery of Faith* about the institution of the Eucharist: "He placed Himself in the order of signs."[11] We can see why Jones found this particular phrase so resonant, since it directly links Christ and the Eucharist to the project of human sign-making: that is, to the project of art and poetry. Similarly, the final section of *The Anathemata*, "Sherthursdaye and Venus Day," takes as its subject de la Taille's argument in *The Mystery of Faith* that "the Supper [on Holy Thursday] and the Cross [on Good Friday] made up one complete sacrifice," a sacrifice that is completed and continued through the Church's regular celebration of the Eucharist.[12] Indeed, Thomas Goldpaugh has shown that *The Mystery of Faith* provides the very structural framework for *The Anathemata*: the poem's complex patterning maps almost perfectly onto de la Taille's argument about the order of the Mass. In other words, de la Taille's theology of the Mass is not just one source among many for *The Anathemata*. It is, in a deep sense, the structural heart of the poem, present at every point even when not alluded to specifically.[13]

This chapter attempts to answer two central questions. First, why did Jones find Catholic sacramental theology so illuminating? And second, how did this theology affect not just Jones's thoughts on the nature and purpose of the Eucharist but also his thinking about, and creation of, poetry? In de la Taille's *The Mystery of Faith*, Jones read that the Eucharist resisted categorization (it was both a thing and an action, a thing that *became* an action) and offered a sense of temporal plenitude and integration. In the celebration of the Eucharist, the past is brought into a millennial present; Christ's sacrifice is not so much reenacted as enacted, made present, fulfilled. Reading Jones's poetry and critical prose, we can see that de la Taille's definition of the Eucharist—"a symbol that effects by itself . . . what it signifies," a material sign that folds time in on itself, making the past present, really and fully—also serves as Jones's definition of poetry.[14] For Jones, both Catholic theologians and modernist artists challenge a referential understanding of signification, in which a symbol (the Eucharist or the artwork) gets its meaning by pointing to something other than itself (God or the subject of the artwork). Instead, Jones claims that Catholics and modernists alike see symbols as, in his language, "re-presentational": the symbol makes present and embodies whatever meaning it might have, and form and substance, past and present, are united as one.

To get at how this sacramental aesthetic plays out in Jones's own poetry—to show, that is, how Jones gives poetic language the temporal extensiveness and efficacy characteristic of the Eucharist—I look at his strange use of participles and verbals. In all of his poetry, from *In Parenthesis*'s depictions of trench warfare to *The Anathemata*'s descriptions of prehistoric geology, Jones wrenches words into new functions with astonishing regularity. Words usually used as nouns become adjectives or verbs; simple present tense verbs shift into the present progressive tense. In a typical passage from *The Anathemata*, Jones describes an ancient Germanic tribe as "shirted, kilted, cloaked, capped and shod."[15] Later, the keel of a ship is "clinkered with lands or flushed with seams. / Raked or bluffed," "Hawse-holed or lathed," "cogginged, tenoned, spiked / plugged or roved / or lashed," "Grommetted, moused; parceled, served."[16] The list could go on. Present participles and verbs in the present progressive aspect also abound. The poem opens with a description of "groping syntax" at the "sagging end" of time, which is heard amidst "the living floriations / under the leaping arches" of Gothic architecture, and it closes with a vision of Christ "riding the Axile Tree."[17] In between, Jones describes a ship's keel as "the trembling tree" and "the quivering elm."[18] Again, the list could go on.

Through this grammatical wrenching, Jones creates a poetics of torsion—a style that is defined by the tension and strain of words stretching beyond their normal functions. By turning nouns into verbs, he blurs the line between thing and action; by finding constant recourse to the progressive tense, he stretches temporal boundaries so that delimited actions become continuous actions. In doing this, Jones makes his poetry presentational rather than propositional. Just as the priest brings the sacred past into the present again in the form of the Eucharist, so for Jones the poet, through grammatical and syntactical contortions, turns static, referential words into active, re-presentative words—words that enact rather than refer, that embody a kind of temporal plenitude that is impossible in everyday language.

In *Sacramental Poetics at the Dawn of Secularism,* Regina Schwartz argues that, at some level, all poetry is sacramental:

> Somehow, a sign seems to inevitably evoke the sacred. But how? First, because it works by evoking something beyond itself, something that transcends the sign. Insofar as it evokes something beyond, the sign participates in transcendence, and transcendence—whether vertical or horizontal, above or beyond our comprehension, control, and use—is the realm of mystery. We can point to it, sign it, and by doing so evoke it, and sometimes even more, manifest it. As Jacques Maritain summarized, for the scholastic philosophers, "sign is that which renders present to knowledge something other than itself." *Signum est id quod repræsentant aliud a se potentiæ cognoscenti. A sign manifests.* And as Augustine

says simply, "Signs, when they pertain to divine things, are called sacraments." Even for Aristotle, a metaphor is not simply ornate language; it bears truth, like riddles that communicate a truth almost incommunicable to human minds.[19]

Likewise, Elaine Scarry argues that all beautiful objects, including poems, are "sacred." The beautiful marks itself as outside our normal perceptual reality, "bound up with the immortal, for it prompts a search for a precedent, which in turn prompts a search for a still earlier precedent, and the mind keeps tripping backward until it at last reaches something that has no precedent, which may very well be the immortal."[20]

Jones certainly would have agreed with Schwartz's claim here: all signs point to something beyond themselves, and in this sense all signs are sacramental. (Indeed, Schwartz begins her book on the cultural effects of the Reformation with a quotation from Jones: "Man is unavoidably a sacramentalist and his works are sacramental in character.")[21] And he likely also would have agreed with Scarry in her claim that beauty consists in a thing or action's otherness, its absolute difference from the ordinary and profane. (*The Anathemata*, recall, begins with the poet/priest "making this thing other.") But what makes Jones's poetry particularly and interestingly sacramental, and what makes it distinctively Catholic, is that Jones looks to the sacramental act not just at the level of theme (although *The Anathemata* does this again and again) or even at the level of structure (as Goldpaugh has shown) but at the very level of grammar and syntax. Jones, we could say, doesn't just want to write sacramental poetry. He wants to make language itself sacramental. Jones alludes to works of contemporary theology, but what is more crucial to notice is how this theological reading informs Jones's writing at the micro-level: the noun shifted into its verbal form; the verb pressed into the progressive tense.

Jones currently occupies a strange place within modernist studies. Even though Eliot and Auden saw Jones as a poetic equal, and even though early critics immediately compared *In Parenthesis* and *The Anathemata* to *The Waste Land* and *Finnegans Wake*, introductions to modernism tend to mention Jones in passing, if at all.[22] Jones's critics are an unusually committed bunch, and there has been excellent work done on Jones by, among others, Kathleen Henderson Staudt and Paul Robichaud. Jones's critics, however, often seem as interested in asserting Jones's greatness as in making arguments about his poetry. Take Thomas Dilworth, the best and most prolific Jones scholar working today. He writes that *In Parenthesis* is "probably the greatest work of British Modernism written between the wars," that the little-known "Epithalamion" is "among the best poems of the middle century," and that *The Anathemata* is the "most aesthetically impressive and rewarding" long poem of the twentieth century.[23]

Jones criticism seems more personal than the criticism of almost any other major modernist figure, and this investment in Jones's status as a great poet means that he is treated more often as an idiosyncratic genius than as part of the modernist period's broader flowering of formal innovation.[24]

Placing Jones alongside modernist peers like Joyce and Pound, however, helps us to see two things: first, that Jones's interest in language that might unite meaning and motion, sign and signified, was one of the defining features of modernist poetics; and second, that, because Jones was a Catholic believer, his claim that poetry can approach the sacramental is an even more radical claim for art's power and importance than his modernist peers were willing to make. Writers like Joyce and Woolf borrow the language of religion in order to understand what happens in the making of art. Jones more dramatically argues that art is, at some deep level, a religious activity.

Poetry as Sacrament, Sacrament as Poetry

Like many other modernists, most notably Eliot and Pound, Jones often used his prose to instruct his readers in how to read his poetry. He wrote essays on modern art and its relation to church history; he supplied extensive notes and long introductions to both *In Parenthesis* and *The Anathemata*; he explicated puzzling allusions, translated arcane bits of Latin or Greek, and let his readers know what literary text or church document might help in their reading. In fact, his texts almost seem to drown in their self-generated secondary material. The 1965 Viking Press edition of *The Anathemata*, for instance, contains a thirty-five-page introduction and footnotes that often take up two-thirds of any given page—all written by Jones himself.

It often is difficult to discern the spirit in which modernist acts of self-explication have been written. Are Eliot's notes to *The Waste Land* genuine, ironic, or some combination of the two? Are Joyce's notes for Stuart Gilbert a legitimate attempt to help the reader, or just another puzzle he teasingly provides for his future interpreters? With Jones, this question never arises: he knows his poetry is difficult, and he wants it to be understood. And why is his poetry so difficult? In part because of its dizzyingly intricate structuring, but mainly because of its endless allusiveness. The first few pages of the last section of *In Parenthesis* offer a good sample. In this small selection, Jones alludes to—and then, in the "General Notes" appended to the end of the poem, provides page citations for—Lewis Carroll's *Hunting of the Snark*, the Welsh epic poems *Y Gododdin* and *Kulhwch ac Olwen*, Shakespeare's *Henry V*, and a particular bugle song played regularly during World War I, among others.[25] Jones most frequently alludes not to other literary works, though, but to religious texts. From the same section of *In Parenthesis*, the "General Notes" list specific references to the Catholic Church's Good Friday liturgy; the "Canonical Hours" that are celebrated daily in the Church's *Divine Office*; a devotion to the "Blessed Virgin Mary" developed by Dominican friars; St. Jerome's Latin translation of the Psalms; and the "Agony and Betrayal" of Christ as narrated in the Gospels.[26]

Jones's poetry was soaked in the liturgy and theology of the Catholic Church, and he knew that his readers would need to familiarize themselves with this liturgy and theology if they were to understand his work. Indeed, at times Jones's work blurs the line between poetry and theology, his footnotes in *The Anathemata* frequently reading like theological essays in miniature. For example, in "Mabinog's Liturgy," the seventh section of *The Anathemata*, Jones describes how different periods of ancient British history have honored the Incarnation. Though the manner and rituals involved in the celebrations might differ, every celebration honors "his body who said, 'DO THIS / for my Anamnesis.' " Jones then offers this footnote:

> Anamnesis. I take leave to remind the reader that this is a key-word in our deposits. The dictionary defines its general meaning as "the recalling of things past." But what is the nature of this particular recalling? I append the following quotation as being clear and to the point: "It (anamnesis) is not quite easy to represent accurately in English, words like 'remembrance' or 'memorial' having for us a connotation of something *absent* which is only mentally recollected. But in the scriptures of both the Old and New Testament *anamnesis* and the cognate verb have a sense of 'recalling' or 're-presenting' before God an event in the past so that it becomes *here and now operative by its effects.*" Gregory Dix, *The Shape of the Liturgy*, p. 161.[27]

Jones believes that the concept of anamnesis—a remembrance that is more powerful, more effective, than our normal sense of the word—is crucial both for his poetry and for Western culture more generally. It was a concept that Jones returned to on other occasions. As Robichaud points out, anamnesis makes another appearance in an essay he wrote on *The Burning Tree*, Glyn Williams's anthology of Welsh poetry. There, Robichaud writes, Jones "compares the memorializing aspect of *Y Gododdin* to the Catholic liturgy . . . observing that it 'does make a kind of *anamnesis* of the personnel of a troop of heavily armed, mounted warriors who ride out from their fort at Dineiddyn (now Edinburgh) to be totally destroyed by a very large concentration of Angles at Catraeth (Catterick) in Yorkshire.' "[28]

Indeed, anamnesis and its description of temporal enfolding were crucial to nearly everything Jones did as a poet: his description of how modern warfare grows out of, and makes active once again, ancient battles; his commitment to the ability of language and sacrament to make the past present. The concept of anamnesis is essential, then, but it also is unfamiliar—at least for the modern secular reader. And so Jones feels compelled to bring the words of a modern theologian, Gregory Dix, into the text to clarify things. Without such an explication, Jones suggests, the reader would not understand the liturgical and sacramental valences of the word, and without these liturgical and sacramental valences, the reader would not understand his poetry. In this instance and in many like it, the theological texts to which Jones alludes are not incidental to the poem's meaning. They help constitute it.

Many other examples of Jones using theological texts to explain his own poetry could be cited. The footnotes of *The Anathemata* in particular act as a running commentary on the theology of the Catholic Mass as understood by Augustine, Irenaeus, de la Taille, and others. But Jones's most sustained examination of sacramental theology, as well as his most sustained examination of his own poetic project, comes in "Art and Sacrament." In this essay, Jones lays out the terms—art, sacrament, and representation—by which he thought his poetry could best be understood.

"Art and Sacrament," later collected in Jones's *Epoch and Artist*, originally appeared in a 1955 book entitled *Catholic Approaches to Modern Dilemmas and Eternal Truths*—a collection that sought to show how traditional Catholic faith could illuminate specifically modern problems.[29] Throughout, Jones borrows the language and conceptual categories of Thomas Aquinas and his neo-Thomist heir Jacques Maritain in order to offer his own account of artistic creation. He begins his essay by carefully distinguishing between art and prudence—the same distinction, we might note, that Maritain draws at the beginning of *Art and Scholasticism*, where he asks, "How is the virtue of Prudence, a virtue at once *intellectual and moral*, to be distinguished from Art, which is an *intellectual* virtue?"[30] Prudence, Jones writes in "Art and Sacrament," is "the tutelary genius who presides over the whole realm of faith, moral, religion, ethic; she is thought of as Holy Wisdom."[31] Prudence is the faculty by which we seek to make our conduct conform to other, higher ends; it is "full of does and don'ts," "concerned with oughts and ought nots."[32]

Art, by distinction, is concerned with the end of the artwork itself. It is, Jones writes, "the sole intransitive activity of man," intransitive here meaning having no end other than itself. Art—or "Ars," as Jones prefers to call it, using the Latin to signal a broader, more capacious and craftsman-like sense of art as making—"concerns a means by which is achieved a 'perfect fit.'"[33] The focus is on craft, on skill, on "means" and "fit"—the finding of the proper, perfect form for the created object. Fit is the only kind of perfection the artist can, or should, seek, and Jones expresses discomfort with any notion of art as a container for ideas or as a didactic tool.[34] Here, Jones echoes Eliot: "The poet makes poetry, the metaphysician makes metaphysics, the bee makes honey, the spider secretes a filament; you can hardly say that any of these agents believes:

he merely does."[35] Leaning heavily on Maritain's *Art and Scholasticism*, Jones defines art as an activity rather than an end, a process and not a product: "Ars has no end save the perfecting of a process by which all sorts of ends are made possible. It *is* that process . . . in so far as art has an end that end is a 'fitting together' and the word art means a fitting together."[36] It is, to use Kantian terms, purposive without purpose.

This contrast between prudence and art leads to Jones's second, related claim: that art is defined by its gratuitousness. As Jones stresses again and again, art sets itself against what he calls, at various times, the "merely utile," the "wholly functional," and the "transitive."[37] Utile things exist for the sake of something else. "War-planes" and "ballistic devices of various kinds" may, through the "play of light on shapes," possess striking beauty. But they are not, and never can be, works of art because they exist *for* something else—in this case, for waging war.[38] Creating a work of art, by contrast, is the exemplary gratuitous act. Nothing demands that a work of art be created; there is no purpose or function that it meets. It is simply a matter of the artist's will being shaped by the artist's skill. In this sense, art is a pure and unmerited gift. As Jones quips, aesthetics "resemble[s] a voyage in uncertain waters" that happens upon "a landfall or two. Perhaps the foreland that suddenly has loomed might be called 'Gratuity Ness.'"[39]

Art, then, is the activity that we engage in when we are creating something for the sake of that something. In this way, art becomes both the activity that uniquely defines humanity (other creatures create beautiful objects, but they create them for use, not for the end of the beautiful object itself) and the activity that brings humanity closest to God. Much as we might like to think so, Jones suggests, the artist does not resemble God in being omnipotent. After all, the artist's will, unlike God's will, is hemmed in by material limitations: the artist must acknowledge and work within the constraints of the medium, whether that be ink and canvas or marble and chisel. Rather, the artist becomes Godlike in the freedom of her creation, in her ability to create because she wants to and not because she has to: "With regard to the gratuitous quality which is said to adhere to Ars it is well to remember that theologians say that the creation of the world was not a necessary, but a gratuitous, act. There is a sense in which this gratuitousness in the operations of the Creator is reflected in the art of the creature."[40] This is, of course, an idea that has a long history in Christian aesthetics: *Paradise Lost* continually shows man imitating God through the creation and cultivation of the beautiful. But, again, Jones gets much of this from Maritain. Notice, for instance, this similar argument made in *Art and Scholasticism*: The artist "is as it were an associate of God in the making of beautiful works; by developing the powers placed in him by the Creator . . . and by making use of created matter, he creates, so to speak, at second remove."[41]

Finally, Jones takes up the issue of representation—or, as he prefers to spell it, "re-presentation." Following modern art critics like Roger Fry and Clive Bell, Jones argues against art as mimesis, wherein the artwork is understood to be the imitation of another thing (say, a tree). Rather, pointing to Post-Impressionist aesthetics as a more accurate account of the artistic process, Jones argues that "a work is a 'thing' and not (necessarily) the impression of some other thing."[42] A good painter must say, " 'This is not a representation of a mountain, it *is* 'mountain' under the form of paint.' "[43] Pointing to Picasso, Jones argues that modern art does not "refer," but re-presents. It is not *about* a subject outside of the work of art but *is* that subject in artistic form.

Here, Jones borrows once again from Maritain. All of Maritain's writing on aesthetics, but especially *Art and Scholasticism*, stress that classical mimesis fails to account for the true nature of artistic representation: "What is required is not that the representation exactly conform to a given reality, but that through the material elements of the beauty of the work there truly pass, sovereign and whole, the radiance of a form—of a form, and therefore of *a truth*."[44] By "radiance of a form," Maritain means that which allows a thing to be understood in the first place—its very truth and essence, what John Trapani calls "the proper principle of a thing's intelligibility."[45] In painting a table with a bowl of oranges on top of it, for example, what is important for Matisse is not that the painting "exactly conform to a given reality"—that it *look like* the table with a bowl of oranges on it—but that the scene's form, its very principle of intelligibility and truth, shine forth. In order to achieve this shining forth, Maritain suggests, certain kinds of distortion need to be used: the artist "can, and he even must, distort in some measure, reconstruct, transfigure the material appearances of nature."[46] In transfiguring the scene before him, Matisse allows the scene to become intelligible, to radiate its true form and reveal this true form to the viewer. In this instance and others like it, Maritain argues, transfiguration does not distract from truthful representation but enables it. Jones agreed. For him, the modern artist seeks not slavish imitation but powerful creation; not representation but re-presentation.[47]

In the most daring move of "Art and Sacrament," Jones explicitly links this Post-Impressionist—we might say modernist—understanding of representation to the Catholic theology of the Eucharist. The Catholic doctrine of transubstantiation states that the bread and wine of the Eucharist make real—that is to say, do not just point towards but actually, really make present—the body and blood of Christ. In this specific way, the re-presentation of the Eucharist is similar to the re-presentation of the modernist artwork. Just as the Post-Impressionist painting of a tree is a showing forth of the tree in a different form, so, Jones writes, "it is said of the eucharistic signs that they are a showing forth of something 'in an un-bloody manner.' "[48] Jones goes on: "That particular instance from the domain of theological definition might, *mutatis mutandis*, be used to help us to understand better something of the function, in general, of Ars as a shower-forth." The striking phrases used here, "showing forth" and "shower-forth," echo Maritain's claim that a radiance of form *passes through* the material elements of a work of art. In both the Eucharist and the artwork, the gap between signifier and signified collapses. The painting actualizes the tree in the form of paint, just as the Eucharist actualizes Christ's saving grace in the form of bread and wine. Jones writes, "nothing could be less 'representa-tional' or more re-presentative or further from 'realism' or more near reality than what is intended and posited" in the Catholic celebration of the Eucharist.[49] Not realism but reality; not representing but re-presenting: for Jones, Post-Impressionist artists like Picasso and Matisse were Catholic sacramentalists, whether they knew it or not.

In a letter, Jones elaborates upon this link between modernist and Catholic re-presentation: "From the doctrinal definition of the substantial presence in the Sacramental Bread, I learnt . . . that a tree in a painting . . . must not be a re-presenting only of a tree, of sap and thrusting wood; it must really be a 'tree,' under the species of paint . . . Certain ideas explicit or implicit in Catholic dogma had a clarifying and a considerably liberating effect."[50] So, for Jones, the Cath-olic Mass is the most perfect distillation of modernist ideas of representation—or, art is modernist insofar as it embodies this Catholic, Eucharistic mode of representation. A poem or painting will never be able to move fully from repre-sentation to sacramental re-presentation; poetry and painting will always, at some level, be referential. But, insofar as the poem or painting is able to approach re-presentation, insofar as it becomes "a recalling, a re-presenting again, anaphora, anamnesis," it is more fully sacramental and therefore more fully modernist.[51] Here, it might be worth recognizing a potential objection: Isn't what Jones is describing here—poetry that re-presents rather than represents, that emphasizes the event or happening of the linguistic event rather than its representational quality—a description of all (or at least all good) poetry? Is Jones's account, in other words, truly an account of the sacramental nature of modernist poetry, or is it just an account of poetry, period? I suspect that Jones would say that his account is about all of poetry (the essay is titled, after all, not "Modern Art and Sacrament" but "Art and Sacrament"), but that modernist poetry displays a higher proportion of sacramentality than other kinds of poetry. And what of the question of belief? For example, would Jones consider John Ashbery a sacra-mental poet despite his nonbelief? After all, Ashbery's poetry also troubles language's referential qualities. I suspect that Jones would say yes, Ashbery is a sacramental poet whether or not he recognizes this fact. What differentiates modernist poetry, or at least Jones's own brand of modernist poetry, isn't just its sacramental quality but also its awareness *of* this sacramental quality.

Representing the Sacraments

So much for Jones's theorizing about the sacramental nature of aesthetic creation. How, though, can we see this vision of art as a sacramental re-presenting play out in his actual poetry? And how does this relate to the specific arguments put forward by de la Taille in *The Mystery of Faith*? The most obvious way Jones creates a sacramental poetics is by regularly featuring sacramental scenes—scenes in which sacraments are actually represented or scenes in which sacramental imagery and language are used.

Jones's first published work, and the first place where we can see him linking poetry to sacrament, was his 1937 epic poem *In Parenthesis*. *In Parenthesis* traces an English-Welsh battalion as it moves through the full-range of World War I experiences. We follow the soldiers and the poem's central figure, private John Ball, from the training grounds to the trenches to the battlefield, even to death. As befits its title, *In Parenthesis* begins in the middle of things.[52] When the poem opens, we are in the midst of the roll call of the fictional 55th Battalion of the Royal Welch Fusiliers:

> '49 Wyatt, 01549 Wyatt.
> Coming sergeant.
> Pick 'em up, pick 'em up—I'll stalk within yer chamber.
> Private Leg . . . sick.
> Private Ball . . . absent.
> 'o1 Ball, 'o1 Ball, Ball of No. 1.
> Where's Ball, 25201 Ball—you corporal,
> Ball of your section.
> Movement round and about the Commanding Officer.
> Bugler, will you sound "Orderly Sergeants."[53]

In a narrative remarkable for all the material that it includes—technical jargon, Christian and pagan allusions, medieval Welsh poetry, mini-essays on modern architecture—the opening is remarkable for what it excludes. We do not know who is speaking; we do not know what group is being addressed; we do not even know where the scene takes place. (Two-thirds of the way through the poem, we learn that the opening location is a training ground at Winnall Down.) The focus, in short, is not on setting or character: infantrymen are identified impersonally by number and surname, and we will not hear from privates Wyatt or Leg for the rest of the narrative. Rather, the focus is on language and movement, and the fact that language brings about movement: Wyatt is called, and immediately he is coming.

The scene, it should be noted, is also about the ways in which language fails to bring about desired movement. Private Ball, after all, is not there to respond to his commanding officer, and his tardiness will be noted: "Take his name take his number—charge him—late on parade—the Battalion being paraded for overseas—warn him for Company Office." But even this apparent failure brings about more and greater activity: "A hurrying of feet from three companies converging on the little group apart where on horses sit the central command."[54] The military world, then, is the world of the speech act, where an act is performed in the saying of it, where enunciation brings about realization.

Many critics have argued that all literary discourse is, at a certain level, a form of performative language.[55] As Jonathan Culler writes, "The beginning of Joyce's *Ulysses*, 'Stately plump Buck Mulligan came from the stairhead bearing a bowl of lather on which a mirror and a razor lay crossed,' does not refer to some prior state of affairs but creates this character and this situation.'"[56] Yet what is most interesting about the beginning of *In Parenthesis* is how Jones relates the efficacious nature of the military command not to literary discourse generally but to the efficacious nature of the sacraments. After the troops have gathered on the parade grounds, the commanding officer, in a priestly fashion, pronounces "the ritual words by virtue of which a regiment is moved."[57] As the words of several commanding officers blend together, as action follows immediately and inexorably upon articulation, Jones looks to the traditional Catholic definition of sacrament: "Words lost, yet given continuity by that thinner command from in front of No. 1. Itself to be wholly swallowed up by the concerted movement of arms in which the spoken word effected what it signified."[58] Here Jones echoes de la Taille, who, in *The Mystery of Faith*, describes a sacrament as that which "effects by itself in the mind what it signifies."[59] In the same section of *The Mystery of Faith*, de la Taille compares sacraments to the royal fiats of old: these royal commands "were words that accomplished what they enunciated, not having merely for object to relate a thing because it had happened, but to say it that it might actually be, and, therefore, to realize it by promulgating."[60] In a certain sense, then, the military command is like the sacrament. To say "come" is to bring about this very action.[61]

There is, of course, a crucial difference between sacrament and military command. If, as de la Taille wrote, a sacrament is a divinely sanctioned "word in action" that speaks of, and therefore brings about, a movement towards grace, then the military command in this poem is a humanly sanctioned "word in action" that speaks of, and therefore brings about, a movement towards death and destruction.[62] Strikingly, we never see a Catholic Mass celebrated in *In Parenthesis*—a surprising omission given that Jones first considered converting to Catholicism after witnessing a priest distributing the Eucharist in an outhouse near the front. When he saw this celebration, Jones remembers, he was struck immediately by "the oneness between the Offerant and those toughs that clustered round him in the dim-lit byre—a thing I had never felt remotely as a Protestant at the Office of Holy Communion."⁶³ In *In Parenthesis*, it seems that the command is the only kind of sacramental language that has a place within the trenches.

Where *In Parenthesis* opens by dramatizing the ways in which war makes language partake of a quasi-sacramental efficacy, *The Anathemata* begins, as noted earlier, with a representation of the efficacy of the Eucharist itself: "We already and first of all discern him making this thing other. His groping syntax, if we attend, already shapes: ADSCRIPTAM, RATAM, RATIONABILEM . . . and by preapplication and for *them*, under modes and patterns altogether theirs, the holy and venerable hands lift up an efficacious sign."⁶⁴ Just as in *In Parenthesis*, the narrative opens *in media res*, with an action already under way. Again, no location is specified, though we gather quickly that we are witnessing a Catholic Mass. Again, we see language "making" things happen, the words of consecration shaping and leading to the efficacious sign being lifted. Here, though, we see not something that is like a sacrament in its efficacy, but the sacrament itself.

In *The Anathemata*, Jones regularly returns to scenes of consecration, scenes in which a thing (here, the bread) is turned into an act of sanctifying grace (here, the Eucharist). As Jones writes in the poem's preface, the word "anathemata" means those things that have been "set up, lifted up, or in whatever manner made over to the gods," and the poem is largely an exploration of this process of "making other."⁶⁵ We move from the opening, in which a modern-day priest lifts the efficacious sign, to Christ himself, as "In the prepared high-room / he implements inside time and late in time under forms indelibly marked by locale and incidence, deliberations made out of time, before all oreogenesis"; to pre-Christian men, "the fathers of those / who forefathered them," who still engage in sacramental activity, as they "set apart, make other, oblate"; and finally, at the poem's conclusion, back to the twentieth-century priest who "does what is done in many places," celebrating the Eucharist "after the mode / of what has always been done."⁶⁶ From start to finish, *The Anathemata* concerns itself with sacrament: how things are made sacramental ("what is done") and what effect this activity has (the "viatic bread shows forth a life").⁶⁷

Yet, in "Art and Sacrament" and in the theological asides that appear throughout his poetry, Jones was not merely saying that art is sacramental when it represents the sacraments—when it gives us a vision of Christ "in the prepared high-room," for instance, or when it illustrates the debased form of sacramental language used on the battlefield. He was saying that art is sacramental when it re-presents anything—when it artistically embodies the particular kind of re-presentation manifested in the Catholic Eucharist. To see exactly how Jones accomplishes this re-presentation in his own work, we need to look at how he deploys language in a sacramental manner even when the sacraments themselves are not being represented.

Re-Presenting Sacramentally

Though critics often focus on the strange content of Jones's poetry—its esoteric allusions, its surprising wedding of Welsh mythology with Catholic theology and modern warfare—Jones's style is arguably stranger. To read a stanza of Jones's poetry is to know, almost immediately, its provenance. Most distinctive is the regularity with which Jones forces individual words into new functions, transforming nouns into verbs and adjectives, descriptions into actions and vice versa. Here is one example of Jones using participles to accomplish this shift, taken from *The Anathemata*. The passage describes the dangers encountered by an ancient ship as it sails past the Scillies, a group of islands just off the coast of Cornwall:

> And did Morgana's fay-light
> abb the warp of mist
> that diaphanes the creeping ebb, or worse
> the rapid flow
> off Scylla's cisted West-site
> screening her felspar'd war
> with the skerry-mill?[68]

Within six lines, Jones coins two verbs ("abb" and "diaphanes") and one adjective ("felspar'd"), none of which is listed in these forms in the *Oxford English Dictionary*. Another word is used in a peculiar manner: the noun "cist," meaning an ancient stone burial chamber, becomes the adjective "cisted." Finally, Jones employs three hyphenated phrases—"fay-light," "West-site," and "skerry-mill"— that bring together two nouns to create a single compound.

In this passage and throughout Jones's poetry, language is under constant pressure. In almost any passage in almost any poem, one finds nouns yoked together through hyphenation to form new compounds, or nouns turned into participles, or the two transformative processes occurring in combination. In *In Parenthesis*, for instance, the trenches are described in this way: "Underearth shorn-up, seeled and propt. Substantial matter guttered and dissolved, sprawled to glaucous insecurity. All sureness metamorphosed."[69] As he often does, Jones here strips his language of verbs of being. By removing the copula and leaving the past participle (not "was guttered and dissolved" but "guttered and dissolved"), Jones blurs the line between adjective and verb. Is "guttered" a description of "substantial matter" or of what that substantial matter did? Probably the first, but indeterminacy is the achieved effect. Jones continually collapses the gap between description and action, between what a thing looks or feels or sounds like and what it does or did. As Robichaud puts it, Jones "significantly does not claim to *represent* the past, but instead suggests that his poetry is an attempt to *express* the past in language."[70] This longing for expression as opposed to representation—or, to again use Jones's own words, re-presentation instead of representation—is not just what Jones wants to accomplish with regards to the past, however. It is what he wants to accomplish with regards to *all* re-presentation, and he does this through the micro-effects of individual lines and words and phonemes.

Jones most frequently accomplishes this blurring of action and description by forcing the noun into the past participle form. In *The Anathemata*, for instance, ancient Celtic soldiers are "caliga'd . . . / torque-wearers," while slightly less ancient Germans appear "half toga'd."[71] A martyr is "tunicled"; hail is "cataracted"; breath is "clovered"; a wife is "wedlocked."[72] In the section entitled "Keel, Ram, Stauros," Jones gives this description of a ship's keel:

> Planked or
>   boarded and above
> or floored, from bilge to bilge.
> Carlings or athwart her
> horizontaled or an-end
>   tabernacled and stepped
> or stanchioned and 'tween decks.[73]

Again, Jones relentlessly excises verbs of being, leaving a passage that is all frenetic action. In each instance, adding an "-ed" to a noun or adjective seems to turn the individual word into a kind of action. Describing a soldier as "caliga'd" rather than "dressed in caliga" turns a caliga into something that can be done to the soldier. Describing a war not as "fought with felspar" but as "felspar'd" animates the mineral, transforming it from an inert object into a process. Mutlu Blasing has described "lyric language" as the place "where sounds must both make sense and remain distinct from sense, so that we can apprehend *the event* of sense in a groundless desire and intention to mean."[74] This is what Jones's grammatical contortions dramatize. We get the event of sense, not its representation, as Jones moves from predication and description and towards enactment.

At one point, describing the origins of pottery in the age between the Paleolithic and Neolithic cultures, Jones writes:

> Searching where the kitchen midden tells of the decline which with the receding cold marked the recession of the Magdalenian splendours.
>
> Yet there he brights fragmented protomorphs
> where lies the rudimentary bowl.[75]

The passage moves away from a decimated culture ("decline," "receding," "recession"), signified by the refuse of the kitchen midden, and towards the unexpected, unexplainable aesthetic impulse itself, signified by the simple, beautiful bowl. Jones signals this cultural shift by a formal shift, from prose to verse. Just as a utilitarian object becomes an artistic one through the process of "brighting," so Jones's language becomes more obviously "poetic" through formal line divisions, which begin with "Yet there he."

Two words in this passage stand out: the single, solitary "yet," which illustrates the gratuitous impulse to create despite sordid cultural and material conditions; and the verb "brights," wherein an adjective is transformed into a verb. "Bright" occurs elsewhere as a verb in *The Anathemata*. For example, when describing another instance of ancient artistry—the prehistoric creation of cave paintings—Jones writes: "And see how they run, the juxtaposed forms, brighting the vaults of Lascaux." Elsewhere, "a sky-shaft brights the whited mole" as a ship approaches the shore; later, Christ cries out in anguish from the Cross while a "dark cloud brights the trembling lime-rock." Towards the beginning of the poem, two more instances occur: "Brighting totally / the post-Pliocene / both Pleistocene and Recent" and "Brighting at the five life-layers / species, species, genera, families, order."[76]

Why does this particular verb so appeal to Jones? His description of brighting the "rudimentary bowl" leads Jones to a series of questions that can help answer this question:

> How else
> *multifariam multisque modis*
> > the splendour of forms yet to come?
> How the dish
> > that holds no coward's food?
> How the *calix*
> > without which
> > how *the* re-calling?[77]

Looking to Christian tradition, we can understand the brighted bowl as a *figura* of the chalice. The bowl receives its ultimate meaning, its fulfillment, in the cup that symbolizes Christ's new covenant with humanity.[78] A straight line runs from the homely, pre-Neolithic bowl to the magical cup that King Arthur must rescue from Hades to the Eucharist itself.[79]

How the dish? How the *calix*? Following Paul de Man, we might read these questions not rhetorically, as they seem to suggest, but literally: How does one get from the "rudimentary bowl" to the sacred "*calix*"?[80] What process initiates the transformation of the purely utilitarian (an unadorned bowl) to the beautiful, salvific cup? The answer, it appears, is the gratuitous process of brighting.

Just as the brighted cup is a *figura* of the sacred *calix*, the act of brighting is a *figura* for the celebration of the sacraments: we can only grasp the full meaning of the protoartist making the bowl "other" when we see the priest making the bread and wine of the Eucharist "other." Indeed, Jones's poetic achievement takes its place in this lineage of sacramental "othering," since the very coining of the verb "brights" partakes of the sacramental process whereby something (here, the adjective "bright") is made other (here, the verb "brights"). "Yet there he brights": for Jones, this is the artistic, and the sacramental, process writ small. We could even say that it is the history of civilization writ small. In the "Rite and Fore-time" section of *The Anathemata*, Jones seems to argue that the history of civilization is largely the history of protosacramentalist artists, all the way from the first visual artist in 20,000 BCE ("man master-of-plastic") to those in modern Vienna who "maze the waltz-forms in gay Vindobona in the ramshackle last phases" (the modern Viennese dancer imitates the ancient Roman maze dance at Vindobona).[81]

Jones's stylistic peculiarities—his tendency to use nouns as adjectives, his love of neologisms and participles—have not gone unnoticed. William Blissett, for instance, has observed that *In Parenthesis*'s "piling up of nouns as adjectives" and its constant recourse to participles were "a fresh response to the [wartime] necessity of conceiving thing and function as one."[82] Paul Robichaud has also pointed out that the verbal noun was a major syntactical feature of the Middle Welsh prose epics that Jones so admired.[83] These critics are correct in drawing such connections. Surely the war brought home to Jones, in horrifying fashion, the ways in which a thing could be turned into a function (a static artillery shell becomes something that kills once it is fired); and surely Jones, who used quotations from the Welsh epic poem *Y Gododdin* as epigraphs to each section of *In Parenthesis*, would have been interested, as Robichaud argues, in combining modernist and medieval models of versification.

But such readings ignore a crucial fact. In Jones's terms, to conceive of thing and function as one is, by definition, to be thinking sacramentally. This is why Jones sees a deep analogy between modernist art and Catholic conceptions of the Eucharist: in both, he writes, "'sign' and 'thing signified' are said to be one."[84] In all modernist art, Jones suggests, whether it be the poetry of Eliot or the painting of Picasso, sign and signified, thing and the effects of this thing, are one. To paraphrase Jones, *The Waste Land* is not a poem about modern despair and futility; it is modern despair and futility under the form of poetry. Picasso's *Les Demoiselles d'Avignon* is not a representation of five prostitutes from Barcelona; it is those prostitutes under the form of painting. Jones sees modernist art as antipropositional—it expresses or presents rather than describes or refers—and, in this precise way, it is sacramental. With this in mind, we can read Jones's own attempts to bring thing and function into a more direct relation, to say that something "brights" rather than "is bright" or that the ground "guttered" rather than "was guttered," as a distinctively modernist and a distinctively sacramental enterprise.

Moreover, as Robichaud notes, Jones first came to realize the potential of noun-verb constructions by his reading of one particular poet, a poet whose antipropositional, expressive, explicitly sacramental verse has led him to be cast as a protomodernist: Gerard Manley Hopkins. In a letter, Jones notes "that the verb-noun thing they go in for in Welsh—and noun-adjective (is it?) seems to have the most valuable . . . influence on the English speech-form" through Hopkins's poetry.[85] The final stanza of Hopkins's *The Wreck of the Deutschland* serves as an excellent example of his use of "the verb-noun thing":

> Dame, at our door
> Drówned, and among oúr shóals,
> Remember us in the roads, the heaven-haven of the reward:
> Our Kíng back, Oh, upon Énglish sóuls!
> Let him easter in us, be a dayspring to the dimness of us, be a
> crimson-cresseted east,
> More brightening her, rare-dear Britain, as his reign rolls,
> Pride, rose, prince, hero of us, high-priest,
> Our héarts' charity's héarth's fíre, our thóughts' chivalry's thróng's
> Lórd.[86]

The alliteration, the hyphenated compounds, the sprung rhythm, the use of a noun, "easter," as a verb: these are all features that Jones borrows from Hopkins at one time or another. As Josephine Miles has written, when Hopkins uses participles as adjectives, he is trying "to catch and fix motion and quality into a more permanent state."[87] And this catching of motion in a single word, this longing to make words not just describe but enact, has a particular theological purpose. In the words of Bernadette Waterman Ward, it "calls out to the reader to recognize the sacramental presence of God in the things of the world."[88] And in the words of the world, too. Jones's regular wrenching of words into new functions has a similar purpose. It is in his poetics of torsion that we see Jones creating a poetry of re-presentation, moving away from description and towards sacramental enactment.

Temporal Integration

In *The Mystery of Faith*, Maurice de la Taille describes the continuous relationship between the Crucifixion, the Last Supper, and the Eucharist: "The work of the Cross completes both sacrifices. The Mass would not be at once a complete sacrifice if the Cross had not gone before; no more than the Supper could attain its sacrificial fulfillment without the Cross intervening."[89] The

Cross, de la Taille writes, sits at the center of "the two sides of the Eucharistic horizon: the side of Christ, looking forward to it, and the side of the Church, looking back upon it."[90] Through the Cross, three events—the Crucifixion, the Last Supper, and the Eucharist—become one, and every celebration of the Eucharist reaffirms and reenacts these three events as one. For de la Taille, to celebrate the Eucharist is to participate in an action—or, more accurately, a relationship—that is always and everywhere already under way.

If de la Taille is a theologian of temporal integration, then Jones is a poet of the same. Where de la Taille affirms the actual unity of the seemingly discrete events that form the Eucharistic horizon, Jones's allusive poetry shows us a world in which there is a continuous, integral relationship between past and present: the present moment points backwards to, and is shaped by, the past, just as it points forwards to, and receives its ultimate meaning and fulfillment in, the future. In his preface to *In Parenthesis*, Jones argues that the soldiers of World War I felt the continuing life of the past in a particularly strong way: "I suppose at no time did one so much live with a consciousness of the past, the very remote, and the more immediate and trivial past, both superficially and more subtly . . . Every man's speech and habit of mind were a perpetual showing: now of Napier's expedition, now of the Legions at the Wall . . . of Wellington's raw shire recruits, of ancient border antipathies . . . of Colen Hên—of the Celtic cycle that lies, a subterranean influence as a deep water troubling, under every tump in this Island, like Merlin complaining under his big rock."[91] Current battles are shaped by past battles; current songs emerge in response to songs from long ago; current sensibilities cannot help but reveal their indebtedness to, indeed their very constitution by, past sensibilities.

Both *In Parenthesis* and *The Anathemata* are brilliant examples of what Joseph Frank calls "spatial form." Like Joyce, Eliot, and other modernists, Jones regularly eschews sequence in favor of simultaneity, asking the reader to, as Frank puts it, "suspend the process of individual reference temporarily until the entire pattern of internal references can be apprehended as a unity."[92] Jones himself conceived of his poetic work in spatial terms (perhaps unsurprising, given that he was such an accomplished visual artist). In the preface to *In Parenthesis*, for example, he writes, "I have only tried to make a shape in words"; "There are passages which I would exclude, as not having the form I desire—but they seem necessary to the understanding of the whole."[93] For Jones, even seeming infelicities are subordinated to the overall shape of the poem; in Frank's words, these seeming infelicities cease to be infelicities when "apprehended as a unity." Both *In Parenthesis* and *The Anathemata* achieve this sense of simultaneity, this shaped unity, in large part through structural means—by having their endings circle back to their beginnings. *In Parenthesis* opens with an act of naming (soldiers are called to attention before they leave the training

grounds), and the poem ends with another act of naming, though of an entirely different kind. After the bloody Battle of the Somme, as soldiers lie dead
or dying in the Mametz Wood, the Queen of the Woods appears. She is a
mythical figure, part Virgin Mary, part pagan goddess. After her divine presence is announced, she goes through the battlefield and distributes flowers to
the dead:

> Some she gives white berries
>> some she gives brown
> Emil has a curious crown it's
>> made of golden saxifrage.
> Fatty wears sweet-briar,
> he will reign with her for a thousand years.
> For Balder she reaches high to fetch his.
> Ulrich smiles for his myrtle wand.
> That swine Lillywhite has daisies to his chin—you'd hardly credit it.[94]

Naming continues, from start to finish, but with a difference. Whereas before
men were identified by their place within the impersonal military order, here
they are given their proper names and recognized in their personhood: each
soldier gets his own specially selected flower. The poem's structure is not so
much circular, then, as it is spiral. The ending of *In Parenthesis* returns to its
beginning, but at a different plane. Whereas we started in the secular world of
the military, we end by approaching the world of eternity. Or, rather, we end at
the meeting point between these two worlds, where details are both this-
worldly (the specificity of individual types of flowers) and signs of transcendent
meaning.

The Anathemata exhibits a similar spiral structure. The poem opens with a
modern-day priest "making this thing other," lifting the Eucharist in the Act
of Consecration, and it ends with another representation of the Eucharist. Here
is the final stanza:

> He does what is done in many places
> what he does other
>> he does after the mode
> of what has always been done.
> What did he do other
>> recumbent at the garnished supper?
> What did he do yet other
>> riding the Axile Tree?[95]

Again, Jones concludes his poem by circling back to the action with which it
began. But again, he ends with a difference: the poem opens in prose, but it

closes in verse. More importantly, where our first sight was of the modern-day priest pronouncing the specific words of consecration ("ADSCRIPTAM, RATAM, RATIONABILEM"), we now end with a deliberately vague description of the priest's actions ("He does what is done in many places"), and with the priest, without warning, transforming into the figure of Christ "riding the Axile Tree." At the poem's conclusion we see how the Eucharistic sacrifice always and everywhere points back towards, and thus makes present again, the original sacrifices of Christ at the Last Supper ("the garnished supper") and Christ on the Cross ("riding the Axile Tree"). It ends, in short, with an assertion of de la Taille's integrated, tripartite sacrifice—a theological statement that is mirrored in the poem's formal integration of beginning and ending.

Describing this concluding stanza, Thomas Dilworth writes, "In the last ten lines, 'He' resolves from triple exposure—the priest at Mass, Jesus at the Supper, Jesus on the Cross—to the single image of the modern Catholic priest."[96] This pushes things a bit too far. As is so often the case, Jones purposefully does not resolve the identity of the speaker, here into "the single image of the modern Catholic priest." Rather, he leaves the referent ambiguous, creating a sign that is suggestive and, ultimately, replete with more than one meaning. As Jones writes in the preface to *The Anathemata*, "The arts abhor any loppings off of meanings or emptyings out, any lessening of the totality of connotation, any loss of recession and thickness through."[97]

What is more important than deciding the specific referent of "he," however, is recognizing that it is *not* the person who is being emphasized in the poem's final stanza, but an action; and, moreover, an action that is itself unspecified. "He does what is done in many places"—this almost tautological statement focuses not on what is done, but on the fact that it is done across space. "He does after the mode / of what has always been done"—again, the "mode" or procedure of doing is kept obscure, with emphasis instead on how this action has been done across time. It should come as no surprise that the poem ends with a verb in the present progressive tense, with Christ "riding the Axile Tree." Christ's crucifixion is not an action that has happened, once and for all, but one that has been and will remain continually active: Christ has ridden the Axile Tree, is riding the Axile Tree, and will ride the Axile Tree. The grammar of the final line reiterates the theological point that the whole poem has made.

It reiterates a poetic point as well. Just as the Eucharistic celebration is the salvific action that is never perfected but always perfecting, so poetry is the artistic action that is never completed but always completing. Jones's work makes this point again and again, most notably in its regular use of the present progressive tense. The poem opens with a priest "making this thing other," closes with Christ "riding the Axile Tree," and throughout uses the "–ing" form to indicate continuous, unfinished action. Jones identifies the modern poet as just the most recent in a seemingly endless line of artists, from the Victorian shipbuilders who "fay that hounding trim and proper—and of the best spruce, to rhyme with her mainmast" to the Paleolithic sculptor "whose man-hands god-handled the Willendorf stone."[98] All of these artists, Jones writes elsewhere, are engaged in the same quest, one that can be added to but never finished: "There is only one tale to tell even though the telling is patient of endless development and ingenuity and can take on a million variant forms."[99] This unending artistic quest points towards eternity: in "Art and Sacrament," Jones writes, "it is on account of the anthropic sign-making that we first suspect that anthropos has some part in a without-endness. Our suspicions may first be aroused by some 'find' from the Pliocene System and they may be heightened when we see some such work as the Demeter of Cnidus or hear sung the *Lauda Sion*."[100] It is the unending nature of artistic production that hints at humanity's eternal nature.

This vision of poetry as development without end is reflected even in Jones's method of composition, which generally consisted of years of tortured writing and rewriting, followed by the publication of the work as a "fragment." For example, "A, a, a, DOMINE DEUS," Jones's most approachable, seemingly straightforward lyric, was really the result of thirty years of struggle, finally appearing in a 1974 volume entitled *The Sleeping Lord and Other Fragments*. The full title of Jones's masterpiece, *The Anathemata: Fragments of an Attempted Writing*, also hints at the necessarily incomplete nature of its achievement, which Jones describes in his preface: "The title-page describes this book as 'fragments of an attempted writing' because that is an exact description of it. It had its beginnings in experiments made from time to time between 1938 and 1945 . . . What is now printed represents parts, dislocated attempts, reshuffled and again rewritten intermittently between 1946 and 1951."[101]

In an undated letter draft, Jones makes clear the connections between his sense of poetry as an always-ongoing project and de la Taille's theology of the always-ongoing salvific action of the Eucharist: "A re-calling of the past, the handing on of what has been received, not by any means to live in the past but to understand that the past lives in us; all such notions are a kind of *anamnesis*, an effectual re-presenting."[102] For Jones, a poetics of temporal integration is, by its very nature, a kind of sacramental poetics; to re-call the past into the present is to engage in a priest-like activity. Just as *The Anathemata* opens with a passage that could be read as a description of both the poet's and the priest's task, so it ends with a similar blurring of the lines between what Jones would call "Sacrament" and "sacrament." Like the priest, the poet "does what is done in many places," doing it "after the mode / of what has always been done."[103] We cannot help but read this final passage as a summary of what Jones has done in the writing of *The Anathemata*: continued in the line of those, like the cave painter and the Roman Catholic priest, who have made things other.

Jones and Modernism

Jones saw his own poetry as sacramental in several crucial senses: in its longing to collapse the distinction between sign and signified; in its desire to create a quasi-efficacious language in which words take on the properties of actions; and, finally, in its sense of time as integrated but always in the process of being completed. How, though, can we relate this vision of poetry as sacrament to modernist aesthetics more broadly speaking? How does Jones's theory of poetry and sacrament change how we read the quasi-sacramental aesthetics of other modernists—Joyce, Yeats, and others?

Perhaps surprisingly, the most pertinent point of comparison can be found in the critical writings of Ezra Pound—surprising because Pound was so harsh a critic of Christianity, claiming at one point that, "after the loss of faith in the Roman Church, the Christian sectaries produced no first-rate theology and little that can be considered intellectually serious."[104] Yet despite this animus, Pound's thinking about the purpose of poetry resembles Jones's explicitly Christian and theological poetics in important ways.

Throughout his career, from the early Imagist days of "In a Station of the Metro" (1913) to his time spent in an American military prison scribbling his cantos on scraps of toilet paper, Pound described poetry as, above all else, a matter of energy and action. In his 1913 essay "The Serious Artist," which appeared a year before the publication of the famous anthology *Des Imagistes*, Pound writes that "the thing that matters in art is a sort of energy, something more or less like electricity or radioactivity, a force transfusing, welding, and unifying."[105] A year later, in an essay on Vorticism, Pound describes the image as "a radiant node or cluster," a "VORTEX, from which, and through which, and into which, ideas are constantly rushing"; it is a "point of maximum energy."[106] Transfusing, welding, and unifying; a point of maximum energy: such descriptions anticipate Jones's own descriptions. Like the sacraments are for de la Taille, like all art is for Jones, good poetry for Pound is a matter of words in action and actions in words.

Pound's casting of poetry as primarily a matter of energy and electricity signals his frustration with the traditional view of language as representational. For Pound, language does not refer to energy; it embodies it, makes it present in the image itself. This is why the node is such an important trope for him. The node is the point at which different forces meet, the location that holds within itself a charge that is then disbursed elsewhere. Pound argues that the best poetry, no matter the time period, is presentational rather than descriptive: "When Shakespeare talks of the 'Dawn in russet mantle clad' he presents something which the painter does not present. There is in this line of his nothing that one can call description; he presents." Likewise, he praises the "definiteness of Dante's presentation."[107] As he writes elsewhere, "All poetic language is the language of exploration. Since the beginning of bad writing, writers have used images as ornaments. The point of Imagisme is that it does not use images *as ornaments*. The image is itself the speech. The image is the word beyond formulated language."[108] Pound's manifestos are attempts to describe a particular kind of poetry that will break down the gap between sign and signified: the image does not point to "the word beyond formulated language," it *is* the word beyond formulated language.

Pound in the early 1910s regularly looked to the discourse of science in order to describe the charged, nonreferential nature of his poetry. In "The Serious Artist," for instance, he writes, "The arts, literature, poesy, are a science, just as chemistry is a science."[109] By the end of the decade, however, Pound had found a new resource to marshal on modernism's behalf: Ernest Fenollosa's writings on the Chinese written language.[110] Chinese ideograms serve as such a perfect image for Pound's modernist poetics because, in Fenollosa's reading, they refuse any separation between thing and action, noun and verb.

Fenollosa argues that, in the natural world, there is no such thing as "a true noun, an isolated thing": "Things are only the terminal points, or rather the meeting points, of actions, cross-sections cut through actions, snap-shots." Neither, however, is there such a thing as pure action: "The eye sees noun and verb as one: things in motion, motion in things."[111] Fenollosa (mistakenly) asserts that the Chinese written character more closely approximates this natural state than any other language because of its pictorial nature: "But Chinese notation is something much more than arbitrary symbols. It is based upon a vivid shorthand picture of the operations of nature. In the algebraic figures and in the spoken word there is no natural connection between thing and sign: all depends upon sheer convention. But the Chinese method follows natural suggestion."[112] When we look at the Chinese symbol for man, Fenollosa claims, we see "the man on his two legs"; when we look at the symbol for horse, we see "the horse on his four legs"; when we look at the sentence "man sees horse," the "group [of symbols] holds something of the quality of a continuous moving picture."[113]

Of course, Pound and Fenollosa were incorrect in this reading of Chinese ideograms as pictographs. George Kennedy, examining the inaccuracies in Fenollosa/Pound's analysis of the Chinese poem "Moon Rays like Pure Snow," writes, "What then is wrong here? For something must be frightfully wrong. Just a complete misunderstanding of what Chinese characters are, how they were created, and how they function as speech symbols."[114] But what matters here is the desire that Pound/Fenollosa felt satisfied by their mischaracterization of

Chinese characters. The Chinese ideogram seems to offer them both the realization of an ancient dream of poets and philosophers alike: that there might be a natural relationship between thing and sign. The Chinese character, and Chinese written language itself, becomes a kind of poetry—immediate, presentational, full of energy, every word the *"verbal idea of an action."*[115] In English poetry, Fenollosa writes, "metaphors are only ways of getting rid of the dead white plaster of the copula."[116] The Chinese ideogram (again, in Fenollosa's misreading) dispenses with the need for the copula altogether: in this language all words, nouns and verbs, adjectives and adverbs, contain within themselves the seed of action.

Pound was not the only modernist to see poetry as a unity of thing and action, sign and signified. As Matthew Mutter writes, Yeats's magical poetics, as well as his esoteric mysticism, consists largely of the quest after a "Unity of Being," which Mutter describes as "a poetic image that has material efficacy in the world," something that "integrates meaning and motion, history and nature."[117] The most famous example of such a poetic "Unity of Being" comes at the end of "Among School Children," where the dancer and the dance become one. Yeats himself points to the analogies between the unity of being, where form and function are perfectly united, and the Catholic Eucharist: "It is still true that the Deity gives us, according to His promise, not His thoughts or His convictions but His flesh and blood . . . We only believe in those thoughts which have been conceived not in the brain but in the whole body."[118]

This link between the modernist "image" and the Eucharist was also made explicit in a debate over the nature of Imagism published in the *Egoist* in 1915. In a special issue devoted to the then-ascendant movement, Harold Monro argued that Imagist poets had merely isolated one unit of traditional verse, the poetic image, stripped it of its surroundings, and acted as if they had started a revolution. What these spare, oftentimes chilly poems actually show, Monro argues, is the inescapable gap between the actual emotions animating a poem and the self-consciously literary images used to represent them: "What [the poet] has observed cannot be reproduced in poetry," and we are left with the sense that the "emotional values of the poem almost escape him."[119]

In the next issue, May Sinclair—poet, novelist, early defender of literary modernism, first critic to use "stream-of-consciousness" to describe the literary representation of the mind at work—responded to these charges. In "Two Notes," Sinclair disputes Monro's reading of Imagist poetry as utterly conventional by pointing to what it is *not*: "It is not Symbolism. It has nothing to do with image-making. It abhors Imagery. Imagery is one of the old worn-out decorations the Imagists have scrapped."[120] What, then, is Imagism? It is above all else a poetics of "Presentation." The image, Sinclair writes, is not "pure form. It is form *and* substance"; "the Image is not a substitute; it does not stand for anything but itself"; "in no case is the Image a symbol of reality (the object); it is reality (the object) itself."[121] Here, Sinclair borrows sacramental language to describe the effects of the image: form *and* substance, a symbol that is somehow something more than a symbol. In the conclusion to her essay, Sinclair draws the sacramental valences of Imagism more explicitly into relief: "For all poets, old and new, the poetic act is a sacramental act with its rubric and ritual. The Victorian poets are Protestant. For them the bread and wine are symbols of Reality, the body and blood. They are given 'in remembrance.' The sacrament is incomplete. The Imagists are Catholic; they believe in Transsubstantiation. For them the bread and wine are the body and blood. They are given. The thing is done. *Ita missa est.* The formula may lead to some very ugly ritual, but that is the fault of the Imagist not of Imagism."[122] Sinclair's claim here—that all poetry is sacramental in nature, and that the poetry of Pound, H. D., and other modernists is specifically Catholic—chimes with Les Murray's claim from "Distinguo": "Poetry is Catholic: / poetry is presence."

What does the fact that several other modernists used the language of the sacraments to describe their own poetics—explicitly in the case of Sinclair and Yeats, implicitly in the case of Pound—tell us about Jones's relationship to the broader modernist moment? First, it shows that Jones's interest in sacramentality was not as idiosyncratic as his critics have often claimed. Modernist aesthetics and sacramental theology share many concerns: the inadequacy of understanding signs as solely referential tools; the longing to make language efficacious so that words become actions and, as Fenollosa/Pound writes, "all speech [becomes] a kind of dramatic poetry";[123] an understanding that the most powerful images wed meaning and motion. Sinclair may exaggerate in saying that Imagists "are Catholic; they believe in Trans-substantiation," but only slightly.

Even modernists who were atheists, like Joyce and Woolf, regularly used the logic and language of the sacraments in their works. *A Portrait of the Artist as a Young Man* ends with Stephen Dedalus, who once considered becoming a priest, instead proclaiming his desire to become "a priest of the imagination, transmuting the daily bread of experience into the radiant body of everliving life," and this "radiant image of the eucharist" helps inspire some of the maudlin verse of the novel's fifth section.[124] *Ulysses* similarly includes a host of "pseudo-Eucharists"—Buck's black Mass, for instance, Bloom's preparation of fried kidneys, and the cup of cocoa in "Ithaca."[125] There is a long critical history of understanding Proust's madeleine as a quasi-Eucharistic symbol. Finally, Richard Kearney has argued that in the works of many modernists we can "discern a grammar of transubstantiation": even Woolf has moments that display a "sacramental aesthetic" in which materials objects and events—a painting or a dinner party—seem to lead to the transcendent.[126]

Of course, Jones's engagement with the sacraments was of a different kind from the engagement of Sinclair, Yeats, or Woolf. Sinclair's essay, for instance, relies upon a facile division between Protestantism and Catholicism, and one need have no familiarity with the finer points of transubstantiation to understand the distinction she is making. The ending of Jones's *The Anathemata*, however, cannot be understood without a familiarity with the tripartite Eucharistic relationship posited by de la Taille. Likewise, the connection between the ancient brighted bowl and the sacred *calix* cannot be grasped without knowing why Jones saw the artist and priest as engaged in similar projects of "making other." Moreover, Jones's interest in the relationship between art and religion is, in many ways, directly counter to this interest in Proust or Joyce. For Jones, it is not a matter of rerouting religion into art; it is a matter of discovering that religion is always and everywhere an artistic enterprise (or, as he would say, a "sign-making" enterprise), and that art is always and everywhere concerned with religious matters.

For Sinclair, Joyce, and others, then, the Eucharist is a trope, a symbol that can be used to better understand art. For Jones, however, the Real Presence of the Eucharist is just that—real—and so to claim that the poet is like a priest is to say something quite radical, perhaps even heterodox, about the power of poetry. In Jones's vision, art is not like a sacrament. In some deep and complex and ultimately unknowable sense, it is sacrament. And, even though the artist must concern himself solely with the end of the artwork itself, in doing so he creates something holy, something that opens up to the divine. At one point in *The Anathemata*, the Lady of the Pool wonders if medieval students studying theology at Oxford were capable of "warming their disputations till frigid syllogism pulses like mother nature."[127] In his poetry, Jones was able to accomplish just this: to show the warm, pulsing life of Catholic sacramental theology, and to show how this vital discourse might shed light on the modernist enterprise.

CHAPTER FIVE

Auden's Meanwhile

Dogmatic theological statements are to be comprehended, neither as logical propositions nor as poetic utterances: they are to be taken, rather, as
shaggy-dog stories: they have a point, but he who tries too hard to get it
will miss it. —W. H. AUDEN, *Secondary Worlds*

In the early months of 1944, W. H. Auden was asked to review the new Oxford
University Press edition of Kierkegaard's *Either/Or* for the *New Republic*—not
Auden's first theological essay for the magazine, nor his last. By this time
Auden's interest in theology generally and in Kierkegaard specifically was well
established. Four years earlier, Auden had written "Leap before You Look," a
modified villanelle that describes the leap of faith that is required if one is to
love another. Composed less than a year after Auden returned to the Christian
faith, the poem borrows both imagery (the "solitude ten thousand fathoms
deep") and ideas (the sense that, in modern, liberal life, it is "fear / That has a
tendency to disappear") from Kierkegaard's work.[1] Other poems from the
early 1940s likewise employ Kierkegaardian tropes: the sonnet sequence "The
Quest" follows the internal, existential adventures of modern man; the epithalamion "In Sickness and in Health" claims that love must "Exist by grace of the
Absurd"; and "Kairos and Logos," mentioned earlier, uses Kierkegaard's idea of
the "aesthetic order" to describe civilization before the Incarnation.[2] Kierkegaard seemed to be the latest in a long line of thinkers—among them Freud,
Jung, Marx, and John Layard—who had become "no more a person / now but
a whole climate of opinion // under whom" Auden lived his life and wrote his
poetry.[3] Indeed, Alan Jacobs has gone so far as to call Kierkegaard the later
Auden's "spiritual master."[4]

In his essay for the *New Republic*, Auden begins by locating Kierkegaard
within an intellectual tradition. Theologically, Auden aligns Kierkegaard with
thinkers like "Augustine, Pascal, Newman and Karl Barth"; philosophically,
he groups him with "existential" thinkers such as Nietzsche, Heidegger, and
William James.[5] Like his intellectual predecessors, Kierkegaard diagnoses humanity's deep unease, even unhappiness, with temporal experience. As Auden
writes, for Kierkegaard "the basic human problem is man's anxiety in time."[6]
Augustine and Barth both expressed this basic human problem from a Christian

perspective: man believes that he is in time but not of time, living his days within the temporal flux even though he feels his deepest self exists above this flux, in eternity. According to Auden, what differentiates Kierkegaard from these thinkers is Kierkegaard's belief that time and temporal existence are not something to be evaded but something to be entered into more fully.[7] As Auden writes in his review, one of Kierkegaard's most radical claims is that "religious significance is, in fact, inseparable from history . . . time is neither escaped nor conquered, but possessed."[8] (Auden's language here, we might note, both echoes and qualifies Eliot's own claim in "Burnt Norton," published five years earlier, that "Only through time time is conquered.")[9]

According to Kierkegaard, because we live in a world of time—that is, because we live in a world of contingency—our lives are defined by choice. Man, Auden writes, is "a being who becomes" and who "must choose of his own free will one out of an infinite number of possibilities which he foresees."[10] Auden sees these claims—that time is not something that we escape from but something that we must pass through; that choice is an anxiety-producing but necessary part of meaningful human existence—as being of special relevance for the period. As Edward Mendelson persuasively claims, Auden believed that much of modern thought was an attempt to escape from personal responsibility. Instead of seeing the self faced with terrifying, inescapable choice, thinkers appealed to "impersonal powers—whether called *élan vital*, the life force, history, social class, psychological archetype, or the shaping power of language and myth—[all of which] denied the reality of individual conscious choice."[11] Auden himself had been seduced, on several occasions, by thinkers who appealed to such impersonal forces, but by the 1940s he displayed a renewed commitment to the essential beauty and reality of free will. In "New Year Letter" (1940), Auden argues that, no matter how much we may wish to bury our individual will in "the bonds of blood or nation," no matter how much we long to "learn our good / From chances of a neighbourhood / Or class or party," individual choice remains a necessity: "Aloneness is man's real condition, / That each must travel forth alone / In search of the Essential Stone, / 'The Nowhere-without-No' that is / The justice of societies."[12] And this, Auden suggests in his Kierkegaard review, is a lesson that the Danish thinker might teach us all.

Towards the end of his essay, Auden shifts focus. While acknowledging the power of Kierkegaard's thoughts on the relationship between time, history, and individual choice, Auden goes on to argue that these ideas are not the primary reason why we should read *Either/Or*. Rather, it is the style in which these ideas are expressed that is most worthy of our attention. Kierkegaard teaches us to see theology and philosophy not simply as a matter of content but also as a matter of form: "Kierkegaard is a dangerous author, because the more he attracts, the more he has the opposite effect to the one he intends, which is to throw the reader back upon his own experience. To become a disciple of Kierkegaard is to betray him, for what he would teach is an approach to oneself, not a conclusion, a style of questioning to apply to all one's experience, including one's experience of reading him."[13] Auden envisions Kierkegaard's philosophical contribution not so much as a series of propositions (history and free will lead to anxiety) as a manner of thinking that enables one to argue towards such propositions through self-questioning and dialectical negation. What is most important is the manner, not the matter, of thought.

This particular way of thinking is dependent upon a particular manner of writing—"a style of questioning" that makes itself felt in the prose itself. A dialectical vision of life, Auden writes, where "fidelity [is not] a single choice . . . made once and for all" but a choice "that . . . is continually rechosen at each successive moment," demands a dialectical style of writing. Kierkegaard argues against the synthesizing, systematic nature of Hegelian philosophy, and his best argument for this position is his own destabilizing, decidedly unsystematic prose.[14] As Auden writes, " 'Either/Or' is a hodge-podge of aphorisms, essays, reviews, journals, letters," and this "lack of systematic form is as intentional as it is in Nietzsche's work."[15] An unsystematic thinker—or, more accurately, an antisystematic thinker—must write in an antisystematic style. Here Auden makes a point that George Steiner has reiterated recently: "In both philosophy and literature style is substance"; just like poetry, philosophy (or, at least, certain kinds of philosophy) is as much built out "of rhythm, of intonation, of grammatical bent" as it is out of ideas.[16]

"The preacher's loose immodest tone"

We have seen this sense of the dialectical, self-negating nature of theological thought and language before, particularly in the work of Karl Barth, who described his own theological writing as "rethinking, 'renewed thinking.' "[17] In my first two chapters, I argue that Barth drew attention to the ways in which theological inquiry must necessarily fail; that, for Barth, all honest theology must end in silence. This account of the incomplete and incompletable nature of theological investigation was part of what attracted Eliot to Barth in the first place—and, of course, part of what attracted Barth to Kierkegaard.

But with Eliot, theology as what Auden calls "a style of questioning" was always balanced by a vision of theology as a coherent, dogmatic system of ideas. Writing on Pascal in 1931, Eliot asserts that the Christian believer "finds himself inexorably committed to the dogma of the Incarnation."[18] The inexorability of this commitment, the firmness of Christian dogma, is crucial to Eliot's understanding of theology and its role in religious poetry. In an essay in *The Sacred Wood*, for example, Eliot argues that Dante is a better philosophical poet than Blake in large part because of the different philosophical schema upon which their works rest. Dante possesses the fixed, "eternal scheme" of Christian dogma whereas Blake, in his heterodox, visionary manner, has jerry-rigged something that resembles "an ingenious piece of home-made furniture."[19] Eliot claims that Dante's dogmatic basis enables him to create "the most comprehensive, and the most *ordered* presentation of emotions that has ever been made" (Eliot's emphasis). By contrast, Blake's heterodoxy—Eliot would more likely term it heresy—gives rise to a poetic "formlessness," a "confusion of thought, emotion, and vision."[20] For Auden, Kierkegaard's "hodgepodge" is something to be praised; for Eliot, Blake's hodgepodge, his "home-made furniture," is something to be lamented. In Eliot's reading, the more solid the metaphysical foundation, the more solid is the poetic achievement. As he writes, "The concentration resulting from a framework of mythology and theology and philosophy" (and by "framework" Eliot means a systematic, authoritative, coherent, and Christian account of the world) "is one of the reasons why Dante is a classic, and Blake only a poet of genius."[21]

Auden certainly admired Christian theology as just such a framework—as a set of authoritative claims about the meaning of nature, grace, and history. In particular, Auden admired Christian theology's willingness to assert that the earthly, physical, temporal world was not something to be condemned or evaded. The theologians who most influenced Auden—Kierkegaard, Reinhold Niebuhr, and Charles Williams—took history, the unfolding of time in this world, as a proper subject for theological inquiry. In *An Interpretation of Christian Ethics*, a book that Auden read and admired, Niebuhr describes two theological tendencies. The first explores the "vertical tension between concrete fact and transcendent source," between the creaturely and the divine. This is the world of revelation and sacrament, of Karl Barth and Maurice de la Taille, of Eliot's *Four Quartets* and Jones's *The Anathemata*. The second theological tendency explores the "horizontal tension between present and future," between the current, fallen City of Man and the future, perfected City of God. This is the world of eschatological hope, of Niebuhr and Williams, and it is the strand of theology Auden explored in his poetry of the 1940s.[22]

Niebuhr highlights the errors to which these two theological tendencies are prone. Theology that focuses on vertical tension—which Niebuhr terms "sacramentalism"—runs the risk of conflating the earthly and the divine: "The sacramentalism of Christian orthodoxy, in which all natural things are symbols and images of the divine transcendence, but in which the tension between the present and the future of prophetic religion is destroyed, is a priestly deflation of prophetic religion." And "prophetic religion," which focuses on the horizontal tension, runs the opposite risk of turning Christ into a "symbol of human goodness and human possibilities without suggestion of the limits of the human and the temporal—in short, without the suggestion of transcendence."[23] But Niebuhr's own theology was clearly of the horizontal kind, concerned with time and history, and so too was Auden's theological poetry. In "For the Time Being," Auden's narrator writes that humankind exists when "The happy morning is over, / The night of agony still to come; the time is noon."[24] It lives, in other words, not in eternity nor in the end of days but in "the moderate Aristotelian city," where "The Time Being is, in a sense, the most trying time of all."[25] Looking to Niebuhr and Williams for guidance, Auden's later poetry explores what it means to live in the "meantime," torn between despair for the present and hope for the future.

If this theological framework was important for Auden's explicitly theological poems—"For the Time Being," "Memorial for the City," and "The Age of Anxiety," among others—then theological style proved just as crucial. More specifically, Auden's reading of Reinhold Niebuhr convinced him that Christian poetry is defined not chiefly by its adherence to dogmatic propositions but by a particular tone and stance taken towards humanity's sinfulness and pride. Niebuhr is the great twentieth-century theologian of irony and, for him, irony has a very specific meaning. It is the surprising gap between intention and consequence that reveals some deep, unconscious, and causal relation between the two. Niebuhr argues that humanity's fall lay in its pride and that this pride ironically arose from humanity's greatest gift: its ability to think above and beyond itself; its capacity for self-reflection and, therefore, self-transcendence. Our capacity for self-transcendence leads to our disavowal of our creaturely nature, which leads to sin, which leads us back towards the creaturely and separates us from God. As James Livingston puts it, Niebuhr believed that "it is not our finitude but our efforts to deny or overcome finitude that is the source of human sin."[26] Original sin is the theological label we give to this tendency towards prideful destructiveness, and Niebuhr argued that it structures all earthly existence. To be human is to fall victim to pride. To be Christian, though, is to recognize this and to open oneself up to God's unmerited, saving love.

For Auden, this theological truth has serious consequences for poetry. If Christian theology shows the irony and absurdity of human existence, then Christian poetry must acknowledge this absurdity, admit humanity's failings, and move towards laughter, pardon, and reconciliation. Theological poetry must be, in short, comic. It must realize that to take oneself too seriously, to have confidence in one's holiness or one's ideas about God, humanity, and the relation between the two, is to give in to the pride and solipsism that Niebuhr so convincingly shows to be humanity's defining feature. In the essay "Words and the Word," Auden has this to say about the particular challenge confronting theological discourse: "The Christian theologian is placed in the difficult position of having to use words, which by their nature are anthropomorphic, to refute anthropomorphic conceptions of God. Yet, when such anthropomorphic conceptions are verbally asserted, he must speak: he cannot refute them by silence. Dogmatic theological statements are to be comprehended, neither as logical propositions nor as poetic utterances: they are to be taken, rather, as shaggy-dog stories: they have a point, but he who tries too hard to get it will miss it."[27] Theology as a shaggy-dog story, as a story with a point, a serious point, but one that will be betrayed if it does not acknowledge its own provisional nature: this is a remarkable vision of theology, and one unlike any other modern poet's. It is no accident that Auden's religious poetry so often focuses on the sacrament of marriage. In Auden's vision, Christian theology teaches that human experience is not a tragedy, as it often seemed to Eliot, but something more like a Shakespearean comedy, ending not with death and despair but with marriage and joy.

There is a long critical tradition of looking at the Christian bent of Auden's later poetry, though this tradition often expresses itself more in lament at Auden's falling off than in an analysis of the uses to which Auden puts Christian images and discourse. Randall Jarrell's polemical 1952 lectures at Princeton offer the sharpest—and most mean-spirited—of these critical readings. There, Jarrell describes the Auden of the 1940s as "a representative neurotic theologian" whose "morals are now, like the Law in Luther or Niebuhr, merely a crutch with which to beat us into submission, to force home to us the realization that there is none good but God, that no works can either save us or make us worth saving."[28] Though Jarrell's lectures provide the vicarious thrill of witnessing one brilliant mind wrestling with another, his reading of both the theology and the poetry is tendentious: "neurotic" is far too reductive a reading of the complex theology expressed in "For the Time Being" and other poems, and Auden regularly reminds us in these poems of the goodness and holiness of creaturely, bodily existence.

In recent years, critics have begun to recuperate Auden's later, explicitly Christian poems. Edward Mendelson, Arthur Kirsch, and Stephen Schuler, for example, have shown just how influential Christianity—its rituals and rites, its dogmas and doctrines—was to Auden's poetry of the 1940s, and they have argued that this influence wasn't, as Jarrell claims, solely deleterious. This chapter expands upon these recuperative projects, offering a more detailed analysis of Auden's specifically theological—and specifically modern—engagement. Instead of analyzing Auden's interest in "Christianity" broadly conceived, as Kirsch does, I offer readings of how specific theological texts (Niebuhr's *The Nature and Destiny of Man*, for instance) influenced specific poems ("For the Time Being"). Kirsch mentions Niebuhr's influence on Auden at several points, but this influence is generally asserted rather than argued. It is telling that he quotes twice from Auden's review of *The Nature and Destiny of Man* but not from the theological text itself. This is typical of most Auden scholarship, which rarely looks in detail at the theology that Auden was consuming and absorbing at the time.

Schuler's excellent *The Augustinian Theology of W. H. Auden* is an exception to this rule, quoting liberally and intelligently from Augustine, Niebuhr, and others. Yet, despite an illuminating section on the importance of Niebuhr's understanding of original sin to Auden's poetry, Schuler's ultimate focus is on Augustinian rather than modern theology. Moreover, in choosing to focus so intensely on Auden's theological reading and writing, Schuler doesn't relate this reading and writing to that of Eliot, Jones, or other of Auden's peers. This singular focus allows for sharp readings of Auden's work, but it also obscures the broader conversation that took place between poetry and theology in the modernist period and Auden's special place within this conversation. After all, part of what makes Auden's achievement in the 1940s so striking is just how different his theological poetry was from that of Eliot or Jones. Not for Auden the Eliotic oscillation between divine transcendence and human despair, nor the Jonesian celebration of poetry's sacramental nature. Auden once described Lord Byron as "the master of the airy manner."[29] It was the genius of Auden to show how theology and airiness might go hand in hand.

Necessity and History

In his 1940 essay "Mimesis and Allegory," Auden describes the delicate balance an artist must strike between belief and art: "Art is not metaphysics any more than it is conduct, and the artist is usually unwise to insist too directly in his art upon his beliefs; but without an adequate and conscious metaphysics in the background, art's imitation of life inevitably becomes, either a photostatic copy of the accidental details of life without pattern or significance, or a personal allegory of the artist's individual dementia, of interest primarily to the psychologist and the historian."[30] Here, Auden echoes Eliot on the aesthetic usefulness of a metaphysical framework. Seeing the world—and, in turn, one's work—through the prism of a defined belief system allows the artist to see meaningful pattern rather than chaos and confusion. The passage also recalls the words of David Jones, who likewise insisted that art and apologia should never be confused with one another. An artist, Auden and Jones suggest, must possess some metaphysical account of the world and its relation to the work of art. Indeed, much of Auden's later criticism offers just such a specifically Christian account of poetic creation.[31] But this metaphysical account, for all three poets, must not itself enter too freely or directly into the poem or painting. As Eliot puts it, "The poet makes poetry, the metaphysician makes metaphysics."[32]

Just like Jones and Eliot, however, Auden often ignored his own warnings against mixing poetry and metaphysics. In the 1940s, Auden's poems frequently take theological ideas as their very subjects: the consequences of the Incarnation for history and the imagination in "For the Time Being," for example, or the nature of revelation and its relation to everyday life in "Kairos and Logos." The 1949 poem "Memorial for the City" is a particularly illuminating example of this tendency. The poem is dedicated to the memory of the theologian, novelist, and poet Charles Williams, and Auden echoes Williams's ideas throughout the work. More specifically, "Memorial for the City" shows Auden working through two theological ideas: first, how, in the Christian vision, humanity finds freedom precisely in its admission of dependence; and second, how human history is the story of Niebuhr's "horizontal tension"—the fitful, hopeful, ultimately impossible attempt to achieve the City of God within human, temporal experience.

The poem begins with a synoptic vision of a classical Greek battlefield:

> The eyes of the crow and the eye of the camera open
> Onto Homer's world, not ours. First and last
> They magnify earth, the abiding
> Mother of gods and men; if they notice either
> It is only in passing: gods behave, men die,
> Both feel in their own small way, but She
> Does nothing and does not care.
> She alone is seriously there.[33]

This opening crystallizes many of Auden's non-Christian concerns. In its panoramic sweep, we hear echoes of early, Hardy-esque poems like "Family Ghosts," where the "longing for assurance takes the form // Of a hawk's vertical stooping from the sky."[34] In its vision of a classical world torn apart by violence, the poem foreshadows the more famous "The Shield of Achilles," which takes place in a world dominated by rape, violence, and voyeurism. In its succinct, painful representation of indifference to human suffering ("Does nothing and does not care"), it recalls "how everything turns away / Quite leisurely" from the suffering of Icarus in "Musée des Beaux Arts."[35]

As the poem proceeds, however, it becomes apparent that Auden's real subject here is theological and political: humanity's attempt to close the gap separating the City of God from the City of Man. The second stanza returns again to a description of the kind of vision afforded by physical distance. When viewed from above, from the perspective of the "crow on the crematorium chimney / And the camera roving the battle," the scene seems to occur in a world "where time has no place."[36] The classical and the modern blend. Though we have been told that this is "Homer's world, not ours," the crematorium recalls the horrors of the Holocaust and the camera's eye–view recalls the opening of Christopher Isherwood's 1939 *Goodbye to Berlin*. In this timeless realm,

isolated experience becomes coherent pattern—"The hard bright light com-
poses / A meaningless moment into an eternal fact"—and singular events are
understood as expressing the eternal, or at least the natural, state of things: "That
is the way things happen; for ever and ever."[37]

In describing the patterned, timeless vision of the battlefield, Auden relies
upon a distinction between the world of nature/necessity and the world of
history/freedom. This distinction, which Auden returns to frequently in his poetry and prose, is most clearly drawn in his essay "The Virgin and the Dynamo."
There, he first defines the "Natural World of the Dynamo": it is "the world of
masses, of identical relations and recurrent events . . . In this world, Freedom is
the consciousness of Necessity and Justice the equality of all before natural
law." This he contrasts with the "Historical World of the Virgin," which is "the
world of faces, analogical relations and singular events . . . In this World, Necessity is the consciousness of Freedom and Justice the love of my neighbor as
a unique and irreplaceable being."[38] In the world of the Dynamo, humans are
seen as purely material beings, buffeted about by physical and natural forces
beyond their control; they are "describable, not in words but in terms of numbers, or, rather, in algebraic terms."[39] In the world of the Virgin, however, humans
are spiritual beings, "describable only in terms of speech"—describable, that
is, by the language that they have themselves created.[40] As is so often the case
with Auden, here the Virgin and the Dynamo offer a way of dividing the world
into binaries: freedom/necessity; the individual face/the undifferentiated masses;
spirit/body. (In another move typical of Auden, though, he sets up these binaries only to show how the truest system—in this case, Christianity—is able to
accommodate both sides.)

Auden borrowed the concepts of the "Virgin" and the "Dynamo" from *The
Education of Henry Adams*, but the ideas expressed about nature, necessity, history, and freedom also derive from his reading of a particular theological text:
Charles Williams's 1939 *The Descent of the Dove: A Short History of the Holy
Spirit in the Church*. Auden admitted his indebtedness to Williams's thinking
on freedom and necessity in his poem "New Year Letter," where he glosses the
striking, aphoristic line—"Where Freedom dwells because it must, / Necessity
because it can"—in this way: "For this quotation, and for the source of many
ideas in this poem, v. *The Descent of the Dove* by Charles Williams."[41] Auden
loved *The Descent of the Dove*, claiming in 1956 that it was "a source of intellectual delight and spiritual nourishment which remains inexhaustible."[42] In
this book, Williams argues that the Christian faith weds nature/necessity and
history/freedom: it offers freedom *from* necessity (that is, freedom from our
natural instincts) in its recognition *of* necessity (our dependence, that is, on the
saving grace of the Holy Spirit). In choosing to accept the gifts of the Holy
Spirit, the church recognizes its insufficiency and its need for divine guidance.

As Williams writes in a quotation that Auden loved, "It is the choice of necessity; it is the freedom of all that is beyond necessity."[43] We choose to acknowledge our dependence on the Holy Spirit. In so doing, we achieve the kind of freedom proper to humanity. The echoes with Kierkegaard—we achieve freedom not in escaping from time and contingency but in facing them most fully—are clear, and this is no accident: by the time Williams wrote *The Descent of the Dove*, he had already worked tirelessly for Oxford University Press on the publication of Kierkegaard's notebooks in English for the first time.

The relation between Christian dependence and Christian freedom would also have been in Auden's mind from his reading of Niebuhr's *The Nature and Destiny of Man*, which the poet described in an earlier review for the *New Republic* as "the most lucid and balanced statement of orthodox Protestantism that we are likely to see for a long time."[44] Niebuhr's book, which offers a theological reading of man's unchanging essence (nature) as well as an account of how this essence shapes, and is shaped by, temporal experience (destiny), opens with the claim that "man has always been his own most vexing problem" because he is both "a child of nature" and thus of necessity and also a "special eminence," whose reason allows him "a degree of transcendence over himself."[45] For both Niebuhr and Williams, Christianity is the one worldview that can account both for humanity's freedom, since it was created in the image of God, and for its insufficiency, since humanity dwells in a fallen world. As James Livingston writes, "Niebuhr believes that the Christian view of the self allows for a unitary conception of human personality that takes into account both our creatureliness and our capacity for self-transcendence." In offering such a synthesizing vision, the Christian view of the self displays a "paradoxically high and low estimate of human nature."[46]

In the opening section of "Memorial for the City," though, we are still firmly situated within the realm of nature and necessity because we are still situated within the mythic, Homeric world—that is, a world defined by nature and divorced from history. In this world, as we gaze down at the battlefield from afar, human tragedy and human romance are both erased by natural processes: "Plum-blossom falls on the dead, the roar of the waterfall covers / The cries of the whipped and the sighs of the lovers."[47] Because we see patterns and not faces, because we act by necessity and not by freedom, Auden writes, "there is no one to blame." A removal from the world of history and time results in a removal from moral responsibility.

Towards the end of the first section, Auden finally offers the criticism of this classical, atemporal perspective that any reader of Williams or Niebuhr would expect. Though the "steady eyes of the crow and the camera's candid eye / See as honestly as they know how," this is not enough: still "they lie."[48] The crow's vision, the camera's vision, the distanced vision, is always by its very nature a limited vision. It can be honest—neither the camera nor the crow means to distort things—but it can never be whole. A world in which no one is to blame is not only not how it should be, Auden claims; it is also not how it is. The temptation to timeless abstraction is certainly a moral error, but it is also a metaphysical error, a misreading of the world's nature. And what is needed to correct this error is human, time-bound vision.

At this moment, the poem shifts to the present, offering us a vision of the bombed-out, violence-ridden German landscape, complete with "a chaos of graves," "barbed-wire" fences, "searchlights," and "loudspeakers."[49] In moving from Homer's world to our "Post-Vergilian City"—in other words, to the modern, Christian city—we realize that "the crime of life is not time." Human action within time, and not time itself, is to blame. As the poem proceeds, narrative and historical change replace static pattern. Modern violence cannot be explained away by Homeric violence. The present is shaped but not determined by the past, and though "our past is a chaos of graves and the barbed-wire stretches ahead / Into our future till it is lost to sight, / Our grief is not Greek." We no longer believe in necessity or the heroism of violence. This acknowledgment of history, of the changes that human decisions have wrought in time, leads to our acknowledgment of moral culpability: "We know without knowing there is reason for what we bear, / That our hurt is not a desertion, that we are to pity / Neither ourselves nor our city." (Auden again rejects the urge to self-pity later in the poem, when he writes of the physical body, "This is the flesh we are but never would believe, / The flesh we die but it is death to pity; / This is Adam waiting for His City.")[50]

It also leads to the poem's second numbered section, which offers another panoramic view—this time not of space, as in the first two stanzas, but of time. Borrowing from Eugen Rosenstock-Huessy's *Out of Revolution: Autobiography of Western Man*, Auden attempts to condense the political history of Christendom into nine sextets, tracing history's changing conceptions of the ideal City.[51] The poem follows these transformations from the time of the Holy Roman Empire (when a "New City rose / Upon" the battle between Emperor and Pope) to the Reformation (when Martin Luther "announced to the Sinful City a grinning gap / No rite could cross") to the French Revolution (when revolutionaries enacted "the Rational City, quick to admire, / Quick to tire") and beyond.[52] In each era, humanity is driven by a particular vision of the good life and the kind of political and social organization that this vision entails. In Reformation-era Germany, it is a vision of the world freed from the papal "machine that so smoothly forgave and saved / If paid"; in revolutionary France, it is a vision of the world of "prelapsarian man," where "mystery" is forsaken and "history marched to the drums of a clear idea."[53] But in each era, this vision fails. History does not march towards perfection but towards "the burnt-out Law Courts and Police Headquarters" of postwar Germany.[54] The "New City," "the Rational City," the "Glittering City": all seem near at hand, but all remain ever distant. The poem's third section ends with humanity still hoping for the advent of a perfect realm that never quite arrives: "This is Adam, waiting for His City."[55]

At this moment, the poem's engagement with the particular vision of history offered by Williams and Niebuhr comes most clearly into focus. The whole argument of *The Descent of the Dove*, Williams claims, is that the Holy Spirit is the means by which God continues to act in and through history—that is, in and through time. As Williams writes, "Christianity is, always, the redemption of a point, of one particular point. '*Now* is the accepted time; *now* is the day of salvation.'"[56] Yet, while Christianity is about a specific and sudden revelation (Christ's entrance into history through the Incarnation), it is also about temporal duration (the Holy Spirit's movement through history). The central question for the church, Williams writes, is, "What are the relations between that *Now* and the consequent *Then*? what are the conditions of the relation—not what ought to be, but what *are*? 'The conversion of time by the Holy Ghost' is the title of the grand activity of the Church."[57] For Williams, though, time is never fully converted by the Holy Spirit. It is in the very nature of time and history to be incomplete, to be in the middle of things: "The Kingdom—or, apocalyptically, the City—is the state into which Christendom is called; but, except in vision, she is not yet the City. The City is the state which the Church is to become."[58]

Niebuhr puts this idea even more forcefully in *An Interpretation of Christian Ethics*. Within human history, Niebuhr writes, the City remains an impossible possibility: the "Kingdom of God is always a possibility in history, because its heights of pure love are organically related to the experience of love in all human life, but it is also an impossibility in history and always beyond every historical achievement."[59] In *The Nature of Destiny of Man*, he makes the same claim: "The idea that history is an 'interim' between the first and second coming of Christ has a meaning which illumines all the facts of human existence. History, after Christ's first coming, has the quality of partly knowing its true meaning."[60] Partly, but not fully: that is the nature of existence in the "interim" that is history. We can sense the City, perhaps even sketch in its outlines, but we can never reach it.

Niebuhr described himself as a Christian realist, which for him meant an antiutopian. As Jason Stevens has argued, Niebuhr's Christian realism defined itself largely in opposition to "perfectionism, the belief that the morality, purity, and concord of the Kingdom of God can be progressively realized as an earthly estate."[61] Like Barth, he urged a refocus on original sin as one of Christianity's most crucial doctrines: crucial because it suggests that humanity is not perfectible and that historical experience is always characterized by the longing for, and frustration of, eschatological hope—the hope that the City can be built in this world.

In his review of *The Nature and Destiny of Man*, Auden recognized the centrality of original sin to Niebuhr's theology of history, and he also recognized how this theology might frustrate political idealists. As he writes, "No Christian doctrine is more unwelcome to the modern liberal than the doctrine of Original Sin."[62] In "Memorial for the City," Auden agrees with the vision of Williams and Niebuhr. At the end of the poem, humanity is left like Adam, "waiting for His City." The poem's shift from nature (classical Greece) to history (the Christian city) has been accomplished, but the fulfillment of nature and history remains a distant hope, Niebuhr's impossible possibility. The poem is eschatological: it looks towards the *eschaton*, towards the fulfillment of peace and the coming of the City, where violence and guilt will be converted to peace and happiness. But it is also skeptical of the *eschaton*'s imminent arrival. In "Memorial for the City," history is not close to being over.

Vertical and Horizontal Tension

As a theological poet, Auden is interested in the meantime, in Adam "waiting for His City" rather than in his achieving it. This is expressed most explicitly in "For the Time Being," a poem whose very title proclaims its fascination with the theology of waiting—with what happens to human history when the Kingdom of Heaven doesn't arrive immediately. The poem moves through the entirety of the Nativity narrative. We see the world preparing itself for the birth of Christ. We listen to Joseph worrying over Mary's fidelity and Herod worrying over the political consequences of the Christian faith. We hear from Wise Men and Shepherds and Angels. All of these characters and events seem to proclaim the same thing: that the Incarnation has done away with the old world and that nothing will ever be the same.

Yet, at the poem's conclusion, the narrator proclaims that, while Christ's birth has indeed changed everything, it has not, as humanity might have hoped, abolished history and established the Kingdom on earth. Humanity is still left to make its way, hopefully but frustratingly, through time: "To those who have seen / The Child, however dimly, however incredulously, / The Time Being is, in a sense, the most trying time of all."[63] The Chorus ends the poem with a hopeful message: "He is the Truth. / Seek him in the Kingdom of Anxiety; / You will come to a great city that has expected your return for years."[64] But the journey towards the City has just started, and "In the meantime / There are bills to be paid, machines to keep in repair, / Irregular verbs to learn, the Time Being to redeem / From insignificance." Auden is just as interested in what happens *after* the Incarnation as he is in what happens *in* the Incarnation. Like

Williams, he is interested in connecting the "now" of Christ's birth to the "then" of subsequent human history.

Auden places Williams's "conversion of time" ("the Time Being to redeem") alongside the boring tasks of daily life (paying one's bills), and, for Auden as for Williams, that is the proper place for it. The task of the Christian is not to inhabit some millennial present but to move towards that millennial present, knowing that it is far off and will not be achieved by human action alone. This is why the first vision of Joseph in "For the Time Being" is of an unremarkable man hurrying to an unremarkable bar, hopeful that he will soon see Mary: "My shoes were shined, my pants were cleaned and pressed, / And I was hurrying to meet / My own true Love."[65] But Mary does not appear, and Joseph is left to wait, passing the time in conversation with the archangel Gabriel. In fact, Joseph's defining feature throughout the poem is his posture of anxious waiting. He waits for Mary, he waits for his Lord ("Where are you, father, where?"), he waits for a theological explanation of Mary's pregnancy: "All I ask is one / Important and elegant proof / That what my Love had done / Was really at your will / And that your will is Love." But the only answer he is given is to continue waiting: "No, you must believe; / Be silent, and sit still."[66] Joseph, like the narrator, must be content to live in Niebuhr's world of horizontal tension.

This is not to say that the poem is uninterested in vertical tension—in the relation between divine transcendence and worldly immanence. In fact, "For the Time Being" shows how Christian theology offers to Auden an account of creaturely embodiment that is both physical and spiritual, immanent and potentially transcendent. As Simeon puts it, Christianity means that "we may no longer, with the Barbarians, deny the Unity, asserting that there are as many gods as there are creatures," but neither can we agree with the philosophers that "God is One who has no need of friends and is indifferent to a World of Time and Quantity and Horror which He did not create."[67] Both pure immanence and pure transcendence are rejected, and Christian theology instead argues for what Auden called "double focus": a reconciling, yet not a conflation, of spirit and body.[68]

With regards to this reconciliation of immanence and transcendence, "Memorial for the City" is again instructive. The poem opens with an epigraph from the medieval mystic Julian of Norwich: "In the self-same point that our soul is made sensual, in the self-same point is the City of God ordained to him from without beginning."[69] This is a very different Julian from the Julian of Eliot's *Four Quartets*. There, Julian takes her place in a tradition of Christian thinkers—St. John of the Cross and Augustine, for instance—who urge self-purgation as a first step towards personal holiness: "Desiccation of the world of sense" and "The intolerable shirt of flame" are necessary, Eliot writes, since "The only hope, or else despair / Lies in the choice of pyre or pyre— / To be redeemed from fire by fire."[70] Auden's Julian, however, makes almost the opposite point. She argues that it is precisely when man is given physical, sensual embodiment, not when the soul is cleansed of the body, that the City of God is vouchsafed to him. For Auden, this is all a consequence of the Incarnation. Christ's taking on of human flesh means that human flesh cannot be, in and of itself, sinful. Rather, just as humanity's salvation comes about through Christ's willingness to enter into creaturely, physical form, so the path to holiness for the sinner lies not away from the creaturely but through it. Later, in "Memorial for the City," Auden gives the physical body itself a voice. The final section, spoken from the perspective of pure body, proclaims its crucial role in humanity's narrative of salvation: "Without me Adam would have fallen irrevocably with Lucifer; he would never have been able to cry *O felix culpa*."[71] Auden's poetry confirms this point again and again: no body, no salvation.

In "For the Time Being," the comical figure of King Herod best expresses the radical changes Christ's birth will bring about for humanity's understanding of both physical embodiment and historical experience. Herod, the poem's exemplar of modern rationalism and do-gooder liberalism, is surely right to see in Christ's birth the frightening introduction of a new order. As Herod complains, all of his social reforms—"soil fertiliser" is now freely available, and "there are children in this province who have never seen a louse"—will be jeopardized by a world in which "Reason will be replaced by Revelation" and "Justice will be replaced by Pity as the cardinal human virtue."[72] And he is also right to emphasize the existential anxiety that such a shift will create within his kingdom: "that once showing them how, God would expect every man, whatever his fortune, to lead a sinless life in the flesh and on earth."[73] Again, Auden emphasizes that the Incarnation does not lead us away from the flesh and away from the earth; it is not a form of philosophical and theological escapism. Rather, it urges a sinless life lived in the flesh and on earth. The creaturely isn't abolished but transformed. As Herod says, his world and his political decisions are determined by "Nature and Necessity," and Christ's entrance into the world threatens the supremacy of these values.[74]

Yet the rest of the poem emphasizes not the apocalyptic shift in worldview ushered in by the Incarnation, but how boring, after this dramatic event, everyday history remains. *Kairos*, or holy time, gives way to *chronos*, or clock time. The contrast is sharp. After Christmas, everything "seems to have shrunk during the holidays. The streets / Are much narrower than we remembered; we had forgotten / The office was as depressing as this."[75] Yet the Christian is asked to make his way through the depressing and ordinary, since this is the only way to get to the epiphanic. Alan Jacobs describes Auden's seeking out of the middle position, somewhere between exultation and despair, in "For the Time Being": "It is not just suffering which cannot, or should not, be represented directly in poetry; the joys of love likewise evade the resources of poetry."[76]

And of theology, too: both poetry and theology exist for Auden in the meantime, in the world of bills and verb conjugations, of hope rather than fulfillment. As Auden writes elsewhere, "Christianity is a way, not a state, and a Christian is never something one is, only something one can pray to become."[77] Consider what a different conclusion Eliot reached in his own Christmas poem, "The Journey of the Magi." There, Christ's birth announces a dramatic ending to the "old dispensation": "this Birth was / Hard and bitter agony for us, like Death, our death."[78] What is left in the wake of the Incarnation for Auden is less like death and more like a hangover—a dull headache that follows the festive celebration, a painful state of affairs that must be endured.

From Apocalypse to the Meanwhile

Auden's claim in "For the Time Being"—that to be human, to be Christian, is to dwell in the meantime, hopeful for the City of God but knowing that it is not immediately on the horizon—reimagines the political eschatology of his earlier political poems, the most famous of which is "Spain." Written in 1937, with the Spanish Civil War raging and ideological fervor at its peak, "Spain" carefully distinguishes all that is past (the religious and wondrous, "the theological feuds in the taverns / And the miraculous cure at the fountain") from all that is future (the secular and scientific, "the gradual exploring of all the Octaves of radiation") from all that is violently, apocalyptically present: "But to-day the struggle."[79] In this apocalyptic present, one constituted by struggle, all kinds of action become possible—even actions that, in ordinary time, might seem evil. It is because the Ideal City seems within reach that moral compromises are seen as "necessary," even just. Take the lines that troubled both Auden and his later readers, lines that describe "the deliberate increase in the chances of death, / The conscious acceptance of guilt in the necessary murder."[80] Such actions can be consciously accepted, can be deliberately chosen, precisely because the time is late, because the Ideal City appears imminent if not yet immanent. The final stanza presents Auden's clearest vision of the apocalyptic context in which these events take place:

> The stars are dead. The animals will not look.
> We are left alone with our day, and the time is short, and
>   History to the defeated
> May say Alas but cannot help nor pardon.[81]

Nature has given way completely to history—or, rather, to History. The stars go out and the animals turn away; time itself seems to be on the verge of abolishment.

Though Auden would eventually repudiate these lines, they are revealing of the poet's understanding of history and historical action at this particular moment. In an earlier poem, "Consider" (1930), Auden offered a similarly eschatological message. "It is later than you think," the speaker exclaims, and things are poised "To disintegrate on an instant in the explosion of mania / Or lapse for ever into a classic fatigue."[82] For the decadent interwar world, two options seem possible: for that decadence to turn explosive or for that decadence to lead to permanent enervation. Here, Auden takes up the mantle of the political and social prophet. Britain is sick, he writes, "seized with immeasurable neurotic dread." The mysterious "supreme Antagonist" is ready to wreak havoc: his message "shall come to be / A polar peril, a prodigious alarm, / Scattering the people, as torn-up paper / Rags and utensils in a sudden gust."[83] The Antagonist's identity is unclear, but it is also largely beside the point. What is crucial is the time's ripeness for violent change: "You cannot be away, then, no / Not though you pack to leave within an hour, / Escaping humming down arterial roads."[84]

When the young Auden wrote these lines, he was convinced—or, at least, his poetic persona seemed convinced—that an old order was on the cusp of passing away forever. Nine years later, after Auden had moved to the United States but right before his return to the Christian faith, the times seemed apocalyptic once again. Where before Auden had seen the imminent collapse of a weakened, neurotic British middle class, now he saw European civilization itself as in danger. In "In Memory of W. B. Yeats," Auden memorably describes the anxious state of prewar Europe: "In the nightmare of the dark / All the dogs of Europe bark, / And the living nations wait, / Each sequestered in its hate."[85] Similarly, once Germany had invaded Poland and the war had started, Auden in "September 1, 1939" again uses the prophetic voice: "We must love one another or die."[86] In "New Year Letter," written in the first months of 1940, Auden opens with a vision of malevolence swiftly moving against European civilization:

The sleepless guests of Europe lay
Wishing the centuries away,
And the low mutter of their vows
Went echoing through her haunted house,
As on the verge of happening
There crouched the presence of The Thing.
All formulas were tried to still
The scratching on the window-sill,
All bolts of custom made secure
Against the pressure on the door,

But up the staircase of events
Carrying his special instruments,
To every bedside all the same
The dreadful figure swiftly came.[87]

In each instance—1930s London, Civil War Spain, a New York dive bar—the cataclysm that is coming seems both inevitable and close at hand, the result of large historical, economic, and psychological forces that cannot be wished away or avoided.

Even within "New Year Letter," however, Auden had begun to shift his attention from apocalyptic necessity and towards individual choice. After dramatically describing the fearful state of the generalized "sleeping guests of Europe," Auden moves to the specific individual: "Yet Time can moderate his tone / When talking to a man alone."[88] Later in the poem, we hear how the millennial dreams of Marxism have proven false: "We hoped; we waited for the day / The State would wither clean away, / Expecting the Millennium / That theory promised us would come: / It didn't."[89] Revolutionary hope is deflated, a deflation that is mirrored in the lines' syntactical unfolding. The hopes are drawn out, lingered over—the first sentence stretches over four lines—only to be suddenly snuffed out by the colon, line break, and short, crisp declaration: "It didn't." The rest of the poem considers what to do, politically and ethically, once the promised revolution has failed to come, when the Millennium remains just as distant and unreachable as ever.

The answers that the poem provides to this question are tentative, but they are Christian and theological rather than Marxist or historical: "true democracy begins / With free confession of our sins. / In this alone are all the same, / All are so weak that none dare claim, / 'I have the right to govern,' or / 'Behold in me the Moral Law.'"[90] Political and social solidarity come about not through the historical dialectic but through Christian humility. As the poem moves towards its conclusion, the Christian allusions—to Charles Williams, to John Donne, to Augustine—begin to pile up, and the entire poem can be read as an attempt by Auden to work through his old philosophical systems (Freudianism and Marxism, most obviously) to arrive at a new, more solid foundation for understanding the relation between history and individual action. "New Year Letter" is a kind of hinge, the poem in which we see Auden's new, Christian vision of history first emerging: gentler, more tempered, hopeful but not apocalyptic.

Auden's sense of an imminent apocalyptic change did not wholly depart from his poetry after 1939. In his 1952 poem "The Age of Anxiety," for instance, the character Emble describes the unquenchable longing for rupture that even those living in the "Middle Way" (deans, financiers, commuters) continue to feel:

   . . . precarious on the
Fringes of their feeling, a fuzzy hope
Persists somehow that sometime all this
Will walk away, and a wish gestates
For explosive pain, a punishing
Demanded moment of mortal change,
The Night of the Knock when none shall sleep,
The Absolute Instant.[91]

Humanity's desire for the "Absolute Instant" does not go away. Humans continue to be, as the poem puts it earlier, "Avid of elseness," wishing to replace "unprivileged time" with "the huge wild beast of the Unexpected."[92]

But this eschatological longing, Auden suggests, must be understood in a different context, a context that is crystallized in the first section of "Memorial for the City":

   . . . As we bury our dead
We know without knowing there is reason for what we bear,
That our hurt is not a desertion, that we are to pity
Neither ourselves nor our city . . . [93]

The line "there is reason for what we bear" can be read in two ways. First, there is reason for what we bear in that we ourselves are the cause of our suffering: we have laid the barbed wire we now find ourselves tangled in, and this is why we should not pity ourselves and our city. Second, though, there is reason for what we bear in that there is a larger, divine narrative in which our suffering makes sense, a narrative that will show that we have not been deserted and thus that "We are not to despair." By this reading, we must reject pity not because we are at fault, though surely we are. Rather, we must reject pity because such a response misinterprets the story in which we find ourselves, reading the present as the ending of a human tragedy rather than as the middle of a divine comedy.

In *The Time That Remains*, Giorgio Agamben differentiates between two ways of understanding time:

But the apostle [Paul] must be distinguished from another figure, with whom he is often confused, just as messianic time is confused with eschatological time. The most insidious misunderstanding of the messianic announcement does not consist in mistaking it for prophecy, which is turned toward the future, but for apocalypse, which contemplates the end of time. The apocalyptic is situated on the last day, the Day of Wrath. It sees the end fulfilled and describes what it sees. The time in which the apostle lives is, however, not the *eschaton*, it is not the end of time. If you want to formulate the difference between

messianism and apocalypse, between the apostle and the visionary, I think you
could say, using a phrase by Gianni Carchia, that the messianic is not the end of
time, but *the time of the end* (Carchia, 144). What interests the apostle is not the
last day, it is not the instant in which time ends, but the time that contracts
itself and begins to end . . . or if you prefer, the time that remains between time
and its end.[94]

This distinction between apocalyptic and messianic time maps quite nicely
onto Auden's own evolving views on time over the course of his career. (And it
also maps quite nicely onto the period's increased interest in Pauline theology.)[95] In the 1930s, under the influence of a Marxist reading of history, Auden
saw time as on the verge of abolishment and/or fulfillment. In the 1940s, under
the influence of a Pauline/Christian reading of history, he saw time as the
meanwhile, as that which remains.

Indeed, Auden's poetry of the 1940s does its most interesting theological
work when it examines what Agamben calls "the time that remains between
time and its end"—when it puts aside the end for the interim. In a 1944 review
of Charles Norris Cochrane's *Christianity and Classical Culture*, Auden claimed
that Christian intellectuals saw in history "not an unfortunate failure of necessity to master chance, but a dialectic of human choice."[96] For Auden, Christian
theology's reading of human history kept the best of Marxism (its utopian vision of the Just City) while eliminating its worst (faith that such a City could
be—by the laws of historical materialism, had to be—achieved in this world,
and soon). In part through his reading of Niebuhr and Williams, Auden came
to believe that time is not short. It is not later than you think, and that is the
challenge: to figure out what to do in the interregnum.

A Theology of Irony

To be a poet of the apocalypse means to be a confident poet—to have confidence that the world is on the verge of sudden, irreversible change and to have
confidence that you can give powerful voice to this reality. To be a poet of the
meanwhile, on the contrary, means to be a tentative poet—to be aware that
you do not know when or how the world will reach its fulfillment or end and
to be wary of those who make claims to such knowledge. To be a poet of the
meanwhile, in short, is to be an ironist.

Auden thought that contemporary Christian theology offered just such an
ironic, self-critical lens on the world and on the self. In "Preface to Kierkegaard," Auden describes Kierkegaard's thinking as dangerous "because the
more he attracts, the more he has the opposite effect to the one he intends,
which is to throw the reader back upon his own experience." The effects of
reading Kierkegaard are, then, ironic: he intends one thing (to throw the reader

back upon his or her own subjective experience and thinking), but the very intellectual and aesthetic power of these arguments causes the opposite (the reader becomes a disciple, following Kierkegaard rather than challenging him). As will become clear below, the word "very" here is crucial. For Kierkegaard, as for Niebuhr, as for Auden, something is ironic not if one's intentions somehow lead to unexpected, even opposite consequences, but if one's intentions causally, through some initially unconscious but ultimately recoverable mechanism, lead to this unexpected conclusion. Kierkegaard would not have been surprised that his rhetorical brilliance, through its very brilliance, brought about the opposite effect of the one he hoped for. His doctoral thesis, after all, was titled *On the Concept of Irony.*

Kierkegaard knew that irony could become a corrosive force, a way of looking at the world that poisons the soul and leads to a deadening of all desire, and Auden knew that Kierkegaard knew this. In *The Living Thoughts of Kierkegaard*, a collection of the philosopher's writings which Auden edited, we read that "irony is an abnormal growth; like the abnormally enlarged liver of the Strasbourg goose it ends by killing the individual."[97] And yet irony, as long as it does not overtake the ironist, still serves a useful, critical purpose.[98] As Kierkegaard argues in *On the Concept of Irony*, there is a deep connection between irony and the growth of subjectivity. In fact, a capacity for irony is one of the defining features of a mature human existence and of consciousness itself: "Just as philosophy begins with doubt, so also a life that may be called human begins with irony."[99] For Kierkegaard, irony makes the dialectic possible. It prevents closure and conclusion; it upsets conventional response; it unsettles and leads to rational, dialectical discourse.

There is no twentieth-century religious thinker more associated with irony than Reinhold Niebuhr. Niebuhr thought and wrote about the irony of human existence—and, more specifically, the irony of the Christian worldview—over the course of his career, though his most explicit analysis came in his 1952 work, *The Irony of American History*. In the preface, Niebuhr carefully outlines the differences between the pathetic, the tragic, and the ironic. In the pathetic situation, Niebuhr writes, the agent "neither deserves admiration nor warrants contrition. Pathos arises from fortuitous cross-purposes and confusions in life for which no reason can be given, or guilt ascribed."[100] This is the world of necessity, the Homeric world from "Memorial for the City," where "There is no one to blame."

The tragic, on the other hand, does involve guilt, since "the tragic element in a human situation is constituted of conscious choices of evil for the sake of good."[101] This is the world of Shakespeare, of Othello choosing vengeance over mercy: he knows that killing Desdemona is an evil act, but he believes that such an act is necessary if justice is to be rendered. Looking to his own moment,

Niebuhr describes the tragic elements of the Cold War, in which "the threat of atomic destruction [is used] as an instrument for the preservation of peace." If questions of morality are irrelevant to the pathetic, then they are both necessary and complex in relation to the tragic, which "elicits admiration as well as pity because it combines nobility with guilt."[102] This is closer to Auden's vision of the "post-Vergilian City," but it is not quite there. Pity has yet to be expunged.

Even more complex than tragedy, and even more crucial (in Niebuhr's argument) to the Christian worldview, is irony:

> Irony consists of apparently fortuitous incongruities in life which are discovered, upon closer examination, to be not merely fortuitous. Incongruity as such is merely comic. It elicits laughter. This element of comedy is never completely eliminated from irony. But irony is something more than comedy. A comic situation is proved to be an ironic one if a hidden relation is discovered in the incongruity. If virtue becomes vice through some hidden defect in the virtue; if strength becomes weakness because of the vanity to which strength may prompt the mighty man or nation; if security is transmuted into insecurity because too much reliance is placed upon it; if wisdom becomes folly because it does not know its own limits—in all such cases the situation is ironic.[103]

Irony is comic but it is not just comic, and the difference lies in causality. In the comic, things that appear incongruous remain just that, incongruous: a stuffy old gentleman slips and falls on a banana peel. In the ironic, things that appear incongruous are actually seen to be causally related: a stuffy old gentleman slips on a banana peel *because* he is walking with his nose in the air. Seeing the world through the lens of irony unmasks the pretensions of the self and the other; flaws that were thought to be strengths are brought into the light. For Niebuhr, irony is about interpretation and right vision—seeing how the world actually is and not how we wish it to be.

As the book's title makes clear, Niebuhr in *The Irony of American History* looks primarily to history—and, more specifically, to the recent foreign policy history of the United States—in order to explore just how frequently and insidiously "virtue becomes vice through some hidden defect in the virtue." "Our age," Niebuhr claims, "is involved in irony because so many dreams of our nation have been so cruelly refuted by history."[104] America believes itself to be pure in motivation, an exceptional nation with an exceptional destiny, and this false sense of purity leads directly and ironically to its imperialist corruption.

But, as Niebuhr argues in the earlier theological works that were so important to Auden, irony is also the mode that best describes the specifically Christian vision of human experience. Man's fall, Niebuhr argues in *The Nature and*

Destiny of Man, was an ironic case of strength leading to weakness: "Man . . . is a sinner not because he is one limited individual within a whole but rather because he is betrayed by his very ability to survey the whole to imagine himself the whole."[105] Elsewhere, Niebuhr describes original sin as "not an inherited corruption . . . but . . . an inevitable fact of human existence, the inevitability of which is given by the nature of man's spirituality. It is true in every moment of existence, but it has no history."[106] Humanity suffers from original sin not because Adam and Eve ate the apple. In fact, Niebuhr believed that too many theologians and believers had committed the "literalistic error of insisting upon the Fall as an historical event."[107] Niebuhr takes great pains to stress that, while he accepts the "doctrine of the inevitability of sin," he does not accept "the dogma which asserted that sin had a natural history"—that is, that all humanity inherits its sinful condition from an event that happened at the beginning of history. Summing up the paradox of original sin, Niebuhr writes that "the Christian doctrine of original sin[,] with its seemingly contradictory assertions about the inevitability of sin and man's responsibility for sin[,] is a dialectical truth which does justice to the fact that man's self-love and self-centeredness is inevitable, but not in such a way as to fit into the category of natural necessity. It is within and by his freedom that man sins."[108] In short, humanity suffers from original sin, remains impure and sinful, because of the inherent irony of its situation. Humans are earthly beings who aspire to become more than earthly and, in doing so, only become more earthly; they are free creatures who, through the practice of this freedom, become sinful and therefore unfree creatures.

This ironic situation would be inescapable were it not for God's divine grace. Niebuhr makes this claim most clearly in *The Nature and Destiny of Man*: "The sinful self must be destroyed from beyond itself because it does not have the power to lift itself out of its narrow interests. It cannot do so because all of its transcendent powers are intimately and organically related to its finiteness."[109] In trying to lift itself out of its self-centeredness, the sinful self succeeds in making its egotism stronger. It is only when the finite opens itself up to the infinite, when the sinful self admits its own insufficiency and gives itself over to grace, that the sinful self can be "destroyed," to use Niebuhr's striking term. And in the destruction of the sinful self, something new and wholly unexpected happens: "When the sinful self is broken the consequence is a new life rather than destruction."[110] New life arises, and so does fuller meaning: "We must recognize that only a divine judgment, more final than our own, can complete the whole structure of meaning in which we are involved."[111] In yet another irony, this fuller meaning, this divine grace, is brought about through another reversal: Christ's seeming defeat in death leads to his ultimate victory and the salvation of humanity. From start to finish, then, the Christian narrative is an ironic one: "The Christian interpretation of ironic failure [the fall] has its counterpart in the conception of ironic success [Christ's redemption of humanity through death]."[112]

Comedy and Theology

If we take irony to mean, as Niebuhr did, a gap between intention and consequence that reveals a deep, underlying, causal relation between the two, then Auden was an ironist from his very first poems. Auden's first dramatic work, *Paid on Both Sides: A Charade*, exhibits several different kinds of irony. There is the dramatic irony by which the Chorus knows things that the characters do not. It knows, for example, that a larger, darker force "Guides the unwilling tread, / The asking breath" of the lives that the play portrays.[113] As Edward Mendelson puts it, Auden in *Paid on Both Sides* "achieved on stage the distant ironic perspective that the modern novel had already achieved, a perspective from which characters are seen as doomed victims of a world whose order they can never understand."[114] Beyond this dramatic irony, there is a situational irony to the play's plot. By seeking to break out of his family's past cycle of violence and reprisal, John Nower only succeeds in bringing this violence and reprisal down upon himself and his betrothed: "But he is defeated; let the son / Sell the farm lest the mountain fall; / His mother and her mother won."[115] Nower is like Oedipus. The more he hopes to avoid his fate, the more he dooms himself. Or, he is like all of humanity in Niebuhr's theological vision. It is the very attempt to escape from sin through one's own power that imprisons the sinful self all the more strongly.

Auden's early poems regularly express the ironic bent of human history in social and political terms. In "Consider," Auden begins by describing the orderly, lifeless festivities of the moneyed class. They attend "the first garden party of the year"; they join each other at the "Sport Hotel," sitting "constellated at reserved tables, / Supplied with feelings by an efficient band."[116] But all of these attempts at order and efficiency only make the way smoother for the "supreme Antagonist," the sower of chaos spreading his message to those who are excluded from such pleasures: "farmers and their dogs / Sitting in kitchens in the stormy fens," workers in "silted harbours, derelict works, / In strangled orchards." In cordoning themselves off, the wealthy guarantee that the "explosion of mania" will come more quickly and more catastrophically.[117]

Similarly, in "A Summer Night," we learn of the social chaos that seems to follow necessarily from attempts at order. Sitting in a ring in an English garden with several other friends, the speaker experiences a mystical feeling of oneness. Danger and death fall away—"The lion griefs loped from the shade / And on our knees their muzzles laid, / And Death put down his book"—and we are left with a vision of Whitmanian democracy:

Now north and south and east and west
Those I love lie down to rest;
   The moon looks on them all,
The healers and the brilliant talkers,
The eccentrics and the silent walkers,
   The dumpy and the tall.[118]

But immediately after this feeling of universal love has been proclaimed, the speaker remembers all that threatens it. The ring of loving equals can exist, the speaker admits, only because "hunger does not move" them.[119] And if mystical oneness is dependent upon freedom from want—an empty stomach, after all, can easily kill off whatever feelings of communal love a person might have—then it is also dependent upon from freedom from larger, historical ills:

And, gentle, do not care to know,
Where Poland draws her eastern bow,
   What violence is done,
Nor ask what doubtful act follows
Our freedom in this English house,
   Our picnics in the sun.[120]

This willed ignorance—of the economic system that leaves the many hungry and the few content; of the international system in which Nazi-ruled Germany threatens neighboring Poland—can create momentary, mystical feelings of community. But it cannot last, and it will only make the ensuing violence more violent. As Mendelson writes, "Auden poses the moral paradox . . . of one's love for the English calm and recognition of its manifest virtues, while at the same time one knows it to be sustained by hidden injustice in colonies and mines."[121] Or, as Alan Jacobs remarks, "This vision of love and community, then, may not be a free gift in which to rejoice, but a dangerous temptation to social quietism: it is at best a 'doubtful act.'"[122] In the following stanza, the present picnic in the sun gives way to future destruction: "Soon, soon, through dykes of our content / The crumpling flood will force a rent." Bourgeois content works as a dyke, concentrating and intensifying the pressure that it withholds; the flood will be all the more "crumpling" because it has been held back.

Auden's early poetry, then, is marked by sociopolitical irony. Feelings of community and oneness lead, ironically but causally, to exclusion and destruction. His later poetry, however, offers something very different: the Niebuhrian sense that creaturely pride leads to weakness, and yet that, through Christ's death, the admission of creaturely weakness opens up the possibility for divine grace. This is made most explicit in Auden's sequence "Horae Canonicae," whose subtitle is "*Immolatus vicerit.*"[123] The words come from the sixth-century

Latin hymn "Pange Lingua Gloriosi Proelium Certaminis," and they mean, "Sacrificed, he will be victorious." They express, in other words, the central irony of the Christian faith: that Christ's suffering and death leads, not indirectly or accidentally but directly and causally, to his ultimate victory. Taken as a whole, the sequence is Auden's most serious examination of original sin, with "Prime" going so far as to assert, in Niebuhrian fashion, that to breathe is to assert the will and, in that assertion, to sin: "I draw breath; that is of course to wish," and "the cost" of this wish "is Paradise / Lost of course and myself owing a death."[124] As Auden puts it in "Nones," the fourth poem in the sequence, "*will* and *kill*" are not "some chance rhyme" but express the deep relation between human desire and human violence that would remain unbreakable were it not for Christ's victory (which victory, of course, is itself ironically brought about through humanity's violence).[125]

"For the Time Being" likewise opens with an expression of the irony of the Christian narrative, this time with a quotation from Romans: "What shall we say then? Shall we continue in sin, that grace may abound? God forbid."[126] Grace leads the way to salvation, but grace is needed in the first place because of sin; it is not humanity's worthiness but its unworthiness that leads to Christ's Incarnation and thus to redemption. In the poem's opening section, "Advent," the Chorus continually intones, "Darkness and snow descend," and it is because darkness and snow descend that the time is ripe for the light and love of Christ.[127] As Auden writes in "Kairos and Logos," the very horrors of human existence—men "placing their lives below the dogs," the "flagrant self-assertions" and the "cuckolded love"—prepare the way for "predestined love" to fall "like a daring meteor into time, / The condescension of eternal order."[128] Here, we see Niebuhr's theology of irony writ small. Randall Jarrell exaggerates, but only slightly, when he writes, "Auden, during most of the 1940s, could say that he taught nothing but guilt, *which is* the escape from guilt."[129]

Auden's innovation, however, lay not in pointing to the ironies inherent in the Christian faith but in treating these ironies in an ironic—that is to say, joking, self-subverting, comical—way. The examples of Auden wedding theological irony (strength leads to weakness, weakness to strength) to comic irony are almost too numerous to count. The final section of "Memorial for the City," for example, begins by expressing the irony of the "happy fall": "Without me Adam would have fallen irrevocably with Lucifer; he would never have been able to cry *O felix culpa*."[130] This is the central theological claim of the poem, one that refers back to the epigraph (where Julian of Norwich connected humanity's sensual nature to its potential for salvation) and to one of the main reasons Auden returned to the Christian faith (its willingness to assert that the creaturely, bodily world could become the place of the holy). And yet, after this line, Auden plays almost every single line for laughs: "With

Hamlet I had no patience," the body declares; "I heard Orpheus sing," it admits, but "I was not quite as moved as they say"; "I was the unwelcome third at the meetings of Tristan and Isolde; they tried to poison me."[131] In "For the Time Being," Auden moves from the solemn theologizing of Simeon ("The Word aroused the uncomprehending depths of their flesh to a witnessing fury, and their witness was this: that the Word should be made Flesh") to the sublimely ridiculous complaints of Herod: "I've tried to be good. I brush my teeth every night. I haven't had sex for a month. I object. I'm a liberal. I want everyone to be happy. I wish I had never been born."[132] "The Age of Anxiety" likewise balances silliness with direct statements of Auden's deepest theological beliefs: Malin's claim, for instance, that God's "Truth makes our theories historical sins, / It is where we are wounded that is when He speaks."[133]

Auden continually treats the central events of the Christian narrative with a comic touch. In "For the Time Being," the narrator explains why a female must be the vessel for humanity's salvation: "For the perpetual excuse / Of Adam for his fall—'My little Eve, / God bless her, did beguile me and I ate,' / For his insistence on a nurse, / All service, breast, and lap."[134] At another point, Joseph is imagined as a modern-day dandy stood up at the bar because his beloved is getting busy, not with a lover but with the Annunciation:

> The bar was gay, the lighting well-designed,
> And I was sitting down to wait
>   My own true Love:
> A voice I'd heard before, I think,
> Cried: "This is on the House. I drink
>   To him
> Who does not know it is too late;"
>   When I asked for the time,
> Everyone was very kind.[135]

Auden here borrows from the tradition of medieval cycle drama, a comic genre that often mined laughter from the Joseph-as-cuckold motif. It is hard to imagine Eliot doing the same. In "The Sea and the Mirror," Auden places the poem's blunt, Kierkegaardian/Barthian sense of humankind's absolute need for divine grace in the mouth of Caliban, a character who speaks in a mesmerizing pastiche of late Henry James: "Yet, at this very moment when we do at last see ourselves as we are, neither cosy nor playful, but swaying out on the ultimate wind-whipped cornice that overhangs the unabiding void—we have never stood anywhere else,—when our reasons are silenced by the heavy huge derision,—There is nothing to say. There never has been,—and our wills chuck in their hands—There is no way out. There never was,—it is at this moment that for the first time in our lives we hear . . . the real Word which is our only *raison d'être.*"[136] Auden's theological poems are never just theological; they are also absurd, and not just in a Kierkegaardian sense but in a (Groucho) Marxian sense—full of camp and comic playfulness. Ursula Niebuhr, Reinhold's wife and a close friend to Auden, put it best. Theological terms "were supposed to be kept in their proper place, in their pigeonholes, or indexed in their files, in the same way that clothes that [theologians] wore on Sunday were kept for their proper uses. But Wystan was taking them out, and scattering the terms— and was wearing Sunday clothes on weekdays."[137]

Critics have pointed to Auden's surprisingly comic treatment of theological material, with Jarrell writing that, in "For the Time Being," "some of the most serious passages have an astonishing bounce and lift; I think [Auden] should have used *Heigh ho, heigh ho, it's off to work we go* (sung in the Seven Dwarfs' cheerfulest tones) as an epigraph for the piece."[138] Kirsch agrees with this sentiment, claiming that "the most compelling characteristic of Auden's [religious] thought is the sense of the comic that informs his dialectic of faith and doubt."[139] For both critics, there is a surprising gap between the theology that Auden is reading (sin-obsessed, guilt-driven) and the style of the poetry that he is writing, a gap that they explain in part as a matter of temperament: Auden loved light verse (he famously edited the 1938 *Oxford Book of Light Verse*), and he enjoyed the technical challenge of writing lightly about the most theologically heavy matters.

Yet Auden's theological reading suggests another reason for his interest in comedy. Auden learned from Niebuhr and Kierkegaard that, to follow Christ, one had to be ever vigilant against complacency and self-importance. For Auden, this meant that the follower of Christ had to be willing to be a comic figure: "The man who takes seriously the command of Christ to take up his cross and follow Him must, if he is serious, see himself as a comic figure, for he is not the Christ, only an ordinary man, yet he believes that the command, 'Be ye perfect,' is seriously addressed to himself."[140] This quotation comes from "Balaam and His Ass," one of Auden's most thoughtful explorations of ethics, art, and the Christian faith. The essay moves through various figures from literary history— Don Giovanni, Prospero, Don Quixote—looking for a saintly embodiment of Christian love. It ends with a surprising choice for this exemplary figure: P. G. Wodehouse's great comic creation, Bertie Wooster. Why conclude with Wooster? Because, Auden writes, he possesses "that rarest of virtues, humility, and so he is blessed." After quoting an exchange between Bertie and his valet Jeeves, Auden concludes the essay: "So speaks comically—and in what other mode than the comic could it on earth truthfully speak?—the voice of Agape, of Holy Love."[141]

In "Balaam and His Ass," to be a "comic figure" means to be willing to be laughed at, to see the absurdity in one's position—a lowly sinner called to be holy. But it also means to recognize that one is part of a comedy—a story that does not end with tragedy and death but leads through tragedy and death towards reconciliation. This is why Auden's Christian poems so often focus on marriage as the central Christian sacrament. In Auden's reading, marriage is a commitment that does not deny the pain involved in intimate relationship but transforms this through faith and devotion. As Auden puts it in his marriage poem "In Sickness and in Health":

> Beloved, we are always in the wrong,
> Handling so clumsily our stupid lives,
>   Suffering too little or too long,
> Too careful even in our selfish loves:
> The decorative manias we obey
> Die in grimaces round us every day,
> Yet through their tohu-bohu comes a voice
> Which utters an absurd command—Rejoice.[142]

For Auden, laughter at the comedy of our existence is only a prelude to the faith, love, and commitment that marriage (and the Christian faith) calls one to. But this laughter is both necessary and joyful. Niebuhr makes a similar point in his "Humour and Faith," where he says, "Humour is, in fact, a prelude to faith; and laughter is the beginning of prayer."[143] Both humor and faith respond to the absurdity of existence, the chasm separating our aspirations from our realities, our dreams from our everyday lives. Auden was not the only interwar poet to recognize these incongruities. He was, however, unique in imagining that laughter was a necessary if insufficient response to these incongruities. In "We Too Had Known Golden Hours," a 1950 poem dedicated to Reinhold and Ursula Niebuhr, Auden half-seriously apologizes for his inveterate use of "the wry, the sotto-voce,/Ironic and monochrome."[144] Yet Auden's poetry of the 1940s shows that there is really no need to apologize. The wry and ironic is, at some deep level, the most theological tone imaginable.

"A Poetics of Belief"

On October 16, 1926, the *Nation and Athenaeum*, a British politics and culture magazine then edited by John Maynard Keynes, published the results of a survey of "the state of religious belief" among its readers.[1] A little over twenty-three years later, in February 1950, the *Partisan Review*, an American politics and culture magazine then edited by Philip Rahv and others, also published the results of a survey, this time of a select group of writers and thinkers, on the dramatic increase in "the number of intellectuals professing religious sympathies, beliefs, or doctrines."[2] These two surveys, the first published at the very height of high modernism and the second at a moment when modernism had begun to give way to something different, tell a fascinating story about the persistence of religious doctrine among the cultured elite; about the increasing respect given to religion as an intellectually defensible—and not simply sociologically interesting—object of study; and about the increasing contact between literary and theological circles in the 1930s and 1940s.

The first survey attempted to gauge the "state of religious belief" among "educated moderns" (more specifically, among the readers of the *Nation and Athenaeum*);[3] the second canvassed a much more select group—individually chosen figures such as Clement Greenberg, Hannah Arendt, Marianne Moore, and W. H. Auden—in an attempt to discern just why there had appeared a "new turn toward religion among intellectuals and the growing disfavor with which secular attitudes and perspectives are now regarded in not a few circles that lay claim to the leadership of culture."[4] The *Nation and Athenaeum* asked respondents a series of simple, yes-or-no questions about religious belief: "Do you believe in a personal God?" for instance, and "Do you believe in transubstantiation?" It also asked about religious practice: "Do you voluntarily attend any religious service regularly?"[5] The *Partisan Review* asked a series of open-ended questions—"What has happened to make religion more credible than it formerly was to the modern mind?"—and asked for long, "discursive comment" in response.[6]

Two surveys, then, of two very different populations with two very different goals. The *Nation and Athenaeum* wanted to determine to what extent the reading public continued to hold certain religious beliefs. The magazine reported the survey's results in a chart with four columns: one for the question, one for the number of yes responses, one for no's, and one for "doubtful or no answer." The survey showed that even "educated moderns" continued to hold religious beliefs in surprising numbers. When asked, "Do you believe in a personal God?," 743 respondents said yes, 1,024 said no, and 82 said they were doubtful or did not give an answer. The magazine also printed a second chart, which reported the results of the same questionnaire being sent to the readers of the *Daily News*. Perhaps unsurprisingly, the wider circulation newspaper had a more faithful readership: to the question of belief in a personal God, 9,991 said yes, 3,686 said no, and 366 did not answer.[7]

If the *Nation and Athenaeum* was most interested in a quantitative description of religious belief, then the *Partisan Review* was most interested in an interpretative description. The *Nation and Athenaeum* wanted to determine the fact of religious belief: how many people believed and how many people did not. The *Partisan Review* wanted to determine the reasons for continued religious belief among the most intelligent, cultured groups. Jacques Maritain's response to being asked whether there might be a "valuable religious consciousness that can be maintained without an explicit credo postulating the supernatural" is typical: "For religion is nothing, or less than nothing, if it does not convey *truth* to us. And there is no attainment of truth if not by means of definite beliefs. Emotional or behavioristic religion, using philosophical or literary aspirin to relieve the lofty anxieties of the superego, is not worth considering. It is but an ersatz concocted by pride: for to *obey* divine Truth speaking to man and in man is exactly what gods like [Malraux and Heidegger] cannot accept."[8] Maritain rejects, clearly and absolutely, any pragmatic account of religion. For him, religious belief must live or die by the truthfulness of its propositions, not by its usefulness. In Maritain's view, religion without content, without specific, doctrinal claims, is not really religion at all but a psychological and social palliative constructed by humanity to relieve its existential anxieties.

As I argue throughout, Maritain's claim—that religion is not something to be used but something to be believed in; that religion is not just "emotional" but also intellectual and doctrinal—was something that interwar poets accepted wholeheartedly. For them, contemporary Christian theology proved such an exciting discipline because it concerned itself with arguing rigorously about matters of the gravest importance: the relationship between transcendence and immanence; the meaning of human history; the nature of temporal experience.

Eliot, Jones, and Auden did not always—even often—agree on what theology had to say about these issues. Eliot admired theologians like Karl Barth, who emphasized the frightening abyss separating divine transcendence from creaturely embodiment, while Auden looked to Charles Williams for an account of how the erotic and the divine, the bodily and the godly, might relate to each other. Jones thought sacramental theology offered a beautiful model for how poets might collapse past and future into a supercharged, millennial present, while Auden saw Niebuhr's work as offering a more persuasive account of the inbetweenness of human history. Eliot saw the Incarnation as the one event that gave hope for human existence, while Jones focused on the Eucharist (and, with the Eucharist, the Last Supper and the Crucifixion). For Eliot, the theological poet had to purge his desires and make himself holy; for Jones, the theological poet had to make something other, imitating and channeling the sacramental function of the Catholic priest; for Auden, the theological poet had to laugh—at himself and at others—and, in laughing, he might move towards pardon and forgiveness.

These three poets continued writing theological verse into the 1950s and beyond. But the moment at which contemporary theology and contemporary poetry seemed to be speaking to each other had largely passed. The shutting down of the *Criterion* in 1939 serves as a turning point. Religion continued to be important to contemporary literature, as evidenced by the *Partisan Review*'s survey, but never again would theology be discussed so regularly—and so intelligently—in the premier literary magazine of the day. Jones rarely referred to theology written after the 1920s and 1930s; Eliot, no longer editing the *Criterion*, seems to have read less and less contemporary theology; and Auden in the 1950s and 1960s looked increasingly to science and physics for the imaginative inspiration that had previously been provided by Barth, Niebuhr, and others. For a time, poetry and theology seemed to be asking the same questions— what is transcendence, and how can human language talk about it intelligently and beautifully?—and, at least in some cases, offering the same kinds of answers. But that time passed relatively quickly.

Of course, this is not to say that literature and religion stopped paying attention to each other after World War II. As Amy Hungerford has shown, the question of belief remained crucial to much post-1945 literary production, especially in the United States. What most interested writers like Don DeLillo and others, however, was not doctrinally specific theology but rather, as Hungerford puts it, "belief without content."[9] With the increasing importance of the "death of God theology" in the 1960s, the dogmatic work of Barth and others seemed less and less in fashion. Barth, it is true, continued to inspire the occasional writer, especially Americans. John Updike, for instance, reviewed several of Barth's works for major publications, placed a Barth scholar at the center of his 1986 novel *Roger's Version*, and praised Kierkegaard and Karl Barth in his 1969 poem "Midpoint." More recently, Marilynne Robinson, another American novelist, has pointed to the importance of Barth's thought to her own writing: one of her characters, John Ames in *Gilead*, even thinks that it would be wonderful to die with Barth's *Epistle to the Romans* by his side so as to recommend it to the living.[10] The recent work of poets like Les Murray, Geoffrey Hill, and Christian Wiman also displays deep theological sophistication.

But in each of these instances, theological interest is largely a matter of personal, idiosyncratic taste. Robinson is regularly hailed as an anachronism, sharing more stylistically and philosophically with nineteenth-century Transcendentalists than with her own contemporaries, and while Updike's lyrical realism influenced many writers in the 1970s and 1980s, few, if any, picked up his love of neo-Orthodoxy. And all of these writers look not to the present but to the *past* for their theological reading: Wiman refers to Barth and Tillich but rarely to his contemporaries; Hill looks even further back. When thinking and writing theologically, these writers look to a former time.

In a recent book, Wiman outlines what he takes to be the needs of twenty-first-century believers: "We need a poetics of belief, a language capacious enough to include a mystery that, ultimately, defeats it, and sufficiently intimate and inclusive to serve not only as individual expression but as communal need."[11] In the 1930s and 1940s, there was what Wiman calls a "poetics of belief"—the sense that real theology had to acknowledge and rejoice in the mystery of belief, in the ultimate frustration all humans must face when trying to reason or write about God. But there was also a theology of poetry—the sense that poetry, and not just individual poets, had something to learn from contemporary theological inquiry. Belief *with* content—specific theological claims about things like the Incarnation and the Eucharist—helped shape what interwar poets thought about the efficacy and sufficiency of human language and the meaning of time and history. For a brief and surprising moment, Christian theology provoked and sustained poetic exploration.

Notes

Chapter 1. A Conversation between Philosophers and Artists

1. Quoted in Mindele Anne Treip, *Allegorical Poetics and the Epic: The Renaissance Tradition to "Paradise Lost"* (Lexington: University Press of Kentucky, 1994), 174, emphasis in original.

2. Of course, the quarrel between truth and trope, philosophy and poetry, has a long history, one that begins long before and extends far beyond the Christian context. In *The Ancient Quarrel between Philosophy and Poetry*, Raymond Barfield shows that, from Plato to Heidegger, Western philosophy "has characterized itself in part by distinguishing how its statements and methods were different from those of the poets and, having made this distinction, what role the work of poetry was to have in philosophy." Barfield, *The Ancient Quarrel between Philosophy and Poetry* (Cambridge: Cambridge University Press, 2011), 1. See also the introduction to Mutlu Blasing, *Lyric Poetry: The Pain and the Pleasure of Words* (Princeton, NJ: Princeton University Press, 2007).

3. Jacques Maritain, *Art and Scholasticism and The Frontiers of Poetry*, trans. Joseph W. Evans (New York: Charles Scribner's Sons, 1962), 4.

4. Ibid., 3; Maritain, *A Preface to Metaphysics: Seven Lectures on Being* (New York: Sheed & Ward, 1939), 63.

5. Maritain, *Art and Scholasticism*, 4.

6. Jacques Maritain, *The Degrees of Knowledge*, trans. Gerald B. Phelan (New York: Charles Scribner's Sons, 1959), 108.

7. Maritain, *Art and Scholasticism*, 53.

8. Rowan Williams, *Grace and Necessity: Reflections on Art and Love* (Harrisburg, PA: Morehouse, 2005), 4.

9. "Transcendence" can be a slippery term. Fergus Kerr's *Immortal Longings*, for instance, shows the shifting valences of "transcendence" in twentieth-century philosophy, from Barth's God, who is the "only absolute there is" and who reveals himself in the form of Jesus Christ, to Martha Nussbaum's (critical) sense of transcendence, "as in the ascent to love in the *Symposium*—the cure for one's vulnerability is to be found in departing altogether from one's humanity into identification with the form of the good." In this book, I use "transcendence" as Barth defined it in *Epistle to the Romans*: as God's radical difference from humanity, a difference that can only be bridged by God's loving and creative action. Fergus Kerr, *Immortal Longings: Versions of Transcending Humanity* (Notre Dame, IN: University of Notre Dame Press, 1997), 162, 18.

10. Jacques Maritain, *Creative Intuition in Art and Poetry* (New York: Pantheon-Bollingen Foundation, 1953), 167, emphasis in original.

11. T. S. Eliot, *The Complete Poems and Plays, 1909–1950* (New York: Houghton Mifflin Harcourt, 1971), 121.

12. Karl Rahner, *Theological Investigations*, vol. 4, trans. Kevin Smyth (London: Darton, Longman & Todd, 1966), 53.

13. Maritain, *Creative Intuition in Art and Poetry*, 30.

14. Recently scholars have begun to offer a far more complicated and particular history of secularism. See, in particular, Charles Taylor's *A Secular Age* (Cambridge, MA: Belknap Press of Harvard University Press, 2007) and Talal Asad's *Formations of the Secular: Christianity, Islam, Modernity* (Stanford: Stanford University Press, 2003). Both works challenge the secularization hypothesis, showing how terms like "the sacred" and "the secular" arose out of long and various intellectual and political histories.

15. See, for instance, Robert Alter, *Canon and Creativity: Modern Writing and the Authority of Scripture* (New Haven, CT: Yale University Press, 2000); Pericles Lewis, *Religious Experience and the Modernist Novel* (New York: Cambridge University Press, 2010); and Stephen Sicari, *Modernist Humanism and the Men of 1914: Joyce, Lewis, Pound, and Eliot* (Columbia: University of South Carolina Press, 2011).

16. A rare and welcome exception to this critical tendency is W. David Soud's *Divine Cartographies: God, History, and* Poesis *in W. B. Yeats, David Jones, and T. S. Eliot* (New York: Oxford University Press, 2016). This book, which adds to and complicates my own earlier essays on T. S. Eliot and David Jones, refreshingly treats the religious interests of these modern poets as sincere, reasoned, and undeniably important for some of the period's best poetry.

17. John Milbank, *Theology and Social Theory: Beyond Secular Reason* (Cambridge, MA: Blackwell, 1990), 260–61. Milbank goes on to contrast this "modern mode of suspicion," which believes that religion can be reduced to a more basic "function" or "means," to "the new, postmodern mode of suspicion," which "claims no ground upon which to decode the hidden truth underlying religion's spurious truth-claims" (261). In other words, the modern critic of religion is a decipherer, finding the truth beneath the surface; the postmodern critic of religion, though, "reveals no secret behind the *mythos*, but merely points to other 'truths,' and shows how these are suppressed or denied by a totalizing perspective."

18. T. S. Eliot, "Henry James," in *Selected Prose of T. S. Eliot*, ed. Frank Kermode (New York: Houghton Mifflin Harcourt, 1975), 151.

19. Ibid., 152.

20. My use of the term "theological modernism" to describe a body of poetry is not to be confused with what Catholics call "theological modernism"—the late-nineteenth- and early-twentieth-century liberal movement that emphasized rationalist and historicist approaches to the Bible and to religious faith.

21. T. S. Eliot, *For Lancelot Andrewes: Essays on Style and Order* (London: Faber & Faber, 1970), 19–20.

22. The resonant phrase "ecstasy of assent" brings to mind John Henry Newman's *Grammar of Assent*. For Eliot's relationship to the thinking of Newman, see Lee Oser, "T. S. Eliot and John Henry Newman," in *T. S. Eliot and the Christian Tradition*, ed. Benjamin G. Lockerd (Madison, NJ: Farleigh Dickinson University Press, 2014), 131–44.

23. See, for instance, Stephen J. Schuler, *The Augustinian Theology of W. H. Auden* (Columbia: University of South Carolina Press, 2013), 59–60, and Edward Mendelson, *Later Auden* (New York: Farrar, Straus & Giroux, 1999), 168–70.

24. Lewis Hyde, *Trickster Makes the World: Mischief, Myth, and Art* (New York: Farrar, Straus & Giroux, 2010), 133.

25. Paul Tillich, *The Interpretation of History*, trans. N. A. Rasetzki and Elsa L. Talmey (New York: Charles Scribner's Sons, 1936), 128.

26. W. H. Auden, *Collected Poems*, ed. Edward Mendelson (New York: Vintage Books, 1991), 305.

27. Ibid., 306.

28. Ibid., 308.

29. Ibid., 309.

30. Ibid., 309, 310.

31. This is not to say that modernist poetry refused to include philosophical speculation, just that someone like Pound or the early Eliot would have blanched at expressing these ideas so directly. Again, Eliot's statement about James is apposite: it's not that Pound or the early Eliot lacked ideas, just that they would have been reluctant to express them in an expository manner. (In their poetry, that is; they were more than happy to elaborate upon their social and literary ideas in critical essays.)

32. David Jones, *The Sleeping Lord and Other Fragments* (London: Faber & Faber, 1995), 9.

33. Quoted in Alison Milbank, *Chesterton and Tolkien as Theologians* (New York: T&T Clark, 2007), 164, where Milbank offers an excellent reading of Jones's poem.

34. See Mark C. Taylor, *After God* (Chicago: University of Chicago Press, 2009). To acknowledge the importance of World War I to the religious revival is not to reduce it to this, and it certainly should not suggest that such a return was, as it were, an intellectual cop-out. As such scholars as Fergus Kerr and Charles Taylor have shown, the modern return to religious and theological questions wasn't a failure of nerve but an attempt to grapple with serious philosophical and ontological questions—philosophical and ontological questions that seemed all the more important given modernity's various cataclysms.

35. John Henry Newman, *Hymns* (New York: E. P. Dutton, 1885), 91.

36. Ibid., 92.

37. Ibid.

38. John Henry Newman, *Apologia Pro Vita Sua*, ed. David J. DeLaura (New York: W. W. Norton, 1968), 50. Newman goes on to state the strongest case against such an anti-dogmatic position: "From the age of fifteen, dogma has been the fundamental principle of my religion: I know no other religion; I cannot enter into the idea of any other sort of religion; religion, as a mere sentiment, is to me a dream and a mockery. As well can there be filial love without the fact of a father, as devotion without the fact of a Supreme Being." Ibid., 51.

39. Newman, *Hymns*, 92.

40. Friedrich Schleiermacher, *On Religion: Speeches to Its Cultured Despisers*, trans. Richard Crouter (Cambridge: Cambridge University Press, 1996), 102; Matthew Arnold, *God and the Bible: A Sequel to "Literature and Dogma"* (London: Smith, Elder, 1884), vii.

41. Matthew Arnold, *Literature and Dogma: An Essay Towards a Better Apprehension of the Bible* (New York: Macmillan, 1883), 107; William James, *The Varieties of Religious Experience* (New York: Penguin Books, 1982), 31.

42. James C. Livingston, *Modern Christian Thought: Enlightenment and the Nineteenth Century*, vol. 1 (Minneapolis: Fortress Press, 2006), 96. Livingston goes on to say that those readers, like Barth and Eliot, who saw Schleiermacher as defining religion solely through intuition and feeling and thus ignoring doctrine are being a bit unfair: "Now it is true that

with Schleiermacher theology undergoes a radical transformation in its notion of theological authority. But it would be erroneous to say that for Schleiermacher the Bible and the Church no longer are theologically normative, for we know that Schleiermacher conceived of doctrine as the true expression of the Christian consciousness *in the Church* at a given time, and that such a consciousness must be a genuine expression of that piety which appears in the New Testament." Ibid., 104.

43. T. S. Eliot, "Arnold and Pater," in *Selected Essays, 1917–1932* (New York: Harcourt, Brace , 1948), 351.

44. Thomas Carlyle, *Sartor Resartus*, ed. Kerry McSweeney (New York: Oxford University Press, 2008), 147.

45. Carlyle, *Sartor Resartus*, 148.

46. Rudolf Otto, *The Idea of the Holy: An Inquiry into the Non-Rational Factor in the Idea of the Divine and Its Relation to the Rational*, trans. John W. Harvey (New York: Oxford University Press, 1958), 29, 13.

47. Ibid., 12.

48. Karl Barth, *The Epistle to the Romans*, trans. Edwyn C. Hoskyns (New York: Oxford University Press, 1933), 27. The second edition of *Epistle to the Romans*, first published in German in 1922 and in English in 1933, was a dramatic revision of the more temperate 1919 edition. In fact, much of what we now understand as "dialectical theology" only appeared in the second edition. For a comparison between these two editions, see Bruce McCormack, *Karl Barth's Critically Realistic Dialectical Theology: Its Genesis and Development, 1909–1936* (New York: Oxford University Press, 1995), 207–88. Recently, Paul Brazier has argued that the 1919 version is a more radical critique of liberal Protestantism than it has been given credit for. See Paul Brazier, "Barth's First Commentary on Romans (1919): An Exercise in Apophatic Theology?" *International Journal of Systematic Theology* 6.4 (2004): 387–403.

49. Livingston notes that Barth's reading of Schleiermacher is at times unfair. Schleiermacher's sense of humanity's absolute dependence upon God—an absolute dependence that we feel and intuit and that serves as the very basis for religious belief and practice—is Barthian; or, perhaps we should say that Barth's sense of humanity's absolute dependence is Schleiermacherian. Where the two part ways is whether we can come to know God through this feeling of absolute dependence. Schleiermacher has confidence that we can; Barth believes that to have such confidence is to make God into something other than God.

50. Barth, *Epistle to the Romans*, 10.

51. Quoted in John McConnachie, *The Significance of Karl Barth* (London: Hodder & Stoughton, 1931), 43.

52. Reinhold Niebuhr, *The Nature and Destiny of Man,* vol. 2 (Louisville, KY: Westminster John Knox Press, 1996), 108.

53. Barth, *Epistle to the Romans*, 85–86.

54. Karl Barth, *Church Dogmatics: Volume 3.3, The Doctrine of Creation*, trans. G. W. Bromiley and R. J. Ehrlich, ed. G. W. Bromiley and T. F. Torrance (New York: T&T Clark, 2006), 293. Barth published a book on St. Anselm, entitled *Anselm: Fides Quaerens Intellectum*, in 1960. In it, he dismisses those who read Anselm as providing an ontological proof for God's existence.

55. Stephen Schloesser, "The Rise of a Mystic Modernism: Maritain and the Sacrificed Generation of the Twenties," in *The Maritain Factor: Taking Religion into Interwar Mod-*

ernism, ed. Rajesh Heynickx and Jan De Mayer (Leuven, Belgium: Leuven University Press, 2010), 34. Elsewhere, Schloesser describes the thought of Maritain and other inter-war Catholic philosophers as "dialectical realism," a bid "to combine, in a dialectical synthesis, both the positivist's observed world as well as something else unseen." Stephen Schloesser, *Jazz Age Catholicism: Mystic Modernity in Postwar Paris, 1919–1933* (Toronto: University of Toronto Press, 2005), 7.

56. Jacques Maritain, *The Existence and the Existent*, trans. Lewis Galantiere and Gerald B. Phelan (Garden City, NY: Image Books, 1956), 31.

57. Martin D'Arcy, *The Nature of Belief* (London: Sheed & Ward, 1931), 237.

58. Eliot, "Arnold and Pater," in *Selected Essays, 1917–1932*, 349.

59. David Jasper, "From Theology to Theological Thinking: The Development of Critical Thought and Its Consequences for Theology," *Literature and Theology* 9.3 (1995): 293–305.

60. James Joyce, *A Portrait of the Artist as a Young Man*, ed. Jeri Johnson (New York: Oxford University Press, 2000), 181.

61. Ibid., 178.

62. M. H. Abrams, for instance, describes how the Romantics and their modernist heirs channeled the religious into the artistic: "The process . . . has not been the deletion and replacement of religious ideas but rather the assimilation and reinterpretation of religious ideas." Likewise, Denis Donoghue argues that Wallace Stevens took "Christian words of faith" and "reduc[ed] them to humanist terms." M. H. Abrams, *Natural Supernaturalism: Tradition and Revolution in Romantic Literature* (New York: W. W. Norton, 1971), 13; Denis Donoghue, *Adam's Curse: Reflections on Religion and Literature* (Notre Dame, IN: University of Notre Dame Press, 2001), 97.

63. Recently, Pericles Lewis, Robert Alter, and Ellis Hanson, among others, have explored more directly modernism's engagement with religion, though these critics remain largely uninterested in, as Jenny Franchot puts it, "engag[ing] intensively with the religious questions of the topic at hand *as religious questions*." Lewis, for instance, explores modernism's interest in the sociology of religion, identifying in the modernist novel "efforts to explain, and provide a substitute for, the sorts of shared normative values that institutional religion no longer adequately supplied." In a slightly different move, Alter finds modernists using the Bible as an exemplary aesthetic object. In his work, he analyzes how Kafka, Joyce, and others mine "the literary force of the biblical text" while simultaneously "undermin[ing] any sense that the Bible is a fixed source of authority." Hanson's work focuses on the Decadents, a group of writers, artists, and composers who, as he writes, found "in Catholicism a romantic cult of the imagination and a spiritualization of eros." Jenny Franchot, "Invisible Domain: Religion and American Literary Studies," *American Literature* 67.4 (1995): 839; Lewis, *Religious Experience*, 19; Alter, *Canon and Creativity*, 17, 95; Ellis Hanson, *Decadence and Catholicism* (Cambridge, MA: Harvard University Press, 1997), 366.

64. A handful of critics has examined modernist interest in theology, but the scope of such critical projects has tended to be either too wide (looking at all of twentieth-century literature) or too narrow (looking at single, isolated modernists). For the first tendency, see Paul Fiddes's *The Promised End: Eschatology in Theology and Literature* (Oxford: Blackwell, 2000); for the second, see nearly all of the (very good) scholarship on Eliot, Jones, and Auden's engagement with religion. Moreover, these theologically inclined critics have tended to look for traces of traditional theologians—Aquinas and Augustine, for instance—in

modernist texts like Joyce's *Ulysses*, ignoring the vibrant theological discussions of the modernist period. See, for instance, two excellent books: John Neary, *Like and Unlike God: Religious Imaginations in Modern and Contemporary Fiction* (Atlanta, GA: Scholars' Press, 1999), and Gregory Erickson, *Absence of God in Modernist Literature* (New York: Palgrave Macmillan, 2007).

65. James A. Pike, ed., *Modern Canterbury Pilgrims and Why They Chose the Episcopal Church* (New York: Morehouse-Gorham, 1956), 41. Although Williams is only a side character in this book, his role in the poetic and theological world of the 1930s is a fascinating one. Working at Oxford University Press, he was almost singlehandedly responsible for Kierkegaard's writing being published in English for the first time. As a poet, his work was just as theological as, if less accomplished than, that of Jones. For Williams's theological aesthetics, see David Mahan, *An Unexpected Light: Theology and Witness in the Poetry and Thought of Charles Williams, Micheal O'Siadhail, and Geoffrey Hill* (Eugene, OR: Pickwick Publications, 2009), 25–88.

66. T. S. Eliot, "Dante," in *The Sacred Wood: Essays on Poetry and Criticism* (London: Methuen, 1976), 167; Eliot, "Blake," in *The Sacred Wood*, 158.

67. Quoted in Agha Shahid Ali, *T. S. Eliot as Editor* (Ann Arbor, MI: UMI Research Press, 1986), 102.

68. Thomas Michael LeCarner has examined the "Buddhist lessons" of *The Waste Land*; Paul Robichaud has argued that Jones's *Anathemata* borrows heavily from pagan religions in order to create "a kind of cultural palimpsest"; and Richard Bozorth has shown how the Jewish philosopher Martin Buber's *I and Thou* (first translated into English in 1937) influenced Auden's "later views of love" as well as his "statements about the dialogic basis of poetic meaning." Thomas Michael LeCarner, "T. S. Eliot, Dharma Bum: Buddhist Lessons in *The Waste Land*," *Philosophy and Literature* 33.2 (2009): 402–16; Paul Robichaud, *Making the Past Present: David Jones, the Middle Ages, and Modernism* (Washington, DC: Catholic University Press, 2007), 126; Richard Bozorth, *Auden's Games of Knowledge: Poetry and the Meanings of Homosexuality* (New York: Columbia University Press, 2001), 219.

69. Karl Barth, in *Revelation*, eds. John Baillie and Hugh Martin (London: Faber & Faber, 1937), 51.

Chapter 2. The "Living Theology" of the *Criterion*

1. T. S. Eliot, *The Letters of T. S. Eliot*, vol. 1, *1898–1922*, rev. ed., ed. Valerie Eliot and Hugh Haughton (New Haven, CT: Yale University Press, 2011), 338–39.

2. Lawrence Rainey, *Revisiting "The Waste Land"* (New Haven, CT: Yale University Press, 2007), 97.

3. Eliot, *Letters of T. S. Eliot*, 1:621.

4. Quoted in Rainey, *Revisiting "The Waste Land,"* 98 and 38.

5. As Rainey argues, Eliot's choice of a specific book publisher was a careful one. Eliot decided to have *The Waste Land* first appear in a commercial edition by Boni & Liveright in 1922, but he then almost immediately released a more prestigious, limited edition with the Hogarth Press in 1923. Rainey describes the balancing act that Eliot was attempting: "Eliot, it is clear, wanted his poem to be successful, yet not too successful. For the prospect of immediate publication by a commercial firm raised prospects that were largely unimaginable within the logic of modernism." Rainey, *Revisiting "The Waste Land,"* 98.

6. Eliot, *Letters of T. S. Eliot*, 1:815.

7. Jason Harding, *"The Criterion": Cultural Politics and Periodical Networks in Inter-war Britain* (New York: Oxford University Press, 2002), 2.

8. In 1930, for instance, Eliot promoted a fight between I. A. Richards and Montgomery Belgion that played out in the *Criterion*'s pages. In the first round, Belgion criticized Richards for supposedly advocating poetry as a "substitute" for religious belief. Richards's response, printed in the *Criterion*, claimed that "the opinions [Belgion] attributes to me are all of his own concoction." Eliot then allowed Belgion a "brief rejoinder." See Montgomery Belgion, "What Is Criticism?," *Criterion*, October 1930, 118–39; I. A. Richards, "Notes on the Practice of Interpretation," *Criterion*, April 1931, 420; and Montgomery Belgion, "Correspondence," *Criterion*, April 1931, 508.

9. Harding quotes a letter from D. H. Lawrence to Murry, after the editor begged Lawrence to contribute to an issue, in which Lawrence urges Murry to give up on the *Adelphi* altogether. Harding, *"The Criterion,"* 36.

10. J. Middleton Murry, "Towards a Synthesis," *Criterion*, June 1927, 312.

11. T. S. Eliot, "Mr. Middleton Murry's Synthesis," *Criterion*, October 1927, 344.

12. This debate has been the subject of much critical attention. The most complete analysis is John Margolis's *T. S. Eliot's Intellectual Development, 1922–1939* (Chicago: University of Chicago Press, 1972), 54–68. Margolis argues that Murry's essay "tried forthrightly to consider the religious implications" of the romanticism versus classicism debate and involved "an extensive discussion of Thomistic thought," but Margolis himself only gestures at these religious implications. Ibid., 63. See also David Goldie, *A Critical Difference: T. S. Eliot and John Middleton Murry in English Literary Criticism, 1919–1928* (New York: Oxford University Press, 1998), 166–80.

13. Murry, "Towards a Synthesis," 297.

14. James Matthew Wilson, "An 'Organ for a Frenchified Doctrine': Jacques Maritain and *The Criterion*'s Neo-Thomism," in *T. S. Eliot and Christian Tradition*, ed. Benjamin G. Lockerd (Madison, NJ: Farleigh Dickinson University Press, 2014), 110.

15. Murry, "Towards a Synthesis," 297.

16. Ibid., 302.

17. Eliot's claim that he was a novice in theological matters is one that he repeated frequently in his letters. In a 1934 letter to Paul Elmer More, for example, he wrote, "I am painfully aware that I need a much more extensive and profound knowledge of theology." Quoted in Barry Spurr, *"Anglo-Catholic in Religion": T. S. Eliot and Christianity* (Cambridge: Lutterworth Press, 2010), 116.

18. Eliot, "Mr. Middleton Murry's Synthesis," 341.

19. Ibid., 345.

20. Ibid., 346.

21. Martin D'Arcy, "The Thomistic Synthesis and Intelligence," *Criterion*, September 1927, 216, 224.

22. Harding gives the most detailed account of how Eliot "consciously prepared the grounds for an ensuing public controversy." Harding, *"The Criterion,"* 36.

23. Eliot, "Mr. Middleton Murry's Synthesis," 346.

24. Harding, *"The Criterion,"* 2.

25. Geoffrey Grigson, *"Criterion* and *London Mercury,"* *New Verse*, May 1939, 62.

26. Denis Donoghue, "Eliot and the *Criterion*," in *The Literary Criticism of T. S. Eliot: New Essays*, ed. David Newton–de Molina (London: Athlone Press, 1977), 38, 39.

27. Ezra Pound, "Criterionism," *Hound and Horn*, October–December 1930, 114.

28. Laura Riding, *Anarchism Is Not Enough* (London: Jonathan Cape, 1928), 90; T. S. Eliot, "A Reply to Mr. Ward," *Criterion*, June 1928, 376. Eliot distanced himself from Maritain's neo-Thomism in his damning-with-faint-praise review of Maritain's *Trois Réformateurs* in the *TLS*. T. S. Eliot, "Three Reformers," *TLS*, November 1928, 818.

29. Critics have tended to overlook both the magazine's final years and the specifics of its theological commitments. David Goldie, for instance, devotes the bulk of *A Critical Difference* to the *Criterion*'s controversies with Murry's *Adelphi* in the mid-to-late 1920s. Harding gives the richest account of the magazine's later years, but even he does not fully grapple with the theology that increasingly dominated the *Criterion*. His chapter on the *Criterion* as "a religiopolitical organ," for instance, focuses primarily on how the magazine "scrupulously avoided party affiliations" and entertained the doctrine of Social Credit. In short, Harding devotes more attention to the political and economic than the religious or theological. Harding, "*The Criterion*," 181.

30. As will become obvious, the Barth who was important to the *Criterion* was the early Barth: the Barth of *The Word of God and the Word of Man* and, more specifically, the Barth of *Epistle to the Romans*. Barth's great systematic theology, as evidenced in the *Church Dogmatics*, did not come until later.

31. Quoted in Bruce McCormack, *Karl Barth's Critically Realistic Dialectical Theology: Its Genesis and Development, 1909–1936* (New York: Oxford University Press, 1995), 369. As W. David Soud puts it, Barth's writing is "apophatic theology minus the mysticism. Every construction makes plain the unreality of the earthly in relation to the eternal. There is no possibility here of human effort leading to a vision of transcendence—only a humble acknowledgement of the unreality of the temporal world under judgment from the eternal." W. David Soud, " 'The Greedy Dialectic of Time and Eternity': Karl Barth, T. S. Eliot, and *Four Quartets*," *ELH* 81.4 (2014): 1376.

32. Marianne Moore, *Selected Letters: Marianne Moore*, ed. Bonnie Costello (New York: Penguin Books, 1998), 379. Though Moore read a bit of theology, especially that of Reinhold Niebuhr, she was not nearly as interested in the discipline as the subjects of this book were. Jennifer Leader has traced the affinities between Moore's "poetics of ontology" and Niebuhr's "ethical ontology," arguing that both poet and theologian sought "to strike a balance between the legitimate claims of a free self and the responsibility to the community or nation at large." As this language makes clear, though, Leader is not particularly interested in Moore's reading of theology as theology. Jennifer Leader, " 'Certain Axioms Rivaling Scripture': Marianne Moore, Reinhold Niebuhr, and the Ethics of Engagement," *Twentieth-Century Literature* 51.3 (2005): 317.

33. Moore, *Selected Letters*, 379.

34. Gilson reviewed Pound's new translation of the poetry of Guido Cavalcanti in October of 1932. In a November 6, 1932, letter, Pound discusses with Gilson the finer points of his review, including whether *consideranza* should be translated as "knowledge" or "contemplation." Maria Luisa Ardizzone, *Guido Cavalcanti: The Other Middle Ages* (Toronto: University of Toronto Press, 2002), 169–71.

35. D'Arcy reviewed Lewis's 1927 *Time and Western Man*; Lewis, in turn, made a charcoal portrait of D'Arcy in 1932.

36. Moore's letters contain other references to theology. A year later, for instance, Moore writes to Bishop, "You and Dr. Niebuhr are two abashing peaks in present experi-

ence for me." In 1946, she tells Ezra Pound that she "wish[es] you would let me tell you something about a sermon that Reinhold Niebuhr preached at church near us two or three weeks ago." Moore, *Selected Letters*, 390, 461–62.

37. Michael Warner, *Publics and Counterpublics* (New York: Zone Books, 2002), 8, 11, 67.

38. Ibid., 68.

39. Describing the public envisioned (and thus created) by the *Spectator*, Warner points out that the magazine "developed a reflexivity about its own circulation," as it "include[d] feedback loops, both in the letters from readers real and imagined and in the members of the club and other devices. Essays refer to previous essays and to the reception of those essays." Warner, *Publics and Counterpublics*, 99.

40. Ibid., 100.

41. A brief list of the *Criterion*'s many attempts to create a public through self-reference would include the multiple-issue romanticism versus classicism controversy; the opening "Commentaries" that sought to differentiate the *Criterion* from other interwar magazines; and the constant reviewing (and advertising) of Faber & Faber writers.

42. As Langdon Hammer argues, for Eliot, marketing and design issues were always, at their root, aesthetic and cultural issues: "Eliot's image of the magazine called 'for a small format and paper, neat but not extravagant and not arty.' This format, avoiding cheap appeals, was meant to confirm the aristocratic bearing announced in Eliot's choice of name." Langdon Hammer, *Hart Crane and Allen Tate: Janus-Faced Modernism* (Princeton, NJ: Princeton University Press, 1993), 17.

43. Eliot often back-loaded the "Books of the Quarter" section with his most prominent reviews and reviewers. In the previous issue, for instance, Auden and Gilson are the last two names listed on the cover. In the issue at hand, Barth's *Epistle to the Romans* is the last specific title mentioned.

44. Norman W. Porteous, "Books of the Quarter," *Criterion*, January 1934, 342; George Every, "Books of the Quarter," *Criterion*, January 1937, 367; Cyril Hudson, "Books of the Quarter," *Criterion*, January 1937, 353.

45. Porteous, "Books of the Quarter," 342–44. Paul Elmer More mentioned Barth in passing in the April 1933 issue, where he includes Barth's *Epistle* among "the three or four imposing productions of combined piety and erudition" that have come out of Germany to puncture the "self-complacent so-called 'liberal theology.'" Paul Elmer More, "Books of the Quarter," *Criterion*, April 1933, 493.

46. Alister E. McGrath, *Thomas F. Torrance: An Intellectual Biography* (Edinburgh: T&T Clark, 1999), 38. The first book-length study in English of Barth's work was John McConnachie's 1931 *The Significance of Karl Barth*, but this was written for a smaller, specialized audience. W. David Soud argues that Barth's thinking found some purchase in the English-speaking world even before the translation of *Epistle to the Romans*, specifically in the figures of J. K. Mozley and Edwyn Hoskyns (Barth's translator). This is true, but it bears repeating: Hoskyns introduced Barth to Anglican theological circles, but Eliot—or at least the *Criterion*—introduced Barth to British *literary* circles.

47. Despite the universal acknowledgment among British theologians of Barth's importance, many were unsympathetic to his work. For instance, Ivor Thomas, a conservative Anglo-Catholic writing for the *TLS*, snidely (and, in hindsight, rather comically) opined that "we may expect that the Barthian theology will be looked upon in years to come as the evanescent product of a troubled age," a mere reflection of the pessimism and

antihumanism of the immediate postwar period. This misreading of Barth was common and frustrated the theologian's defenders. Ivor Thomas, "Karl Barth's Theology," *TLS*, September 14, 1933, 600.

48. Porteous, "Books of the Quarter," 343.

49. Ibid., 343.

50. For Kierkegaard's influence on Eliot, see Paul Murray, *T. S. Eliot and Mysticism: The Secret History of "Four Quartets"* (London: Macmillan, 1991), 103–24.

51. Porteous, "Books of the Quarter," 343.

52. Ibid., 344.

53. Ibid., 342.

54. Every, "Books of the Quarter," 366.

55. Ibid., 367.

56. Ibid.

57. Charles Taylor, *Sources of the Self: The Making of Modern Identity* (Cambridge, MA: Harvard University Press, 1989), 215.

58. Every, "Books of the Quarter," 367.

59. Ibid., 367.

60. T. S. Eliot, "The Metaphysical Poets," in *Selected Prose of T. S. Eliot*, ed. Frank Kermode (New York: Houghton Mifflin Harcourt, 1975), 64. Eliot himself related the problem of dissociated sensibility to theology. In his preface to *The Idea of a Christian Society*, Eliot writes that the idea of a "religious revival . . . seems to me to imply a possible separation of religious feeling from religious thinking which I do not accept—or which I do not find acceptable for our present difficulties." T. S. Eliot, *Christianity and Culture* (New York: Houghton Mifflin Harcourt, 1960), 4.

61. Every, "Books of the Quarter," 367.

62. Charles Smyth, "Books of the Quarter," *Criterion*, July 1935, 717.

63. Karl Barth, *The Epistle to the Romans*, trans. Edwyn C. Hoskyns (New York: Oxford University Press, 1933), 29. For a discussion of the misappropriation of Barth by Smyth, see Maurice Cowling, *Religion and Public Doctrine in Modern England* (New York: Cambridge University Press, 1980), 91–95.

64. Michael de la Bédoyère, "Books of the Quarter," *Criterion*, July 1936, 712.

65. Arthur N. Prior, "Books of the Quarter," *Criterion*, October 1938, 142–43.

66. Hudson, "Books of the Quarter," 354.

67. Christopher Dawson, "Religion and the Totalitarian State," *Criterion*, October 1934, 3. In this same issue, in a different essay, Dawson reviews Reinhold Niebuhr's *Reflections on the End of an Era*. While Dawson criticizes aspects of Niebuhr's book, such as the fuzziness with which he uses the term "orthodoxy," he sees the American theologian as "an interesting sign of the times" and his book as an indication that the "days of liberal Protestantism are numbered." Christopher Dawson, "Books of the Quarter," *Criterion*, October 1934, 131.

68. Dawson, "Religion and the Totalitarian State," 5.

69. Ibid., 13.

70. Christopher Dawson, *Essays in Order 3* (New York: Macmillan, 1931), 122. Dawson's social thinking was an important influence on Eliot—a debt that Eliot acknowledged in the introduction to *The Idea of a Christian Society*. Dawson believed, like Eliot, that much of modern intellectual and social history had been a movement towards secularized

thinking, atomization, and unthinking materialism (in both the philosophical and more colloquial senses). How could this drift be corrected? By a return to what Dawson called "historical Christianity": namely, the traditions and heritage of Roman Catholicism. For more on Eliot and Dawson, see Benjamin Lockerd, "Beyond Politics: T. S. Eliot and Christopher Dawson on Religion and Culture," in Lockerd, *T. S. Eliot and Christian Tradition*, 217–38.

71. Dawson, "Religion and the Totalitarian State," 15.

72. Ibid., 15–16.

73. Ibid., 16.

74. E. W. F. Tomlin, "Books of the Quarter," *Criterion*, October 1935, 135.

75. This sentiment is echoed by *Criterion* contributor V. A. Demant, who in 1939 wrote that "Totalitarian tendencies find their ultimate enemy in the existence of the Church, because the Church insists upon a super-political ground of human life." V. A. Demant, *The Religious Prospect* (London: Frederick Muller, 1939), 55.

76. Alec Randall, "German Periodicals," *Criterion*, October 1934, 170–71.

77. V. A. Demant, "Dialectics and Prophecy," *Criterion*, July 1935, 559. Demant greatly influenced Eliot's own *The Idea of a Christian Society* (1939) and was singled out for praise in two of Eliot's *Criterion* "Commentaries." See "Commentary," *Criterion*, January 1932, 271–73, and "Commentary," *Criterion*, January 1934, 276–77.

78. Demant, "Dialectics and Prophecy," 562.

79. Ibid., 570–71.

80. Randall Jarrell echoes this (mis)characterization of Barth as a Manichean thinker years later. In his lectures on Auden, he claims that Barth, along with Niebuhr and Kierkegaard, sees existence as fundamentally evil and corrupt: "We are damned not merely for what we do, but for doing anything at all—and properly damned, for what *we* do is necessarily evil: *Do not, till ye be done for* is our only possible slogan . . . everything (except the Wholly Other, God) is evil; for Auden, like Niebuhr, accepts the Fall not merely as a causal myth, but as the observed essence of all experience." This is an unfair reading of Barth, for whom Christ's Incarnation shows the real meaningfulness and holiness of existence. But it is a reading that continues to plague his reputation. Randall Jarrell, *Randall Jarrell on W. H. Auden*, ed. Stephen Burt with Hannah Brooks-Motl (New York: Columbia University Press, 2005), 88.

81. T. S. Eliot, "The Idea of a Literary Review," *New Criterion*, January 1926, 3. In magazines that exhibit a tendency rather than a dogmatic "programme," Eliot writes, "editor and collaborators may freely express their individual opinions and ideas, so long as there is a residue of common tendency, in the light of which many occasional contributors, otherwise irrelevant or even antagonistic, may take their place and counteract any narrow sectarianism." Ibid., 2.

82. Herbert Read, "Books of the Quarter," *Criterion*, January 1926, 191.

83. Douglas Lane Patey, *The Life of Evelyn Waugh: A Critical Biography* (London: Wiley-Blackwell, 2001), 39.

84. Goldie, *A Critical Difference*, 140. In this same passage, Goldie summarizes the position of Catholic Modernists like George Tyrell—those who favored historical criticism of the Bible and believed that dogma must change in substance over time. For these religious liberals, Thomism was, as Goldie writes, "too crude a systematization" of the "empirical nature of their faith."

85. Quoted in Arthur H. Dakin, *Paul Elmer More* (Princeton, NJ: Princeton University Press, 1960), 269. This claim—that Eliot's reading of Maurras directly led to his conversion—has been challenged by many scholars in recent years, most convincingly by Lyndall Gordon and Barry Spurr. Eliot's interest in Christianity (though "interest" is too pallid a word for something that was more like a haunting) was lifelong. He had what appears to have been a visionary experience while at Harvard, for instance, where he also read a great deal on mysticism, including Dean Inge's *Studies of English Mystics* and Julian of Norwich's *Revelations of Divine Love*. See Spurr, *"Anglo-Catholic in Religion,"* 1–34.

86. For Eliot's complicated relationship with Maurras and Action française, see, among others, Kenneth Asher, "T. S. Eliot and Charles Maurras," *American Notes and Queries* 11.3 (1993): 20–29, and Anthony Julius, *T. S. Eliot: Anti-Semitism and Literary Form* (Cambridge: Cambridge University Press, 1995), 214–17.

87. Gerald A. McCool, *The Neo-Thomists* (Milwaukee: Marquette University Press, 1994), 40. Brian Shanley likewise emphasizes that "twentieth-century Thomism is not monolithic but comprises instead various ways of perpetuating the thought of Aquinas." Brian Shanley, O.P., *The Thomist Tradition* (Boston: Kluwer Academic Publishers, 2013), 21.

88. D'Arcy wrote sixteen reviews for the magazine, ranging from a long review of Husserl's *Ideas* and phenomenology more generally to a review of I. A. Richards's *Menicus on the Mind*. D'Arcy admired Thomism for, among other reasons, the lens that it offered onto the problems of Catholic Modernism (again, "modernism" here meaning theological and not literary modernism).

89. Martin D'Arcy, "Books of the Quarter," *Criterion*, October 1933, 130–31.

90. Ibid., 164–65.

91. In almost every review, D'Arcy draws attention to the writer's clarity (or lack thereof). In his review of Husserl, for instance, D'Arcy calls the phenomenologist "the most difficult writer to follow since Kant," complaining that "time and again sentences have to be re-read, and even then their meaning is not always clear." In reviewing R. G. Collingwood, D'Arcy cites Collingwood's own interest in nontechnical language: "Even Mr. Collingwood himself is not immaculate, though it is a pleasure to read his prose after striving with the barbaric technical terms of a Kant and Whitehead and Husserl." Martin D'Arcy, "Books of the Quarter," *Criterion*, January 1932, 339; D'Arcy, "Books of the Quarter," *Criterion*, April 1934, 501.

92. Frederic Hood, "Books of the Quarter," *Criterion*, January 1938, 343.

93. For Belgion's many literary dustups, see Harding, *"The Criterion,"* 143–57.

94. Montgomery Belgion, "Art and Mr. Maritain," *Dublin Review*, October–December 1930, 201.

95. Horton Davies, *Worship and Theology in England*, vol. 5 (Princeton, NJ: Princeton University Press, 1965), 184. For an extensive examination of Dawson's relationship to the English literary scene of the interwar period, see Adam Schwartz, *The Third Spring: G. K. Chesterton, Graham Greene, Christopher Dawson, and David Jones* (Washington, DC: Catholic University of America Press, 2005).

96. Montgomery Belgion, "Books of the Quarter," *Criterion*, October 1933, 145.

97. Ibid., 146.

98. Ibid., 145.

99. Robert Scholes and Clifford Wulfman, *Modernism in the Magazines: An Introduction* (New Haven, CT: Yale University Press, 2010), 53.

100. Roberts, famous mostly for his work as an anthologizer (he edited the 1936 *Faber Book of Modern Verse*), contributed thirty-two reviews, mainly of poetry, and helped solicit original verse from other young poets.

101. Michael Roberts, "Books of the Quarter," January 1937, 378, 379.

102. Michael Roberts, *The Modern Mind* (London: Faber & Faber, 1937), 276.

103. T. S. Eliot, "Michael Roberts," *New English Weekly*, January 13, 1949, 164.

104. Algar Thorold, "Books of the Quarter," *Criterion*, October 1933, 170.

105. Etienne Gilson, "Books of the Quarter," *Criterion*, October 1932, 109. Gilson's description in this review of Cavalcanti as a *"natural dimostramento,"* or natural philosopher, would affect Pound's relationship to Cavalcanti in his later poetry. See James Wilhelm, *Ezra Pound: The Tragic Years, 1925–1972* (University Park: Pennsylvania State University Press, 1994), 66–68.

106. Shanley, *The Thomist Tradition*, 11.

107. Evelyn Underhill, "Books of the Quarter," *Criterion*, January 1935, 342, 340.

108. Robert Sencourt, "St. John of the Cross," *Criterion*, July 1931, 643.

109. Eliot, "Three Reformers," 818.

110. Quoted in Harding, *"The Criterion,"* 71.

111. T. S. Eliot, "Commentary," *Criterion*, May 1927, 189.

112. T. S. Eliot, "Bruce Littleton Richmond," *TLS*, January 13, 1961, 17. Statistics for the *TLS* found in Derwent May, *Critical Times: The History of the "Times Literary Supplement"* (New York: HarperCollins, 2001), 213.

113. In a tribute to Richmond, Eliot wrote: "Bruce Richmond was a great editor. To him I owe a double debt, first for the work he gave me to do and for the discipline of writing for him, and second for illustrating, in his conduct of the weekly, what editorial standards should be—a lesson I tried to apply when I came to edit the *Criterion*." Eliot, "Bruce Littleton Richmond," 17.

114. *Does Civilization Need Religion?* (1928), *Moral Man and Immoral Society* (1933), and *An Interpretation of Christian Ethics* (1936) all received short reviews in the *TLS*.

115. Ivor Thomas, "The Christian View of Man: From Anxiety to Sin," *TLS*, January 24, 1942, 40.

116. Thomas, "Karl Barth's Theology," 600.

117. Ivor Thomas, "A Modern Defender of John Knox: Karl Barth's Gifford Lectures," *TLS*, November 26, 1938, 752.

118. T. S. Eliot, "The Life of Prayer," *TLS*, June 21, 1928, 460.

119. Ibid., 460.

120. Eliot, "Three Reformers," 818.

121. In 1931, Murry reviewed Maritain's *Essays in Order* and *The Things That Are Not Caesar's*; in 1938, *Questions de conscience*; in 1939 *True Humanism* and *Anti-Semitism*; and in 1940 *Science and Wisdom*. In 1939, nearly half of Murry's contributions to the *TLS* were on religious books.

122. W. H. Auden, "The Means of Grace," *New Republic*, June 2, 1941, 765.

123. W. H. Auden, "Tract for the Times," *Nation*, January 4, 1941, 25.

Chapter 3. T. S. Eliot, Karl Barth, and Christian Revelation

1. Eliot planned to read this text as part of a lecture tour of Italy organized by the British Council. The tour was to take place in the spring of 1940 but was canceled due to

international unrest. The text of the lecture can be found in the T. S. Eliot Collection, King's College, Cambridge University. For a summary of the lecture, see Lesley Higgins, "T. S. Eliot and the Poetry of Gerard Manley Hopkins," in *T. S. Eliot: Essays from the Southern Review*, ed. James Olney (Oxford: Clarendon Press, 1988), 138–43. In the undelivered lecture, Eliot offers a summary of the history of English religious poetry, moving from the mysticism of fourteenth-century figures like Julian of Norwich and Richard Rolle, to the Renaissance lyrics of Donne, Herbert, and Vaughan, all the way up to the work of Tennyson and Hopkins.

2. Quoted in Ronald Bush, *T. S. Eliot: A Study in Character and Style* (New York: Oxford University Press, 1983), 224.

3. T. E. Hulme, *Speculations: Essays on Humanism and the Philosophy of Art* (New York: Harcourt, Brace, 1924), 118.

4. Bush, *T. S. Eliot*, 224.

5. T. S. Eliot, *The Complete Poems and Plays, 1909–1950* (New York: Houghton Mifflin Harcourt, 1971), 117. As Christopher Ricks and Jim McCue note, these lines echo at least two religious sources: the fourteenth-century mystical text *The Cloud of Unknowing*, which exemplifies the apophatic mode of theology that the rest of *Four Quartets* will so brilliantly embody; and Lancelot Andrewes's 1619 Ash-Wednesday Sermon. *The Poems of T. S. Eliot*, vol. 1, ed. Christopher Ricks and Jim McCue (Baltimore: Johns Hopkins University Press, 2015), 908.

6. As Leonard Diepeveen writes, "Eliot shapes his audience in order to refocus its horizon of expectations, to recreate it in a more useful form." Leonard Diepeveen, "'I Can Have More Than Enough Power to Satisfy Me': T. S. Eliot's Construction of His Audience," in *Marketing Modernisms: Self-Promotion, Canonization, Rereading*, ed. Kevin J. H. Dettmar and Stephen Watt (Ann Arbor: University of Michigan Press, 1996), 40. This was a common modernist strategy, similar to Virginia Woolf's claim in "Modern Fiction," just a few years before she wrote *Mrs. Dalloway*, that the modern novelist must describe everyday consciousness.

7. Steve Ellis, *The English Eliot: Design, Language and Landscape in "Four Quartets"* (New York: Routledge, 1991), 132.

8. Pericles Lewis, "Religion," in *A Companion to Modernist Literature and Culture*, ed. Kevin J. H. Dettmar and David Bradshaw (Oxford: Blackwell, 2006), 22.

9. W. David Soud, "'The Greedy Dialectic of Time': Karl Barth, T. S. Eliot, and *Four Quartets*," *ELH* 81.4 (2014), 1365, 1376, 1365. In many ways, my reading of *Four Quartets* resonates with Soud's essay. We are both interested in how Barth's self-negations provide a theological model for Eliot's poetry: both poet and theologian display what Soud describes as the "devastating recognition of one's nonbeing confronted with the hyperessentiality of God" (1383). We also both examine the idea of the "moment" in *Four Quartets* and how this relates to, and departs from, Barth's vision of "the *Moment* of human-divine encounter" (1365). Finally, we both end by looking at the conclusion of "Little Gidding," which holds out the hope of a reconciliation that can only happen outside of time. Where I depart from Soud, however, is in my focus on the tension between Eliot's desire to be a sacramental/Catholic poet and the fact that, at the level of form, Eliot *is* a dialectical/Protestant poet. I also argue that Eliot's engagement with Barthian theology must be understood within the context of modern poetry's broader engagement with then-contemporary theological discourse.

10. Almost every major Eliot critic of the past fifty years could be cited on this critical/poetic divide, but Ronald Bush offers the most compelling account, arguing that the oppositional relationship of Eliot's prose (romanticism versus classicism) becomes a dialectical relationship in his poetry. Eliot's power "comes from an almost unbearable tension between romantic yearning and intellectual detachment" and is the "result not of feeling and intellect working hand-in-glove but of powerful emotion held in powerful check." Bush, *T. S. Eliot*, x, xi.

11. Many critics have identified Eliot's conflation of order and religion. John Xiros Cooper, for instance, argues that Eliot's vision of the ontological stability offered by religion replaced his earlier, modernist aesthetic of fragmentation: "The comfort of belief in the twentieth century lies precisely in believing that the ontological link between the symbolic order and things cannot be broken." John Xiros Cooper, *T. S. Eliot and the Ideology of "Four Quartets"* (New York: Cambridge University Press, 1995), 21.

12. Eliot, *Complete Poems and Plays*, 122, 145.

13. Eliot, *Complete Poems and Plays*, 136.

14. William Blissett, "T. S. Eliot and Catholicity," in *T. S. Eliot and the Christian Tradition*, ed. Benjamin G. Lockerd (Madison, NJ: Farleigh Dickinson University Press, 2014), 34.

15. David Tracy, "T. S. Eliot as Religious Thinker: *Four Quartets*," in *Literary Imagination, Ancient and Modern: Essays in Honor of David Grene*, ed. Todd Breyfogle (Chicago: University of Chicago Press, 1999), 271.

16. Willa Cather, *Not under Forty* (New York: Alfred A. Knopf, 1936), v.

17. Michael North, *Reading 1922: A Return to the Scene of the Modern* (New York: Oxford University Press, 1999), 4.

18. *1922: Literature, Culture, Politics*, ed. Jean-Michel Rabaté (New York: Cambridge University Press, 2015) is the latest book to show how 1922 seemed to signal a shift in art, politics, religion, philosophy, and other areas. As Rabaté puts it, "What was looming was less the perception of the new as a break with the past, and more so the wish to reconsider and reconfigure the entire system, a system of values to which one would often give the name 'culture'" (3).

19. In fact, North opens his account with Ezra Pound's typically hyperbolic claim that, as North writes, "the Christian era ended on October 30, 1921, when James Joyce wrote the final words of *Ulysses*." North, *Reading 1922*, 3.

20. Quoted in Soud, "The Greedy Dialectic," 1364.

21. Mark C. Taylor, *After God* (Chicago: University of Chicago Press, 2007), 186, 192.

22. Friedrich Schleiermacher, *On Religion: Speeches to Its Cultured Despisers*, trans. Richard Crouter (Cambridge: Cambridge University Press, 1996), 132.

23. Karl Barth, *The Epistle to the Romans*, trans. Edwyn C. Hoskyns (New York: Oxford University Press, 1933), 80.

24. Ibid., 27.

25. M. Chaning-Pearce, "Karl Barth as a Post-War Prophet," *Hibbert Journal* 35 (1936–37), 369.

26. Ibid., 370.

27. Ibid., 369.

28. Ibid., 374.

29. Eliot's affinities with Barth are even deeper than Chaning-Pearce could have known. As Lyndall Gordon relates, the young Eliot was dissatisfied with his family's soft Unitarianism

due to his "sense of man's unlikeness, his distance from an unknowable deity." Of course, Barth was hardly the first religious thinker to affirm the infinite qualitative distinction between God and man: Gordon relates Eliot's religious inclinations to those of an earlier New Englander, Jonathan Edwards. Barth, in other words, with his focus on original sin and his vision of a world desperately in need of God's shattering grace, was part of a particular religious tradition to which Eliot felt himself drawn. Lyndall Gordon, *T. S. Eliot: An Imperfect Life* (New York: W. W. Norton, 1998), 20.

30. Pascal and Hulme both emphasized the radical disjuncture between nature and grace. In his introduction to Pascal's *Pensées*, Eliot indicated that he agreed with the French philosopher's "analysis of the *three orders*: the order of nature, the order of mind, and the order of charity. These three are *discontinuous*; the higher is not implicit in the lower as in an evolutionary doctrine it would be." Eliot likewise admired Hulme's assertion that there exists an "*absolute discontinuity* between vital and religious things." T. S. Eliot, "The *Pensées* of Pascal," in *Selected Essays* (London: Faber & Faber, 1951), 416, emphasis in original; Hulme, *Speculations*, 11, emphasis in original.

31. Hans Urs Balthasar, *The Theology of Karl Barth*, trans. John Drury (New York: Holt, Rinehart & Winston, 1971), 69–70.

32. For Barth's relationship to German expressionism, see Ian R. Boyd, *Dogmatics among the Ruins: German Expressionism and the Enlightenment as Contexts for Karl Barth's Theological Development* (New York: Peter Lang, 2004), and Stephen H. Webb, *Re-Figuring Theology: The Rhetoric of Karl Barth* (Albany: State University of New York Press, 1991), 1–18.

33. Balthasar, *The Theology of Karl Barth*, 70.

34. This is one of the central questions of Eliot's religious poetry as well. Take "Ash-Wednesday," for instance: "Still is the unspoken word, the Word unheard, / The Word without a word, the Word within / The world and for the world." Or "Burnt Norton" (these lines immediately precede mention of "the Word"): "Words strain, / Crack and sometimes break, under the burden, / Under the tension, slip, slide, perish, / Decay with imprecision, will not stay in place, / Will not stay still." Eliot, *Complete Poems and Plays*, 65, 121.

35. Barth, *Epistle to the Romans*, 65.

36. Ibid., 380, 227, 49.

37. Kierkegaard is the other famously paradoxical Christian thinker of the modern period, and it is not an accident that Kierkegaard is everywhere present in *Epistle to the Romans*. Midway through the book, Barth praises the Danish thinker's "dialectical audacity," and the whole book might be read as a homage and reviving of Kierkegaard's dialectical style and method. Ibid., 252.

38. Ibid., 231.

39. Ibid., 99.

40. David Tracy, "Fragments: The Spiritual Situation of Our Times," in *God, the Gift, and Postmodernism*, ed. John D. Caputo and Michael J. Scanlon (Bloomington: Indiana University Press, 1999), 172.

41. Webb, *Re-Figuring Theology*, 148.

42. This rhetorical, image-based, exclamatory theology is very different from Barth's later work, especially the *Church Dogmatics*. This is an irony of Barth's reception in the English-speaking world: by the time *Epistle to the Romans* was first translated into English in 1933, Barth had dramatically altered both his theology (becoming more Christocentric)

and his style (less violent, more classically restrained). In fact, Barth's theological and stylistic progression maps quite nicely onto Eliot's own movement from the tortured Expressionism of "Preludes" and "Rhapsody on a Windy Night" to the classic reserve of *Four Quartets*.

43. Eliot, *Complete Poems and Plays*, 14.

44. Ibid., 12.

45. Ibid., 12, 15.

46. Ibid., 38.

47. Ibid., 37.

48. Barth, *Epistle to the Romans*, 5–6.

49. Eliot, "The Metaphysical Poets," in *Selected Prose of T. S. Eliot*, ed. Frank Kermode (New York: Houghton Mifflin Harcourt, 1975), 65, emphasis in original.

50. Barth, *Epistle to the Romans*, 521.

51. Webb, *Re-Figuring Theology*, 145.

52. Franco Moretti, *Modern Epic: The World-System from Goethe to García Márquez* (London: Verso, 1996), 227.

53. Terry Eagleton, *Wittgenstein: The Terry Eagleton Script, the Derek Jarman Film* (London: British Film Institute, 1993), 5.

54. Barth's literary tastes were decidedly middlebrow. His abiding love was for detective fiction, and he claimed to have learned English from reading the mystery novels of Dorothy Sayers. Still, his writing displays some familiarity with literary modernism. In *Epistle to the Romans*, for instance, he glosses Paul with this quotation from *The Brothers Karamazov*: "Each one of us is utterly guilty in the presence of all; and, more than all others, I am guilty." He also sprinkles his work with allusions to Kierkegaard and Ibsen. Barth, *Epistle to the Romans*, 185.

55. Interestingly, where *The Waste Land* resembles Barth's *Epistle to the Romans* in its style, I would argue that it is still a profoundly Catholic work in its theology (insofar as it has a theology). Throughout the poem, there is confidence that the spirit, if it dwells within the world at all, dwells immanently within long-lasting institutions and places like the Magnus Martyr and the Roman Catholic tradition. In other words, Eliot seems to see grace as dwelling within history (Catholic) as opposed to entering it unbidden from beyond (Protestant). I am indebted to conversations with Frank Farrell for this reading of *The Waste Land*'s theological implications. For more on this, and how Eliot might be read productively as a Hegelian thinker, see Frank Farrell, *Why Does Literature Matter?* (Ithaca: Cornell University Press, 2004), 183–86.

56. George Hunsinger, *How to Read Karl Barth: The Shape of His Theology* (New York: Oxford University Press, 1991), 77.

57. John Baillie, Preface, *Revelation*, ed. John Baillie and Hugh Martin (London: Faber & Faber, 1937), x.

58. Ibid., xi.

59. T. S. Eliot, Introduction, *Revelation*, 1.

60. T. S. Eliot, "Mr. Middleton Murry's Synthesis," *Criterion*, October 1927, 340.

61. Eliot, Introduction, *Revelation*, 2.

62. Baillie, Preface, *Revelation*, xviii.

63. Ibid., xv.

64. Ibid., xvi.

65. Ibid., xix.

66. Eliot himself puzzled over the relationship between Christian and non-Christian revelation throughout his career. In *The Waste Land*, Eliot draws upon both Western and Eastern traditions, sharply juxtaposing, for instance, the Buddha's Fire Sermon with Augustine's *Confessions*. Similarly, in "The Dry Salvages," Eliot seems to hint at some deep connection between the teachings of Christ and the teachings of Krishna. The question of how to relate Christian to non-Christian revelation, however, is beyond the scope of this chapter and this book. For an illuminating look at this problem, see A. David Moody, *Tracing T. S. Eliot's Spirit* (New York: Cambridge University Press, 1991), 18–38.

67. Barth, in *Revelation*, 42.

68. Ibid., 44.

69. Ibid., 63. In a later essay in the collection, the Russian Orthodox theologian Sergius Bulgakoff posits, contra Barth, "a certain reciprocity, or *a likeness between the image of God and man*, in fact, their correlatedness." This correlatedness makes possible natural revelation: the world's beauty, moral law, man's conscience—all are signs of God's revelation. Bulgakoff, in *Revelation*, 129.

70. Barth, in *Revelation*, 42.

71. Eliot, *Complete Poems and Plays*, 64.

72. Barth, in *Revelation*, 51.

73. Barth, *Epistle to the Romans*, 29. Eliot in "The Dry Salvages" will describe the same moment as "the point of intersection of the timeless / With time." Eliot, *Complete Poems and Plays*, 136.

74. Barth, *Epistle to the Romans*, 29.

75. Martin D'Arcy, in *Revelation*, 181.

76. Ibid., 183.

77. Quoted in Balthasar, *The Theology of Karl Barth*, 39.

78. D'Arcy, in *Revelation*, 221.

79. Ibid., 202.

80. Ibid., 218–19.

81. Ibid., 217.

82. David Tracy, *The Analogical Imagination: Christian Theology and the Culture of Pluralism* (New York: Crossroad, 1981), 408, 415, 408, 413.

83. Ibid., 417.

84. In *Like and Unlike God*, for instance, John Neary channels Tracy to offer a typology of the modernist imagination, placing Joseph Conrad and James Joyce within the dialectical-analogical schema. Neary argues that Conrad, with his focus on indecipherability and the inadequacy of language, falls within the dialectical camp, while Joyce's *Ulysses*, in showing that "the worldly is the transcendent; the farcical is the profound," exhibits faith in the power of the analogical imagination. John Neary, *Like and Unlike God: Religious Imaginations in Modern and Contemporary Fiction* (Atlanta, GA: Scholars' Press, 1999), 104.

85. Tracy, *Analogical Imagination*, 303.

86. Eliot, *Complete Poems and Plays*, 21, 22.

87. Tracy, "Fragments," 175.

88. Susan K. Wood, "The Liturgy and Sacraments," in *The Blackwell Companion to Catholicism*, ed. James Buckley, Frederick Christian Bauerschmidt, and Trent Pomplun (Malden, MA: Blackwell, 2007), 340.

89. This is not to say that Hopkins was a purely analogical poet; far from it. The "dark sonnets" in particular are among the most haunting evocations of the despair associated with the dialectical imagination in the English language. Still, "God's Grandeur" serves well as an example of the analogical mode.

90. Gerard Manley Hopkins, *The Major Works*, ed. Catherine Phillips (New York: Oxford University Press, 2002), 128.

91. Ibid., 139.

92. Ibid., 140. This is in stark contrast to Eliot's own Marian poem, "Ash-Wednesday," where Eliot provides a vision not of ecstatic profusion but of dramatic purgation (indeed, the lines echo Dante's *Purgatorio*): "Under a juniper-tree the bones sang, scattered and shining / We are glad to be scattered, we did little good to each other, / Under a tree in the cool of the day, with the blessing of sand, / Forgetting themselves and each other, united / In the quiet of the desert." Eliot, *Complete Poems and Plays*, 62–63.

93. T. S. Eliot, *After Strange Gods* (London: Faber & Faber, 1934), 47.

94. Eliot, "Baudelaire," in *Selected Prose*, 232.

95. Higgins, "T. S. Eliot," 141.

96. Eliot, *Complete Poems and Plays*, 136.

97. Ibid., 130.

98. Ibid.

99. Ibid., 131.

100. A. David Moody, *Thomas Stearns Eliot, Poet* (New York: Cambridge University Press, 1994), 224, 225.

101. Charles Taylor, *A Secular Age* (Cambridge, MA: Belknap Press of Harvard University Press, 2007), 284. Taylor elaborates at greater length upon the idea of "ontic logos" in *The Sources of the Self*, where he argues that to be modern is, at some level, to feel the loss of a universe that, by its very nature and in its every part, possesses meaning, beauty, and plenty.

102. Eliot, *Complete Poems and Plays*, 133–34.

103. Ibid., 127, 125.

104. Ricks and McCue, *The Poems of T. S. Eliot*, 1:882.

105. Donald Davie, "T. S. Eliot: The End of an Era," in *T. S. Eliot: "Four Quartets": A Casebook*, ed. Bernard Bergonzi (London: Macmillan, 1969), 156–57. Other critics have repeated the claim that, in many moments, *Four Quartets* lapses into undisciplined banality. As I will argue, though, these moments of undisciplined banality should be read as radically intentional, serving an important function in the sequence's larger strategy of rhythmic and theological contrast.

106. Ricks and McCue, *The Poems of T. S. Eliot*, 1:882.

107. Eliot, *Complete Poems and Plays*, 141.

108. T. S. Eliot, "The Music of Poetry," in *Selected Prose*, 113.

109. Eliot, *Complete Poems and Plays*, 136, 138.

110. Ibid., 136.

111. Ibid., 107.

112. Ibid., 108.

113. Ibid., 107, 108.

114. Ibid., 108, 109.

115. Ibid., 122.

116. Lee Oser, "Coming to Terms with *Four Quartets*," in *A Companion to T. S. Eliot*, ed. David E. Chintz (Malden, MA: Wiley-Blackwell, 2009), 219.

117. Barth, in *Revelation*, 51.

118. In the above quotation, it is important to note that Barth does not say that all the things of this world—earth and animals and humanity—lack dignity. Rather, he says that these things lack *divine* dignity. He is not claiming, in other words, that this world is evil; he is claiming that this world is not God.

119. Eliot, *Complete Poems and Plays*, 118.

120. Ibid.

121. In a recent essay, Kevin Hart offers a phenomenological reading of the rose garden scene, arguing that the sequence teaches us not to seek out or hold too dear such privileged moments: "If our reading of 'Burnt Norton' inclines us to think of this fragment as prizing the Christian revelation over common human wisdom, a reading of *Four Quartets* may well edge us toward another interpretation: we should follow the path of mere Christianity and not seek special revelation or private spiritual consolation." Kevin Hart, "Eliot's Rose Garden: Some Phenomenology and Theology in 'Burnt Norton,'" *Christianity & Literature* 64.3 (2015): 259.

122. Mutlu Blasing, *Lyric Poetry: The Pain and the Pleasure of Words* (Princeton, NJ: Princeton University Press, 2007), 115. To note that the flesh is often sinful, though, is not to say that the flesh *is* sinful for Eliot. As his best critics argue, such a view does not do justice to the complex relationship Eliot's poetry bears to this world. As Jewel Spears Brooker writes, "Eliot is no Manichean. He does not believe the world is evil and nature is unwholesome." Brooker, *The Placing of T. S. Eliot* (Columbia: University of Missouri Press, 1991), 115.

123. T. S. Eliot, "The Social Function of Poetry," *Adelphi*, July–September 1945, 154, emphasis in original.

124. F. R. Leavis, *The Living Principle: "English" as a Discipline of Thought* (New York: Oxford University Press, 1975), 253.

125. Eliot, *Complete Poems and Plays*, 144–45. As Jed Esty puts it, *Four Quartets* "remains attached to local dimensions of history ("Now . . .") and geography (". . . and in England"), but cannot meaningfully dwell in those dimensions without aspiring to grasp larger patterns of time (eternity) and space (the universe). The poem recognizes that historical time only has meaning in relation to worldly entities like the nation or the person." Jed Esty, *A Shrinking Island: Modernism and National Culture in England* (Princeton, NJ: Princeton University Press, 2004), 136.

126. Eliot, *Complete Poems and Plays*, 125, 119.

127. Laura Riding, *Anarchism Is Not Enough* (London: Jonathan Cape, 1928), 90.

128. Eliot, *Complete Poems and Plays*, 145, 143.

Chapter 4. Sacramental Theology and David Jones's Poetics of Torsion

1. Les Murray, *Dog Fox Field* (Manchester, UK: Carcanet, 1991), 84.

2. *Catechism of the Catholic Church*, 2nd ed. (Washington, DC: United States Catholic Conference, 2000), 896.

3. Jonathan Culler, *Theory of the Lyric* (Cambridge, MA: Harvard University Press, 2015), 137; Mutlu Blasing, *Lyric Poetry: The Pain and the Pleasure of Words* (Princeton, NJ: Princeton University Press, 2007), 2.

4. Missy Daniel, "Poetry Is Presence: An Interview with Les Murray," *Commonweal*, May 22, 1992, 10.

5. David Jones, Preface, *Epoch and Artist* (London: Faber & Faber, 1959), 13.

6. Jones, "Art and Sacrament," in *Epoch and Artist*, 167.

7. David Jones, *The Anathemata* (New York: Viking Press, 1965), 49.

8. Jones, Preface, *The Anathemata*, 36–37.

9. Ibid., 37.

10. Thomas Dilworth, *Reading David Jones* (Cardiff: University of Wales Press, 2008), 170.

11. Jones, "Art and Sacrament," 179.

12. Maurice de la Taille, *The Mystery of Faith and Human Opinion Contrasted and Defined*, trans. J. B. Schimpf (London: Sheed & Ward, 1930), 232.

13. In "Mapping the Labyrinth: The *Ur-Anathemata* of David Jones," *Renascence* 51.3 (1999): 253–80, Goldpaugh offers a reading of the intricate layering of *The Anathemata*'s various parts. In more recent work, including a paper given at the "David Jones: Christian Modernist?" conference at Oxford in September 2014, Goldpaugh linked this layering to de la Taille's analysis of the Catholic Mass.

14. de la Taille, *The Mystery of Faith*, 201.

15. Jones, *The Anathemata*, 62.

16. Ibid., 174–75.

17. Ibid., 49, 244.

18. Ibid., 173.

19. Regina Schwartz, *Sacramental Poetics at the Dawn of Secularism: When God Left the World* (Stanford: Stanford University Press, 2008), 4.

20. Elaine Scarry, *On Beauty and Being Just* (Princeton, NJ: Princeton University Press, 1999), 23, 30.

21. Quoted in Schwartz, *Sacramental Poetics*, 3.

22. Peter Nicholls does not mention Jones in *Modernisms: A Literary Guide* (Houndmills, Basingstoke: Macmillan, 1995), while Pericles Lewis's *The Cambridge Introduction to Modernism* (New York: Cambridge University Press, 2007) briefly connects Jones's epic poems to the work of Joyce before moving on to more prominent American modernists like Marianne Moore and William Carlos Williams.

23. Dilworth, *Reading David Jones*, 1, 99, 2.

24. Exceptions to this include Paul Robichaud's *Making the Past Present: David Jones, the Middle Ages, and Modernism* (Washington, DC: Catholic University Press, 2007) and Kathleen Henderson Staudt's *At the Turn of a Civilization: David Jones and Modernist Poetics* (Ann Arbor: University of Michigan Press, 1994). In his work, Robichaud "explores how Jones transforms Victorian medievalism through the stylistic alchemy of Anglo-American modernism, producing a poetry that has strong thematic continuities with the Victorian period but is aesthetically and formally modernist" (5). In other words, Robichaud argues that Jones brings together a medievalist ethos (a longing for the coherence and beauty of the medieval world) to modernist form. My argument is that Jones saw modern interpreters of medieval theology (Maritain, de la Taille, etc.) as offering aesthetic and philosophical justification *for* modernist form. It is not so much, as Robichaud writes, that Jones saw "how earlier aesthetic practices could be adapted to the formal demands of twentieth-century writing" (154). Rather, in Jones's view, the long tradition of Catholic theology provided the very basis for the formal experiments of twentieth-century writing. Staudt's work is excellent through and through, though she focuses primarily on Jones's connection with modernism not through his poetics but through his way of "imagining history." In other

words, she shows how Jones uses "linguistic texture and etymology to demonstrate 'how then became now'" (137), and how, "Like Eliot and Pound, David Jones believes that the culture of his generation is fundamentally contrary to the poet's impulse" (12).

25. David Jones, *In Parenthesis* (New York: New York Review Books, 2003), 220.

26. Ibid., 220.

27. Jones, *The Anathemata*, 205.

28. Robichaud, *Making the Past Present*, 61.

29. Other essays in the collection include "Physics and Philosophy," "The Church and Sex," and "An Approach to Africa." Again, the implicit claim of the volume is that Catholicism and Catholic theology might speak not just to purely theological issues but to the whole panorama of human existence. Elizabeth Longford, ed., *Catholic Approaches to Modern Dilemmas and Eternal Truth* (London: Weidenfeld & Nicolson, 1955).

30. Jacques Maritain, *Art and Scholasticism and The Frontiers of Poetry*, trans. Joseph W. Evans (New York: Charles Scribner's Sons, 1962), 3.

31. Jones, "Art and Sacrament," 145.

32. Ibid., 146.

33. Ibid., 149, 150.

34. Jones will not go so far as to say that art has no moral bearing, however. As he ends up saying, "Man could not belong to Prudentia except as an artist and he could not be an artist but for that tie-up with Prudentia." This may seem to fly in the face of Jones's art-prudence distinction. Jones has an argument, borrowed from Maritain, for why this is not so; that argument, however, is beyond the scope of this chapter. Jones, "Art and Sacrament," 150.

35. T. S. Eliot, "Shakespeare," in *Selected Essays, 1917–1932* (New York: Harcourt, Brace, 1948), 118.

36. Jones, "Art and Sacrament," 151.

37. Jones, "The Utile," in *Epoch and Artist*, 180.

38. Ibid., 181.

39. Jones, "Art and Sacrament," 149.

40. Ibid., 153.

41. Maritain, *Art and Scholasticism*, 60.

42. Jones, "Art and Sacrament," 172.

43. Ibid., 170.

44. Maritain, *Art and Scholasticism*, 56–57, emphasis in original.

45. John Trapani, *Poetry, Beauty, and Contemplation: The Complete Aesthetics of Jacques Maritain* (Washington, DC: Catholic University of America Press, 2011), 124. In his chapter on Maritain's understanding of the perception of beauty, Trapani summarizes what Maritain means by aesthetic "clarity or radiance": "Naturally, this splendor will impart a certain delight in the senses, but sensual delight is only an accompanying good—the real splendor is the splendor of intelligibility" (123).

46. Maritain, *Art and Scholasticism*, 60.

47. Jones and Maritain here foreshadow Cleanth Brooks, who famously claimed that we can't paraphrase a poem's meaning because the poem's very form *is* its meaning. Jones here likely also borrowed from the influential arguments of Roger Fry and Clive Bell, both of whom urged a focus on the artwork's formal relations and not its subject matter or social context.

48. Jones, "Art and Sacrament," 169.

49. Ibid., 170.

50. Quoted in Elizabeth Ward, *David Jones: Mythmaker* (Dover, NH: Manchester University Press, 1983), 36.

51. Jones, "Art and Sacrament," 167.

52. In the preface, Jones describes the many meanings of this title: "This writing is called 'In Parenthesis' because I have written it in a kind of space between—I don't know between quite what—but as you turn aside to do something; and because for us amateur soldiers (and especially for the writer, who was not only an amateur, but grotesquely incompetent, a knocker-over of piles, a parade's despair) the war itself was a parenthesis—how glad we thought we were to step outside its brackets at the end of '18—and also because our curious type of existence here is altogether in parenthesis." Jones, Preface, *In Parenthesis*, xv.

53. Jones, *In Parenthesis*, 1.

54. Ibid.

55. For a synoptic view of the relationship between speech act theory and literary discourse, see especially J. Hillis Miller, *Speech Acts in Literature* (Stanford: Stanford University Press, 2002).

56. Culler, *Theory of the Lyric*, 126.

57. Jones, *In Parenthesis*, 3.

58. Ibid.

59. de la Taille, *The Mystery of Faith*, 201.

60. Ibid., 203.

61. There is a long history of relating sacramental theology to J. L. Austin's theory of speech-acts. For a particularly illuminating analysis, see Denys Turner, *Faith, Reason, and the Existence of God* (New York: Cambridge University Press, 2004), 68–73. As Timothy Gould insists, however, Austin's "performative utterance" is also, in some deep sense, anti-sacramental: "Austin insisted that the utterance does not refer to some inward, invisible act, for which the words would then be taken as an outward and visible—but still descriptive—sign." Still, as I emphasize throughout, Jones saw the sacraments as a kind of performative language, language that, in its very articulation, *does* something. Timothy Gould, "The Unhappy Performative," in *Performativity and Performance*, ed. Andrew Parker and Eve Kosofsky Sedgwick (New York: Routledge, 1995), 21.

62. de la Taille, *The Mystery of Faith*, 202.

63. Quoted in David Jones, *Dai Greatcoat: A Self-Portrait of David Jones in His Letters*, ed. René Hague (Boston: Faber & Faber, 1980), 249.

64. Jones, *The Anathemata*, 49.

65. Jones, Preface, *The Anathemata*, 29.

66. Jones, *The Anathemata*, 53, 64, 244.

67. Ibid., 244.

68. Ibid., 100.

69. Jones, *In Parenthesis*, 76.

70. Robichaud, *Making the Past Present*, 158, emphasis in original.

71. Jones, *The Anathemata*, 185.

72. Ibid., 127, 141, 194, 198.

73. Ibid., 174.

74. Blasing, *Lyric Theory*, 119, emphasis in original. Blasing uses these words to describe the effect of the ending of *The Waste Land*, where the thunder speaking "DA" shows us the abyss separating human from divine language: "The distance between natural

sounds, God's word or syllable, which we cannot hear except as it resounds in nature, and meaningful human language is absolute" (118–19).

75. Jones, *The Anathemata*, 78.

76. Ibid., 60, 108, 237, 77, 74.

77. Ibid., 78–79.

78. Erich Auerbach defines figural interpretation as "establish[ing] a connection between two events or persons in such a way that the first signifies not only itself but also the second, while the second involves or fulfills the first." Erich Auerbach, *Mimesis: The Representation of Reality in Western Literature*, trans. Willard R. Trask (Princeton, NJ: Princeton University Press, 1953), 73.

79. Of the cup, Jones writes in a footnote, "In Welsh mythology, when Arthur goes to raid the Celtic hades one of the spoils he has to recover is a vessel from which no coward can eat or drink." Jones, *The Anathemata*, 79.

80. De Man famously reads the final line of Yeats's "Among School Children" not as a rhetorical question but as a literal question. When read in this way, "the question can be given a ring of urgency, 'Please tell me, how *can* I know the dancer from the dance?' " Paul de Man, *Allegories of Reading: Figural Language in Rousseau, Nietzsche, Rilke, and Proust* (New Haven, CT: Yale University Press, 1982), 12.

81. Jones, *The Anathemata*, 59. See Dilworth, *Reading David Jones*, 124.

82. William Blissett, "The Syntax of Violence," in *David Jones: Man and Poet*, ed. John Mathias (Orono, ME: National Poetry Foundation, University of Maine, 1988), 200.

83. Robichaud, *Making the Past Present*, 22.

84. Quoted in William Blissett, *The Long Conversation: A Memoir of David Jones* (New York: Oxford University Press, 1981), 46.

85. Quoted in Thomas Dilworth, *The Shape of Meaning in the Poetry of David Jones* (Toronto: University of Toronto Press, 1988), 33–34.

86. Gerard Manley Hopkins, *The Major Works*, ed. Catherine Phillips (New York: Oxford University Press, 2002), 118–19.

87. Josephine Miles, "The Sweet and Lovely Language," in Kenyon Critics, *Gerard Manley Hopkins* (New York: New Directions, 1945): 64.

88. Bernadette Waterman Ward, *World as Word: Philosophical Theology in Gerard Manley Hopkins* (Washington, DC: Catholic University of America Press, 2002), 24.

89. de la Taille, *The Mystery of Faith*, 232, 90.

90. Ibid., 242–43.

91. Jones, Preface, *In Parenthesis*, xi.

92. Joseph Frank, *The Idea of Spatial Form* (New Brunswick, NJ: Rutgers University Press, 1991), 15.

93. Jones, Preface, *In Parenthesis*, x.

94. Jones, *In Parenthesis*, 185.

95. Jones, *The Anathemata*, 244.

96. Dilworth, *Reading David Jones*, 176.

97. Jones, Preface, *The Anathemata*, 24.

98. Jones, *The Anathemata*, 120, 59.

99. Jones, Preface, *The Anathemata*, 35.

100. Jones, "Art and Sacrament," 156.

101. Jones, Preface, *The Anathemata*, 14–15.

102. Quoted in Adam Schwartz, *The Third Spring: G. K. Chesterton, Graham Greene, Christopher Dawson, and David Jones* (Washington, DC: Catholic University of America Press, 2005), 348. Schwartz writes, "Jones's verse seeks to render various prior eras as concurrent facets of a vital present just as the Eucharist makes the historical events of Christ's Supper and Passion actual at each Mass." Ibid., 348.

103. Jones, *The Anathemata*, 244.

104. Ezra Pound, "Religio," in *Selected Prose: 1909–1965*, ed. William Cookson (New York: New Directions, 1973), 68.

105. Ezra Pound, "The Serious Artist," in *Early Writings: Poems and Prose*, ed. Ira B. Nadel (New York: Penguin Books, 2005), 242.

106. Pound, "Vorticism," in *Early Writings*, 289, 278.

107. Pound, "A Retrospect," in *Early Writings*, 255–56, 257.

108. Pound, "Vorticism," in *Early Writings*, 285.

109. Pound, "The Serious Artist," 234. In this way, Pound anticipates the scientific discourse of T. S. Eliot, who, in his 1921 essay "Tradition and the Individual Talent," famously claims that artistic depersonalization "may be said to approach the condition of science" and compares the artistic process to "the action which takes place when a bit of finely filiated platinum is introduced into a chamber containing oxygen and sulfur dioxide." T. S. Eliot, "Tradition and the Individual Talent," in *The Sacred Wood: Essays on Poetry and Criticism* (London: Methuen, 1976), 53.

110. Pound first published Fenollosa's "The Chinese Written Character as a Medium for Poetry" in 1919, though he made such extensive revisions, insertions, and deletions to the document that it is perhaps best understood as Pound's essay.

111. Pound, "The Chinese Written Character as a Medium for Poetry," in *Early Writings*, 310.

112. Ibid., 308–9.

113. Ibid., 309.

114. George A. Kennedy, "Fenollosa, Pound and the Chinese Character," in *Selected Works of George A. Kennedy*, ed. Li Tien-yi (New Haven, CT: Far Eastern Publications, 1964), 456.

115. Pound, "The Chinese Written Character," 309, emphasis in original.

116. Ibid., 328.

117. Matthew Mutter, "'The Power to Enchant That Comes From Disillusion': W. H. Auden's Criticism of Magical Poetics," *Journal of Modern Literature* 34.1 (2010): 74.

118. W. B. Yeats, "Certain Noble Plays of Japan," in *The Collected Works of W. B. Yeats*, vol. 4, *Early Essays*, ed. Richard J. Finneran and George Bornstein (New York: Simon & Schuster, 2007), 172–73.

119. Harold Monro, "The Imagists Discussed," *Egoist*, May 1915, 74.

120. May Sinclair, "Two Notes," *Egoist*, June 1915, 88.

121. Ibid.

122. Ibid., 89.

123. Pound, "The Chinese Written Character," 312.

124. James Joyce, *A Portrait of the Artist as a Young Man*, ed. Jeri Johnson (New York: Oxford University Press, 2000), 186.

125. Richard Kearney offers a reading of these "pseudo-Eucharists" in *Anatheism: Returning to God after God* (New York: Columbia University Press, 2011), 103–9.

126. Kearney, *Anatheism*, 118–32.

127. Jones, *The Anathemata*, 129.

Chapter 5. Auden's Meanwhile

1. W. H. Auden, *Collected Poems*, ed. Edward Mendelson (New York: Vintage Books, 1991), 314, 313. Auden returns to this image in, among other places, "The Sea and the Mirror," where Prospero describes the existential terrors that remain even when we are in our dotage: while trying to enjoy retirement in seclusion and peace, the elderly magician feels he is really "Sailing alone, out over seventy thousand fathoms" (409). This later poem is drenched in Kierkegaardian imagery and ideas. In fact, as several critics have argued, "The Sea and the Mirror" as a whole—and certainly Caliban's speech to the audience—can be read as a description of the Kierkegaardian movement from the aesthetic stage of existence to the ethical stage of existence to the religious stage of existence. See, for instance, Rachel Wetzsteon, *Influential Ghosts: A Study of Auden's Influences* (New York: Routledge, 2007), 98.

2. Auden, *Collected Poems*, 319, 305.

3. Ibid., 275.

4. Alan Jacobs, *What Became of Wystan? Change and Continuity in Auden's Poetry* (Fayetteville: University of Arkansas Press, 1998), 29. As Jacobs shows, many of Kierkegaard's central claims—"that in relation to God we are always in the wrong" (78), for example—prove crucial for Auden's theological/existential poetry.

5. W. H. Auden, "A Preface to Kierkegaard," *New Republic*, May 14, 1944, 683.

6. Ibid.

7. This idea—that, for the Christian theologian, time is the enemy—has been misattributed to Augustine and Barth for a long time. G. C. Berkouwer, one of Barth's first critics, believed that Barth privileged eternity over time absolutely. As George Hunsinger writes, "In reading Bath, Berkouwer imagines an original separation of eternity from time such that time never really has a chance. Time is thought to be so overpowered by an a priori eternity that it is effectively 'eternalized,' being monistically absorbed, as it were, into God." This is not the case, though. Hunsinger again: "For Barth the human existence of Jesus is accorded not only epistemological but ontological priority." George Hunsinger, *How to Read Karl Barth: The Shape of His Theology* (New York: Oxford University Press, 1991), 16.

8. Auden, "A Preface to Kierkegaard," 686.

9. T. S. Eliot, *The Complete Poems and Plays, 1909–1950* (New York: Houghton Mifflin Harcourt, 1971), 120.

10. Auden, "A Preface to Kierkegaard," 683.

11. Edward Mendelson, *Later Auden* (New York: Farrar, Straus & Giroux, 1999), 19.

12. Auden, *Collected Poems*, 238; 238–39.

13. Auden, "A Preface to Kierkegaard," 686.

14. Ibid.

15. Ibid., 685.

16. George Steiner, *The Poetry of Thought: From Hellenism to Celan* (New York: New Directions, 2011), 37.

17. Quoted in Bruce McCormack, *Karl Barth's Critically Realistic Dialectical Theology: Its Genesis and Development, 1909–1936* (New York: Oxford University Press, 1995), 288.

18. T. S. Eliot, introduction to Blaise Pascal, *Pensées*, trans. W. F. Trotter (New York: E. P. Dutton, 1932), xii.

19. T. S. Eliot, "Dante," in *The Sacred Wood: Essays on Poetry and Criticism* (London: Methuen, 1976), 167; Eliot, "Blake," in *The Sacred Wood*, 156.

20. Eliot, "Dante," 168; Eliot, "Blake," 156, 158.

21. Eliot, "Blake," 158.

22. Reinhold Niebuhr, *An Interpretation of Christian Ethics* (San Francisco: Harper & Row, 1963), 20.

23. Ibid., 18, 9.

24. Auden, *Collected Poems*, 400.

25. Ibid., 399.

26. James C. Livingston, *Modern Christian Thought: Enlightenment and the Nineteenth Century*, vol. 2 (Minneapolis: Fortress Press, 2006), 179.

27. W. H. Auden, *Secondary Worlds* (New York: Random House, 1968), 136. In this same essay, Auden contrasts the necessarily shaggy-dog style of theological discourse with God's necessarily sober style of speaking: "Since the Word was made Flesh, it is impossible to imagine God as speaking in anything but the most sober prose. If Blake was right in saying that Milton was of the Devil's party without knowing it, this is because, while it is perfectly credible that Lucifer should speak in a high style, to give God admirable speeches to deliver is to turn him into a Zeus without Zeus's vices. As the German pietist Hamann rightly observed; 'If, when God said "Let there be light", the angels had applauded, wouldn't God have said, "Did I say anything particularly silly?" ' " Ibid., 136.

28. Randall Jarrell, *Randall Jarrell on W. H. Auden*, ed. Stephen Burt with Hannah Brooks-Motl (New York: Columbia University Press, 2005), 99, 89.

29. Auden, *Collected Poems*, 97.

30. W. H. Auden, "Mimesis and Allegory," in *Prose: 1939–1948*, vol. 2, ed. Edward Mendelson (Princeton, NJ: Princeton University Press, 2002), 87.

31. See, for instance, "Words and the Word," where Auden gives his most elaborate account of how Christian belief might inform and complicate poetic creation. In this essay, Auden goes so far as to claim that belief in the Christian God might call into question the very act of writing poetry. Echoing Eliot's lines about the word and the Word in "Ash-Wednesday," Auden writes, "if God is the word, then men are forbidden all pagan idolatry of words," and what is poetry but an idolatry of words—a belief that words possess truth and beauty independent of God's divine Word? Auden, *Secondary Worlds*, 134.

32. T. S. Eliot, "Shakespeare," in *Selected Essays, 1917–1932* (New York: Harcourt, Brace, 1948), 118.

33. Auden, *Collected Poems*, 591.

34. Ibid., 41.

35. Ibid., 179.

36. Ibid., 592.

37. Ibid.

38. W. H. Auden, "The Virgin and The Dynamo," in *The Dyer's Hand*, ed. Edward Mendelson (New York: Vintage Books, 1989), 61–62.

39. Ibid., 61.

40. Ibid.

41. Quoted in Jacobs, *What Became of Wystan?*, 142.

42. W. H. Auden, "Charles Williams: A Review Article," *Christian Century* (May 2, 1956), 553. Auden was attracted to *The Descent of the Dove* in part because he so esteemed Williams. In 1956, Auden wrote that, when he first met Williams shortly after returning from his disastrous experience in the Spanish Civil War, "for the first time in my life [I] felt myself in the presence of personal sanctity . . . I felt transformed into a person who was incapable of doing or thinking anything base or unloving." James A. Pike, ed., *Modern Canterbury Pilgrims and Why They Chose the Episcopal Church* (New York: Morehouse-Gorham, 1956), 41.

43. Charles Williams, *The Descent of the Dove: A Short History of the Holy Spirit in the Church* (Grand Rapids, MI: William B. Eerdmans, 1980), 6–7.

44. W. H. Auden, "The Means of Grace," *New Republic*, June 2, 1941, 766.

45. Reinhold Niebuhr, *The Nature and Destiny of Man*, vol. 1 (Louisville, KY: Westminster John Knox Press, 1996), 1.

46. Livingston, *Modern Christian Thought*, 2:178.

47. Auden, *Collected Poems*, 592.

48. Ibid., 592.

49. Ibid.

50. Ibid., 595.

51. For Auden's channeling of Rosenstock-Huessy's strange work of political philosophy, see John Fuller, *W. H. Auden: A Commentary* (Princeton, NJ: Princeton University Press, 1998), 417–20.

52. Auden, *Collected Poems*, 592, 593, 594.

53. Ibid., 593, 594.

54. Ibid., 594.

55. Ibid., 595.

56. Williams, *Descent of the Dove*, 14.

57. Ibid., 15.

58. Ibid.

59. Niebuhr, *An Interpretation of Christian Ethics*, 19.

60. Niebuhr, *The Nature and Destiny of Man*, 2:51.

61. Jason Stevens, *God-Fearing and Free: A Spiritual History of America's Cold War* (Cambridge, MA: Harvard University Press, 2010), 31.

62. Auden, "The Means of Grace," 766.

63. Auden, *Collected Poems*, 399.

64. Ibid., 400.

65. Ibid., 362.

66. Ibid., 363, 364.

67. Ibid., 389.

68. In "New Year Letter," Auden criticizes "the devil who controls / The moral asymmetric souls, / The either-ors, the mongrel halves / Who find truth in a mirror" and instead lauds "the gift of double focus, / That magic lamp which looks so dull / And utterly impractical / Yet, if Aladdin use it right, / Can be a sesame to light." Auden, *Collected Poems*, 220.

69. Ibid., 591.

70. Eliot, *Complete Poems and Plays*, 120, 144.

71. Auden, *Collected Poems*, 595.

72. Ibid., 391, 393.

73. Ibid., 394.

74. Ibid., 390.

75. Ibid., 399.

76. Jacobs, *What Became of Wystan?*, 89.

77. Auden, *Prose: 1939–1948*, 250.

78. Eliot, *Complete Poems and Plays*, 69.

79. W. H. Auden, *Selected Poems*, ed. Edward Mendelson (New York: Vintage Books, 2007), 55, 57.

80. Ibid., 57.

81. Ibid.

82. Auden, *Collected Poems*, 62.

83. Ibid., 61, 62.

84. Ibid., 62.

85. Ibid., 248.

86. Auden, *Selected Poems*, 97.

87. Auden, *Collected Poems*, 199.

88. Ibid.

89. Ibid., 218.

90. Ibid., 241.

91. Ibid., 473.

92. Ibid., 463, 473.

93. Ibid., 592.

94. Giorgio Agamben, *The Time That Remains: A Commentary on the Letter to the Romans*, trans. Patricia Dailey (Stanford: Stanford University Press, 2005), 62.

95. The influence of Barth's *Epistle to the Romans* led to a renewed interest in Pauline thought among other theologians as well. To take one example: as Charles Lemert has argued, "Niebuhr's study of the Swiss theologians led him to reconsider Pauline theology, which in turn opened up a fresh line of inquiry that led to his so-called orthodoxy." Charles Lemert, *Why Niebuhr Matters* (New Haven, CT: Yale University Press, 2011), 104. Besides Barth, Walter Benjamin and his friend Gershom Scholem also introduced the idea of messianic time back into midcentury political and religious discourse. For Benjamin's understanding of time and its relation to the messianic as opposed to the apocalyptic, see Peter Fenves, *The Messianic Reduction: Walter Benjamin and the Shape of Time* (Stanford: Stanford University Press, 2010).

96. W. H. Auden, "Augustus to Augustine," *New Republic*, September 25, 1944, 374.

97. Søren Kierkegaard, *The Living Thoughts of Kierkegaard*, ed. W. H. Auden (New York: New York Review of Books, 1999), 48.

98. Ibid., 47.

99. Søren Kierkegaard, *The Concept of Irony with Continual References to Socrates*, ed. and trans. Howard V. Hong and Edna Hong (Princeton, NJ: Princeton University Press, 1992), 6.

100. Reinhold Niebuhr, *The Irony of American History* (Chicago: University of Chicago Press, 2008), xxiii.

101. Ibid.

102. Ibid., xxiii–xiv.

103. Ibid., xxiv.

104. Ibid., 2.

105. Niebuhr, *The Nature and Destiny of Man*, 1:17.

106. Niebuhr, *An Interpretation of Christian Ethics*, 55.

107. Niebuhr, *The Nature and Destiny of Man*, 1:267–68.

108. Ibid., 263.

109. Niebuhr, *The Nature and Destiny of Man*, 2:113.

110. Ibid., 113–14.

111. Reinhold Niebuhr, *Discerning the Signs of the Times: Sermons for Today and Tomorrow* (New York: Charles Scribner's Sons, 1946), 14.

112. Niebuhr, *The Irony of American History*, 161.

113. Auden, *Collected Poems*, 5.

114. Edward Mendelson, *Early Auden* (New York: Farrar, Straus & Giroux, 2000), 63.

115. Auden, *Collected Poems*, 26.

116. Ibid., 61.

117. Ibid., 62.

118. Ibid., 117.

119. Ibid., 118.

120. Ibid.

121. Mendelson, *Early Auden*, 169.

122. Jacobs, *What Became of Wystan?*, 56.

123. Auden, *Collected Poems*, 627.

124. Ibid., 628.

125. Ibid., 634.

126. Ibid., 347.

127. Ibid., 349.

128. Ibid., 306. In this poem and elsewhere, Auden also borrows ideas from the German theologian Paul Tillich. For Auden's reading of Tillich, see Mendelson, *Later Auden*, 53.

129. Jarrell, *Randall Jarrell on W. H. Auden*, 100.

130. Auden, *Collected Poems*, 595.

131. Ibid., 596, 595, 596.

132. Ibid., 387, 394.

133. Ibid., 535.

134. Ibid., 364.

135. Ibid., 362.

136. Ibid., 444.

137. Quoted in Arthur Kirsch, *Auden and Christianity* (New Haven, CT: Yale University Press, 2005), xvi.

138. Jarrell, *Randall Jarrell on W. H. Auden*, 130.

139. Kirsch, *Auden and Christianity*, 176.

140. Auden, "Balaam and His Ass," in *The Dyer's Hand*, 135.

141. Ibid., 145.

142. Auden, *Collected Poems*, 319.

143. Niebuhr, *Discerning the Signs of the Times*, 111.

144. Auden, *Collected Poems*, 622.

Conclusion. "A Poetics of Belief"

1. "The Questionnaire: Final Results," *Nation and Athenaeum*, October 16, 1926, 75.

2. *Religion and the Intellectuals: A Symposium* (New York: Partisan Review, 1950), 5.

3. In an earlier 1926 issue, Leonard Woolf had described the "liberal scepticism, atheism, or agnosticism which is characteristic of the majority of educated moderns." This offhand comment provoked a backlash from the *Nation and Athenaeum*'s believing readers, and the survey was designed to test whether the majority of the magazine's readers did in fact believe, "in the words of the late Mr. Clutton-Brock, [that] 'the universe is cold, indifferent, and meaningless' to us." For these quotations and a more in-depth examination of the genesis and results of the survey, see Elyse Graham and Pericles Lewis, "Private Religion, Public Mourning, and *Mrs. Dalloway*," *Modern Philology* 111.1 (2013): 88–106. See also R. B. Braithwaite, *The State of Religious Belief: An Inquiry Based on 'The Nation and Athenaeum' Questionnaire* (London: Hogarth Press, 1927).

4. *Religion and the Intellectuals*, 5. In the editorial statement that opens *Religion and the Intellectuals*, we read that "there is no doubt that the number of intellectuals professing religious sympathies, beliefs, or doctrines is greater now than it was ten or twenty years ago, and that this number is continually increasing or becoming more articulate."

5. "The Questionnaire," 75.

6. *Religion and the Intellectuals*, 6.

7. "The Questionnaire," 76.

8. *Religion and the Intellectuals*, 96–97, emphasis in original.

9. Amy Hungerford, *Postmodern Belief: American Literature and Religion Since 1960* (Princeton, NJ: Princeton University Press, 2010), xiii.

10. Marilynne Robinson, *Gilead* (New York: Picador, 2006), 110.

11. Christian Wiman, *My Bright Abyss: Meditation of a Modern Believer* (New York: Farrar, Straus & Giroux, 2013), 124.

Suggested Further Reading

For a long time, scholars were relatively uninterested in the continued presence of Christianity within the modernist period. Happily, the landscape has changed within the past decade or so. There hasn't been a better, more fruitful moment for critics, like myself, who are interested in Eliot *and* Augustine, Woolf *and* Barth, Joyce *and* Maritain.

Erik Tonning's *Modernism and Christianity* (2014) offers perhaps the most synoptic overview of the subject matter, with a particularly good section on how modernists such as Eliot and Jones saw the Church as a potentially (and productively) disruptive force; not merely something to provide intellectual and spiritual comfort but something that might call social, philosophical, and aesthetic conventions into question. Those interested in how literary modernists understood the relationship between religion and sociality will find much to admire in Pericles Lewis's *Religious Experience and the Modernist Novel* (2010). In a very different vein, Ellis Hanson's *Decadence and Catholicism* (1997) examines the queer energies offered to Decadent artists—protomodernists, really—by Roman Catholicism. Beautifully written and clearly argued, *Decadence and Catholicism* remains a first-rate work of scholarship on religion and literature, gender and sexuality, and aesthetics more generally. Though Siobhan Phillips's *The Poetics of the Everyday: Creative Repetition in Modern American Verse* (2010) doesn't concern itself solely, or even primarily, with religion, it elegantly shows how the poems of Elizabeth Bishop, Wallace Stevens, and others both grew out of, and departed from, Christian understandings of temporality and ritual.

In the specific area of modernist poetry and theology, the scholarly conversation remains more muted. In the years since I first began researching and publishing on the subject, however, several significant works have appeared. Kierkegaard is a regular reference point in Phillips's *The Poetics of the Everyday*, for instance, and *The Maritain Factor: Taking Religion into Interwar Modernism* (2010), edited by Rajesh Heynickx and Jan De Maeyer, shows the importance of Maritain and neo-Scholasticism to European modernism. Gregory Erickson's *The Absence of God in Modernist Literature* (2007) convincingly traces connections between modernist aesthetics, Death of God theology, and deconstruction. It is a rare scholar who can write equally as intelligently about Proust, Altizer, and Derrida; Erickson is such a one. Finally, W. David Soud's recent book, *Divine Cartographies: God, History, and Poesis in W. B. Yeats, David Jones, and T. S. Eliot* (2016), argues persuasively for the importance of mystical theology to the modernist moment.

Part of the purpose of this book is to show how theology was an essential imaginative and intellectual resource for an important strand of modern poetry, not just for individual poets, but also for the entire body of work I have called theological modernism. For those looking to read about the theological commitments and interests of individual poets, though, there are many admirable studies from which to choose. Lyndall Gordon's biography *T. S. Eliot: An Imperfect Life* (1998) remains one of the best. Its sections on Eliot's early reading in, and experience of, mysticism are particularly strong. Barry Spurr's *Anglo-Catholic in Religion: T. S. Eliot and Christianity* (2010) is deeply versed in the history and controversies of Anglo-Catholicism, using these as a way to understand Eliot's entire career, not just his explicitly Christian work. The recently published *T. S. Eliot and Christian Tradition* (2014), edited by Benjamin D. Lockerd, offers a multifaceted account of Eliot's Christian sensibility.

For readers interested in David Jones, Thomas Dilworth's *Reading David Jones* (2008) is the essential text. Jones fans wait eagerly for Dilworth's forthcoming biography of the poet/artist. Kathleen Henderson Staudt's *At the Turn of a Civilization: David Jones and Modern Poetics* (1993) contains an excellent account of how Jones's sacramental poetry relates to structuralist and poststructuralist accounts of language, while Paul Robichaud's *Making the Past Present: David Jones, the Middle Ages, and Modernism* (2007) convincingly sees Jones's medievalism as a response to a European culture in crisis. Finally, the best critic on Auden's religious sense is also the best Auden critic, period: Edward Mendelson. *Later Auden* (1999) in particular offers an unparalleled examination of the intellectual and existential stakes of Auden's return to Christianity, an examination that Arthur Kirsch's more recent *Auden and Christianity* (2005) contributes to as well. Alan Jacobs, one of the strongest living critics on religion and literature, published an earlier book, *What Became of Wystan: Change and Continuity in Auden's Poetry* (1998), which remains illuminating for its insight into Auden's shifting faith and its implications for his poetry.

In conclusion, I would be remiss not to recommend the many superb books that look beyond the modernist period to talk about poetry and theology more generally. All of Rowan Williams's criticism is brilliant, but the grace with which he moves between theology and literature is particularly impressive in *Grace and Necessity: Reflections on Art and Love* (2005) and *Dostoevsky: Language, Faith, and Fiction* (2008). David Mahan's outstanding *An Unexpected Light: Theology and Witness in the Poetry and Thought of Charles Williams, Micheal O'Siadhail, and Geoffrey Hill* (2009), shows how poetry might, in certain modes, actually "do theology." Speaking of which: one of the great spurs to this project was a book not from the world of modernists but from the world of medievalists—Jim Rhodes's *Poetry Does Theology: Chaucer, Grosseteste, and the "Pearl"-Poet* (2001). I first heard about this book from my wife, a medievalist, whose own dissertation, "Speculation and Time in Late Medieval Visionary Discourse," offers a lovely account of the medieval period's blending of poetry and theology. All of these books served the first function of literary criticism: they urged me to read more sensitively and to think more deeply. I hope that this book has done the same for its readers.

Index

Credits

Excerpts from Gerard Manley Hopkins's *Gerard Manley Hopkins: The Major Works*, edited by Catherine Phillips (Oxford World's Classics, 2000, 2008). Used by permission of Oxford University Press.

Excerpts from T. S. Eliot's "The Waste Land," "The Rock," "The Journey of the Magi," and "Preludes" from *Collected Poems 1909–1962*. Copyright 1936 by Houghton Mifflin Harcourt Publishing Company. Copyright © renewed 1964 by Thomas Stearns Eliot. Used by permission of Houghton Mifflin Harcourt Publishing Company and Faber and Faber Ltd. All rights reserved.

Excerpts from W. H. Auden's "Musée des Beaux Arts," "In Memory of W.B. Yeats," and "In Memory of Sigmund Freud," copyright © 1940 and renewed 1968 by W. H. Auden; "Paid on Both Sides," copyright © 1934 by The Modern Library and renewed 1962 by W. H. Auden; "New Year Letter" and "Kairos and Logos," copyright © 1941 and renewed 1969 by W. H. Auden; "The Age of Anxiety," copyright © 1947 by W. H. Auden and renewed 1975 by the Estate of W. H. Auden; "For the Time Being," copyright © 1944 and renewed 1972 by W. H. Auden; "The Shield of Achilles," copyright © 1952 by W. H. Auden and renewed 1980 by The Estate of W. H. Auden; "Memorial for the City," copyright © 1951 by W. H. Auden and renewed 1979 by The Estate of W. H. Auden; "Leap Before You Look" and "In Sickness and In Health," copyright © 1945 and renewed 1973 by W. H. Auden; "Consider," copyright © 1934 and renewed 1962 by W. H. Auden; "A Summer Night," copyright © 1937 by Random House, Inc. and renewed 1965 by W. H. Auden; "Prime (Horae Canonicae: 1)," copyright © 1951 by W. H. Auden and renewed 1979 by The Estate of W. H. Auden; and "Family Ghosts," from *W. H. Auden Collected Poems* by W. H. Auden, copyright © 1976 by Edward Mendelson, William Meredith and Monroe K. Spears, Executors of the Estate of W. H. Auden. Used by permission of Random House, an imprint and division of Penguin Random House LLC, and Curtis Brown, Ltd. All rights reserved.

Excerpts from W. H. Auden's "Spain 1937" and "September 1, 1939," copyright © 1940 and copyright renewed 1968 by W. H. Auden, from *Selected Poems* by W. H. Auden, edited by Edward Mendelson. Used by permission of Vintage Books, an imprint of the Knopf Doubleday Publishing Group, a division of Penguin Random House LLC, and Curtis Brown, Ltd. All rights reserved.

Excerpts from David Jones's *The Anathemata* (Faber and Faber, 1952), *In Parenthesis* (Faber and Faber, 1937), and *The Sleeping Lord and Other Fragments* (Faber and Faber, 1974). Used by permission of Faber and Faber Ltd., and the trustees of the Jones Estate.

Excerpt from Les Murray's "Distinguo" from *Dog Fox Field* (Carcanet, 1992). Used by permission of Farrar, Straus & Giroux, Inc., Carcanet Press Limited, and Margaret Connolly & Associates.